RESOLUTE

ALSO BY MARTIN W. SANDLER

Lost to Time: Unforgettable Stories That History Forgot

The Letters of John F. Kennedy

Atlantic Ocean: The Illustrated History of the Ocean That Changed the World

Against the Odds: Women Pioneers in the First Hundred Years of Photography

America: A Celebration!

The Story of American Photography: An Illustrated History for Young People

YOUNG READERS (SELECTED TITLES)

Shipwrecked! Diving for Hidden Time Capsules on the Ocean Floor

Picturing a Nation: The Great Depression's Finest Photographers Introduce America to Itself

Race through the Skies: The Week the World Learned to Fly

Imprisoned: The Betrayal of Japanese Americans During World War II

1919 The Year That Changed America (2019 National Book Award winner)

The Whydah: A Pirate Ship Feared, Wrecked, and Found

Apollo 8: The Mission That Changed Everything

Iron Rails, Iron Men, and the Race to Link the Nation: The Story of the Transcontinental Railroad

What Was America's Deadliest War?: And Other Questions About the Civil War (Good Question!)

The Impossible Rescue: The True Story of an Amazing Arctic Adventure

Inventors, Civil War, Immigrants, Cowboys, and Pioneers (Library of Congress series)

America Through the Lens: Photographers Who Changed the Nation

Secret Subway: The Fascinating Tale of an Amazing Feat of Engineering

Trapped In Ice!: An Amazing True Whaling Adventure

Flying over the USA: Airplanes in American Life (Transportation in America)

Island of Hope: The Story of Ellis Island and the Journey to America

Photography: An Illustrated History

REVISED EDITION

RESOLUTE

JOHN FRANKLIN'S LOST EXPEDITION AND THE DISCOVERY OF THE QUEEN'S GHOST SHIP

MARTIN W. SANDLER

UNION
SQUARE
& CO.

NEW YORK

UNION
SQUARE
& CO.

NEW YORK

UNION SQUARE & CO. and the distinctive Union Square & Co. logo
are trademarks of Sterling Publishing Co., Inc.

Union Square & Co., LLC, is a subsidiary of Sterling Publishing Co., Inc.

First hardcover edition published in 2006 by Sterling Publishing Co., Inc.

ISBN 978-1-4549-6021-8
ISBN 978-1-4549-6022-5 (e-book)

For information about custom editions, special sales, and premium purchases,
please contact specialsales@unionsquareandco.com.

Printed in Canada

2 4 6 8 10 9 7 5 3 1

unionsquareandco.com

Cover design by Jared Oriel
Original interior design by Russell Hassell,
revised interior design by Rich Hazelton

For picture credits, see page 311.

DEDICATION

THIS BOOK IS DEDICATED to seekers everywhere, a sentiment never better expressed than by Kenneth Roberts, who wrote: "On every side of us are men who hunt perpetually for their personal Northwest Passage, too often sacrificing health, strength, and life itself to the search; and who shall say they are not happier in their vain but hopeful quest than wiser, duller folks who sit at home, venturing nothing."

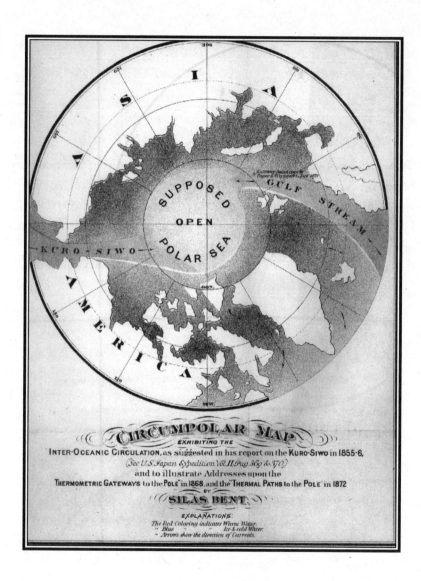

CIRCUMPOLAR MAP

EXHIBITING THE

INTER-OCEANIC CIRCULATION, as suggested in his report on the KURO-SIWO in 1855-6,

(See U.S. Japan Expedition Vol. II. Pag. 369 & 370.)

and to illustrate Addresses upon the

THERMOMETRIC GATEWAYS to the POLE in 1868, and the THERMAL PATHS to the POLE in 1872

BY

SILAS BENT.

EXPLANATIONS:

The Red Coloring indicates Warm Water.
" Blue " Ice & cold Water.
" Arrows show the direction of Currents.

CONTENTS

LIST OF MAPS

DRAMATIS PERSONAE

ALEXANDER ARMSTRONG, doctor aboard the *Investigator*, among the first to view the final link in the Northwest Passage.

HORATIO AUSTIN, commander of the five-vessel fleet sent in search of John Franklin in 1850.

GEORGE BACK, artist and explorer, accompanied John Franklin on his first two Arctic expeditions, led 1833 expedition in search of John Ross, commander of 1836 expedition in search of the Northwest Passage.

JOHN BARROW, second secretary of the Admiralty, and the "father of Arctic exploration."

FREDERICK BEECHEY, 1825–28 commander of the *Blossom*, a supply ship for the Parry and Franklin passage-seeking expeditions.

EDWARD BELCHER, commander of five-vessel fleet, including the *Resolute*, organized in 1852–54 to search for lost Franklin expedition; court martialed for abandonment of the fleet.

JOSEPH RENÉ BELLOT, French naval officer, member of William Kennedy's 1851 search for John Franklin, drowned on the Edward Inglefield expedition while attempting to bring supplies to the Belcher rescue fleet.

DAVID BUCHAN, commander of 1818 expedition in search of the North Pole.

JAMES BUDDINGTON, New London whaling captain of the *George Henry* and discoverer of the abandoned *Resolute*.

RICHARD COLLINSON, commander of the *Enterprise* in 1850 search for John Franklin.

SAMUEL CRESWELL, artist and lieutenant aboard the *Investigator* sent in search of Franklin in 1850.

PETER DEASE, co-leader (with Thomas Simpson) of 1837 expedition in search of the Northwest Passage.

EDWIN DE HAVEN, commander of the 1850 U.S. expedition in search of John Franklin.

JANE FRANKLIN, wife of John Franklin, leading instigator of the search for her husband.

JOHN FRANKLIN, commander of the 1845 *Erebus-Terror* expedition in search of the Northwest Passage; object of the most prolonged search and rescue effort in history.

CHARLES FRANCIS HALL, American leader of two expeditions (1860 and 1864) in search of John Franklin, leader of 1871 expedition in quest of the North Pole.

HENRY J. HARTSTENE, American naval captain, commander of the crew that returned the *Resolute* to Great Britain.

ISAAC HAYES, American surgeon on Elisha Kent Kane's 1853 search for John Franklin, leader of 1860 search for the North Pole.

WILLIAM HOBSON, second-in-command to Leopold M'Clintock on 1857 *Fox* expedition; discover of only written evidence of lost Franklin expedition.

EDWARD INGLEFIELD, commander of the *Isabel*, sent by Lady Franklin in 1852 in search of her husband; commander of the *Phoenix*, supply ship for Belcher expedition.

JOE (EBIERBING), Inuit who served as guide and helpmate to Charles Francis Hall and Frederick Schwatka on their Arctic expeditions; husband of Tookoolito (Hannah).

ELISHA KENT KANE, surgeon on the 1850 U.S. expedition in search of John Franklin, and leader of the 1853 Franklin-seeking expedition aboard the *Advance*.

HENRY KELLETT, commander of the *Plover* on an 1848–51 Franklin search, and commander of the *Resolute* on the Belcher expedition.

WILLIAM KENNEDY, commander of the Lady Franklin-funded search for her husband in the *Prince Albert*, in 1851–52.

GEORGE FRANCIS LYON, second-in-command on Edward Parry's second search for the Northwest Passage.

LEOPOLD M'CLINTOCK, officer on James Clark Ross's 1848 Franklin search, officer on Horatio Austin's 1850 search, commander of the *Intrepid* during Belcher-led 1852 search, and commander of the 1859 Lady Franklin-financed search in the Fox that led to the discovery of the most conclusive evidence of John Franklin's fate.

ROBERT MCCLURE, mate on George Back's 1836 passage search, officer of James Clark Ross's 1848 search for John Franklin, commander of the *Investigator*, and discoverer of the last link in the Northwest Passage.

GEORGE NARES, second mate on the *Resolute*, commander of the ground-breaking *Challenger* oceanographic expedition in the early 1870s, commander of the 1875 search for the North Pole

SHERARD OSBORN, commander of the *Pioneer* during Horatio Austin's 1850 search and Edward Belcher's 1852 search for John Franklin.

EDWARD PARRY, commander of the *Alexander* on John Ross's 1818 Northwest Passage search, commander of three expeditions (1819, 1821, 1824) in quest of the passage, commander of 1827 search for the North Pole.

WILLIAM PENNY, whaling captain, commander of the *Lady Franklin* and the *Sophia* in the 1850 Franklin search.

BEDFORD PIM, lieutenant aboard the *Resolute*, rescuer of Robert McClure and the crew of the *Investigator*.

W. J. S. PULLEN, lieutenant on the *Plover* and *Herald* expedition sent in support of the search for John Franklin, 1848–51.

JOHN RAE, surgeon/explorer for the Hudson's Bay Company, second-in-command on John Richardson's 1848 search for John Franklin, and discoverer, in 1853, of Franklin relics and Inuit reports of cannibalism among Franklin's men.

JOHN RICHARDSON, surgeon/naturalist/explorer, member of John Franklin's first and second overland Arctic expeditions, commander of 1848 Franklin search.

JOHN ROSS, commander of 1818 passage-seeking expedition, commander of 1829 search for the passage, commander of 1850 private search for John Franklin.

WILLIAM SCORESBY, early Arctic expert and renowned whaleman.

THOMAS SIMPSON, co-leader (with Peter Dease) of 1837 expedition in search of the Northwest Passage.

TOOKOOLITO (HANNAH), Inuit woman who served as guide and helpmate to Charles Francis Hall on his Arctic expeditions, wife of Joe (Ebierbing).

FREDERICK SCHWATKA, American leader of the 1878 expedition in search of the records of the Franklin expedition.

PARKER SNOW, member of Lady Franklin's privately funded 1850 expedition in search of her husband in the yacht *Price Albert*.

FOREWORD

One finds a very limited number of events in history that not only encapsulate the spirit of an age, but tremble on the edge of possibility: That Troy, whose topless towers stirred the West's first and greatest epic verse, could actually be found and excavated; that, on a Christmas night in the midst of the worst trench warfare the world had yet seen, British and German troops could gather together, exchanging whiskey and cigars; that three or four small rips in her hull could bring the unsinkable Titanic to the bottom of the ocean in little more than two hours.

The Arctic—where time itself is among the things susceptible to freezing—where, as the inimitable Rudolf Erich Raspe described in his Munchausen tales, sentences spoken in the winter could not be heard until they thawed out the next summer—has seen more than its share of such tales. Writers of fiction and poetry have found it an ideal landscape in which to unfold the extremities of human endeavor; the efforts of a man "to build a fire" in Jack London's story of that name, or the comfort found in a fiery furnace by the eponymous hard-luck prospector of Robert W. Service's "The Cremation of Sam McGee," could, it seems, have happened nowhere else. And yet it is the Arctic, more than any other place upon Earth, where the adage that "truth is stranger than fiction" finds its most dramatic embodiment, and as the great number of recent books on Arctic explorers testifies, the romance of those "unknown regions of eternal frost" remains strong to this day.

Yet throughout this revival of interest in the history of Arctic exploration, one of its greatest and strangest stories has gone almost completely untold: That of the loss, and uncanny re-appearance, of the British exploration vessel HMS *Resolute*. Here is surely one of the most singular events in the history of exploration—that a ghost ship, abandoned in the utmost reaches of the Arctic archipelago, could pilot itself to freedom, recovered as a "floating Pompeii" even as the officers who once strode its decks still lived—and yet it became far more than that. By setting the singular story of the *Resolute* in the context of the great international drama of the search for Sir John Franklin's lost Arctic expedition, and setting that story itself within the complex history of national sympathies sometimes divided, sometimes joined by the Atlantic Ocean, Martin Sandler has restored to its entirety a chapter of our history which hitherto has been told only in a piecemeal fashion. It is a story in which ships are as much characters as men, a story of bravery, generosity, and sacrifice, a story of bonds of friendship forged upon an icy anvil. Though long relegated to the periphery of history, the HMS *Resolute* lives on at its very center, as her timbers still stand today before the seat of power of a great nation, witness to decisions and commands its original officers could never have imagined.

Ralph Waldo Emerson once remarked that many of the most important discoveries are of things already known—by which he meant, I believe, that history can only live if one recovers its strangeness, its singularity, even its shock. In this book Martin Sandler has accomplished just that: He has given us anew something we had almost forgotten we possessed—the history of the timbers of a stout ship, in which, at the peak of a great international Arctic drama, all that is best about our nation once set sail.

—Russell A. Potter
Rhode Island College

O n May 5, 1845, the "Commissioners for executing the office of High Lord Admiral of the United Kingdom of Great Britain and Ireland" issued a twenty-three part set of orders to Sir John Franklin, the most revered of all the British naval explorers, which began by stating:

> *Her Majesty's government having deemed it expedient that*
> *further attempt should be made for the accomplishment of a*
> *north-west passage by sea from the Atlantic to the Pacific Ocean,*
> *of which passage small portion only remain to be completed,*
> *we have thought proper to appoint you to the command of the*
> *expedition to be fitted out for that service, consisting of Her*
> *Majesty's ship "Erebus" under your command, taking with you*
> *Her Majesty's ship "Terror," her Captain (Crozier) having been*
> *placed by us under your orders.*

As far as both the Admiralty and the British public were concerned, Franklin's endeavor would, they were certain, be the successful culmination of a quest that had become a national obsession, a quest that had become akin to the search for the Holy Grail—to find the fabled Northwest Passage. It would not turn out as planned. Instead, John Franklin's voyage would be the pivotal development in one of the most remarkable and enduring sagas in history.

It is an epic tale—an adventure, mystery, and detective story all rolled into one, played out against the harshest backdrop in the world. Most of all, it is the story of a unique breed of men, the astronauts of their day, willing to sail into the unknown, willing to risk all for glory, for country, and, truth be known, for the sheer adventure of it all. "They cannot help it, these Arctic fellows; it is in their blood." That is how Roderick Murchison, the president of the Royal Geographical Society described the scores of nineteenth-century explorers who went searching for the Northwest Passage. The same could have been said for the hundreds of Englishmen and Americans who took part in the thirty-nine expeditions that went seeking those who had disappeared in their search for the passage. What is most astounding is that they did it all under circumstances that we today can hardly imagine. Boldly they ventured into the harshest environment in the world, knowing they would have to spend at least one or even two or three long, dark winters trapped in the ice waiting for the all-too-brief periods when conditions would allow them to resume their search before becoming trapped again. Removed from loved ones and out of touch with the rest of the world for years at a time, they lived with the knowledge that death, in any one of a number of forms, could come at any time. As the American explorer and doctor Isaac Hayes, wrote in 1867:

> *A heavy line of icebergs was discovered to lie across our course; and, having no alternative, we shot in among them. . . . As the last streak of the horizon faded from view between the lofty bergs behind us, the steward (who was of a poetical turn of mind) came from the galley, and halting for an instant, cast one lingering look at the opening, and then dropped through the companion scuttle, repeating from the Inferno: "They who enter here leave hope behind."*

And they did it all with what we today would regard as the most inadequate of accoutrements—no cell phones, no global positioning systems, no snowmobiles, no helicopters, no synthetic tents or parkas. Instead, they searched treacherous, ice-filled waters armed with what were more sketches than maps, and navigational instruments that would cause modern mariners to shake their heads in dismay. They trudged thousands of miles over the barren, frozen wasteland, hauling their heavy sledges behind them in temperatures that fell to seventy degrees below zero, and often camped on the ice in simple canvas tents. No wonder that the expeditions of the day engendered unprecedented heroics. No wonder that they also spawned deception, intrigue, colossal blunders, outright lunacy, and even murder and cannibalism.

The drama of the search for the passage and for Franklin's lost expedition is made even more compelling and relevant by a new dimension to the saga that, until now, has never really been told in full. In 1962, newspapers throughout the world carried a now-iconic photograph of a young John F. Kennedy Jr. peering out from beneath a magnificent desk in the White House's Oval Office while his father worked above. It was a charming, human portrayal of the popular president and his equally popular son. Few who viewed the photograph could have realized that the desk in the picture was directly connected to the John Franklin saga. The circumstances of this surprising, unlikely connection present their own fascinating story, one that includes what has been referred to as arguably the "most miraculous voyage ever to take place." Perhaps most important, it is a story of developments that, in the end, linked America and Great Britain in friendship and provided both nations with a tangible symbol of goodwill that remains until this day.

What remains also are the lessons in courage and determination given to the world by those who lived out the Arctic adventure. Theirs is a story that has never ended, filled with mysteries that are still unsolved. As long as these mysteries endure, there will be modern-day searchers who will seek answers to riddles that continue to captivate us more than 150 years after they first emerged. And there will continue to be men and women determined to follow in the footsteps of Edward Parry, John and James Clark Ross, Elisha Kent Kane, Leopold M'Clintock, Frederick Schwatka, and so many of the others who people this book.

They challenged the unknown. They pushed back the frontiers. They endowed future generations of daring souls with the inspiration to become explorers. They made themselves immortal by inscribing their names forever on the Arctic chart. Their motivation is perhaps best explained by astronaut Michael Collins, a member of the first expedition to reach the moon. "Man," Collins stated, "has always gone where he has been able to go. It's simple. He will continue pushing back his frontier, no matter how far it takes him from his homeland."

—Martin W. Sandler
Cotuit, Massacusetts

OPPOSITE: These engravings from the book *The Frozen Zone and Its Explorers* ... (1874) by Alexander Hyde et al. envision the *Erebus* and the *Terror* stuck in the ice, and the funeral of Sir John Franklin.

THE EREBUS AND TERROR IN THE ICE-STREAM.

FUNERAL OF SIR JOHN FRANKLIN.

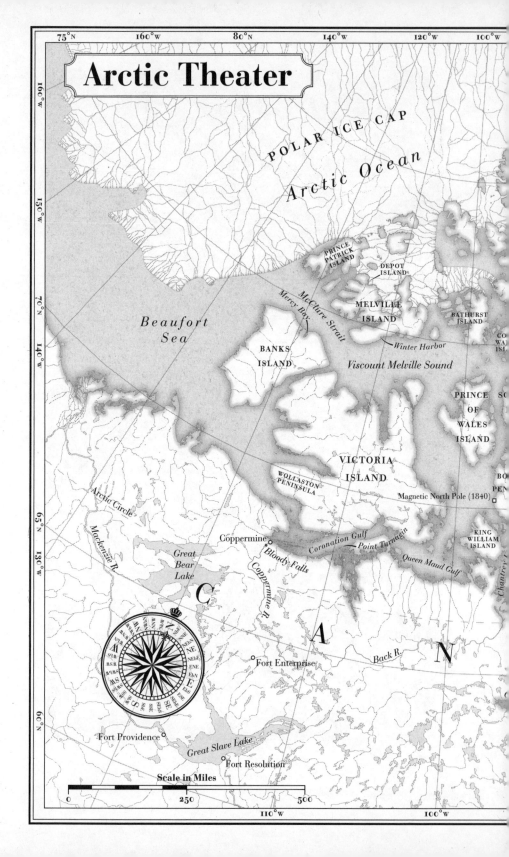

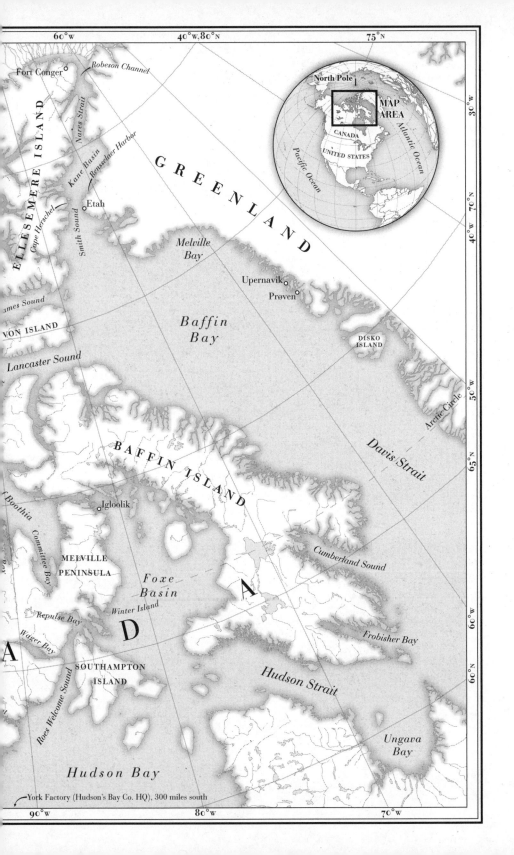

CHAPTER 1

The

Arctic Prize

"It is still the only thing left undone, whereby a
notable mind might be made famous and remarkable."
—Sixteenth-century explorer MARTIN FROBISHER

THE ARCTIC WEATHER could not have been much worse that fall
of 1855. It was only September 10, yet as the whaleship *George
Henry* made its way through the Davis Strait it was continually being struck by floating packs of ice. The temperature had
continued to fall, threatening to turn the rapidly moving ice into one
impenetrable mass. The intermittent fog and the howling winds made
navigation, at times, nearly impossible.

For thirty-eight-year-old Captain James Buddington it was the
latest of the challenges and near disasters that had plagued his vessel
and its twenty-five-man crew ever since they had left New London,
Connecticut, four months earlier. It was not that he was unaccustomed
to the hardships of Arctic whaling. Lean, powerfully built, and known
for his colorful vocabulary and his love of swapping yarns, Buddington
had been at sea since the age of seventeen, when he had stolen away

from his family farm one night and shipped aboard a whaler. Known also for his willingness to take risks in pursuing his mammoth prey, he had been enormously successful, continually returning home with his hold filled to capacity with barrels of precious whale oil, his deck crammed with bundles of equally valuable whalebone.

But this voyage had been different. Almost from the moment that the men of the *George Henry* had entered the northern whaling grounds, they had run into trouble. They had been in the Arctic for only sixteen days when they were struck by an ice floe, which tore a huge hole in the vessel's bow. Fortunately, the damage was above the waterline and they had been able to put into a nearby Greenland port for repairs.

Once back underway, Buddington found that the inlets that led to the richest whaling areas were totally impassable. Somehow they were able to capture a few whales but, by August, conditions had deteriorated even further and the continual snow and fog made it almost impossible to sight whales, let alone hunt them down. Realizing that the situation was becoming hopeless, Buddington made the decision that all whaling captains dreaded having to make. Reluctantly, he decided that even though his hold was far from full of oil and bone, he would put the safety of the ship and its crew ahead of the wrath of the *George Henry*'s owners that he was certain to face, and head for home.

Within a week of their turning back, everyone aboard knew that the captain had made the right decision. With the ice continuing to mount and waves pounding angrily over their deck, even those crewmen who were most disappointed at having to return with so empty a vessel looked forward to escaping the Arctic's clutches. But suddenly they were startled by a shrill cry from the lookout perched high in the *George Henry*'s masthead. The whaler's bellow was not the usual welcome shout of "Thar she blows" or "There go flukes." Instead, it was a shrill announcement that another ship had been sighted some fifteen miles in the distance.

Was it another whaleship, Buddington wondered? Whatever type of vessel it was, he welcomed the opportunity of exchanging news with its captain. But it would be a while, he knew, before he got that opportunity. The water between the two ships was filled with grinding ice and it would take time for him to make his way close enough to the other vessel to hail her. Conditions were so bad, in fact, that it took five days. Finally, on September 16, using all the skill and experience at his command, Buddington was able to finish maneuvering the *George Henry* through the floes until only a single large mass of ice separated the two ships. One thing became instantly clear: The other vessel, whoever she was, was no whaleship. She was huge, at least six hundred tons, with its entire hull sheathed to cut through ice. Immediately, Buddington ran up a signal flag indicating that he wished to speak with the other captain. There was no reply. *George Henry*'s crew then gathered at the rail and began shouting across the ice pack to the other vessel. Still there was no response.

Now mystified, Buddington ordered his two mates, John Quayle and Norris Havens, and two of his seamen, George Tyson and a whaler known only as Tallinghast, to walk across the ice pack and board the silent ship. It was not an easy crossing. The four men were forced to struggle over huge mounds of ice and to use ice rafts to carry them over open stretches of water. "As we approached within sight," Tyson later wrote, "we looked in vain for any signs of life. Could it be that all on board were sick or dead? What could it mean? Surely if there was any living soul on board, a party of four men traveling toward her across the hummocky ice would naturally excite their curiosity. But no one appeared."

Finally reaching the vessel, they climbed aboard. Spying a nameplate, they discovered that they were now standing on the deck of the HMS *Resolute*. Moving ahead, they encountered the unmanned pilot's wheel. Inscribed in brass letters around it were the words "England expects that every man will do his duty." This was no whaling vessel. This was a ship of the British navy. But where were her sailors? Nowhere on deck was there a person to be seen. What they found, Tyson later recounted, was "a deathlike silence and a dread repose."

Spotting the cabin door, they kicked it in, went below, and were astounded by what greeted them. Lamps and vases rested on small tables. Plates, glasses, knives, forks, and spoons were arranged on a much larger table as if the ship's occupants were about to begin a meal. In what was obviously one of the officers' cabins, books lay open, giving the impression that their owners had just stepped out of the room and would return momentarily to resume their reading. The captain's epaulets were draped over a chair. Clothing, toiletries, and scores of other personal items lay neatly about the crew's quarters. Tin playing cards were laid out, indicating that a game had been in progress. A quick check of the galley revealed dozens of shelves of canned meat waiting to be opened. But there was absolutely no member of the *Resolute* aboard. Not a soul. Who were they? Where had they come from? What had happened to them? The men of the *George Henry* had discovered a ghost ship.

Their orders were to report back to Buddington as soon as they had identified themselves to the officers and crew of the mystery ship. Anxious as they were to convey their startling news to the captain, they realized that daylight was rapidly fading. To risk making the return crossing in the dark was to court disaster. They would spend the night where they were.

They awoke to a raging snowstorm, one that kept them aboard the Resolute for the next three days. Not that they minded. There were plenty of diversions aboard the spacious vessel to amuse men who had spent the last four months confined aboard their cramped whaleship. "Among other things," Tyson recorded in his journal, "we found some uniforms of the officers, in which we arranged ourselves, buckling on the swords, and putting on the cocked hats, treating ourselves as British officers . . . Well, we had what sailors call a 'good time,' getting up an impromptu sham duel; and before those swords were laid aside one was cut in twain, and the others were hacked and beaten to pieces, taking care, however, not to harm our precious bodies, through we did some hard fighting."

Not surprisingly, all of the high jinks were accompanied by the drinking of wine that they had found almost as soon as they had entered the living quarters. Later, Tyson would recall the event that followed his first tasting of that wine as the most memorable incident of his initial encounter with the great English ship. "The decanters of wine, with which the late officers had last regaled themselves, were still sitting on the table, some of the wine still remaining in the glasses, and in the rack around the mizen-mast were a number of other glasses and decanters,"Tyson wrote. "Some of my companions appeared to feel somewhat superstitious, and hesitated to drink the wine, but my long and fatiguing walk made it very acceptable to me, and having helped myself to a glass, and they seeing it did not kill me, an expression of intense relief came over their countenances, and they all, with one accord, went for that wine with a will and there and then we all drank a bumper to the late officers and crew of the *Resolute.*"

It was a poignant moment, hardened whalemen paying tribute to a mysterious crew. Yet before the third quarter of the nineteenth century was over, it would be but one of many similarly remarkable happenings that would take place in a foreboding land which, when the century began, was still mostly a vast blank on the map. This immense, uncharted region would provide the backdrop for one of history's most compelling stories, a saga that would include unforgettable characters, murder, intrigue, cannibalism, unprecedented heroics, triumph and tragedy, and the greatest mystery of the age. It began with the obsession to find the Northwest Passage.

As the second decade of the nineteenth century began, England, having established itself as the ruler of the seas, was about to embark on a new age of discovery, motivated in great measure by the desire to advance scientific discovery. Unknown waters waited to be charted. Unexplored coastlines and the land beyond them needed to be explored and mapped. The inhabitants of these lands needed to be found and their surroundings and ways of life encountered and recorded. Geographical puzzles needed to be solved. What was the source of the Nile? Was the Congo a separate entity or did it join up with the Nile, making them one great river? Could the North Pole be reached?

But there was another, even more deep-rooted, motivation for discovery as well. In a world where trade was paramount to prosperity, failure to discover new routes to coveted markets meant being left behind. And in early nineteenth-century England that meant, above everything else, finding a shorter route to the Orient. Since before Christianity, spices from Asia had been at the core of world trade. But acquiring the pepper, cinnamon, cloves, nutmeg, and other exotic spices meant either dealing with price-gouging Venetian merchants or making the long, expensive, and dangerous voyage around Cape Horn or the Cape of Good Hope. For more than four hundred years, Europeans had sought a shorter, safer route, one that would allow them to travel directly from the Atlantic to the Pacific by sailing through the Arctic, north of Canada. But did such a passageway exist? That was the big question, one that would make the quest for a Northwest Passage nothing short of akin to the search for the Holy Grail. (The quest for a commercial passage occupied the hearts and minds of men for centuries; see note, page 269.)

None of the earlier searches for the passage had even come close to succeeding. Whatever place names existed on the sketchy Arctic map—those of Cabot, Foxe, Hudson, Frobisher, Baffin, and others— were names of men who had tried and failed. Throughout the sixteenth, seventeenth, and eighteenth centuries, as ships disappeared and explorers failed to return, interest in the passage first waned and then all but vanished. By the nineteenth century, however, England had become a much different nation than that from which the pioneer Arctic explorers had sailed. England's Industrial Revolution, combined with a series of ringing military victories, had imbued the country with unprecedented national pride, a confidence that anything, including the discovery of the passage, could be accomplished.

Yet, despite all this, it is safe to say that the renewed effort to find the coveted route would never have taken place when it did had it not been for the determination and efforts of one man. His name was John Barrow and he was unquestionably the father of Arctic exploration.

Barrow's early life gave little indication of how far he would rise or how much influence he would eventually have on future events. He was born in 1764 in the small northern English village of Ulverston where his father was a journeyman farmer. His formal education ended

John Barrow devoted more than forty years of his life to organizing the search for the Northwest Passage.

at the age of thirteen when he left school and went to work as a clerk in a Liverpool iron foundry. When he was sixteen, he joined a whaling expedition to Greenland.

Humble beginnings indeed but, from the first, Barrow, a dark-haired, moon-faced young man, had demonstrated a high intelligence, a thirst for knowledge, and an appetite for work. Although his education was brief, he had, by the time he left school, proved himself unusually skilled at mathematics and had learned to read and write both Latin and Greek.

During his whaling voyage, he had developed a deep interest in navigation and astronomy and had become fascinated with the frigid areas of the far North.

And somehow he had an inborn talent for recognizing opportunity and taking advantage of it. After returning from his whaling venture, he used his mathematical aptitude to get a job teaching the subject in Greenwich. He also earned extra money by tutoring, an activity that unexpectedly changed his life and fortunes. One of the young men he tutored was the son of a wealthy English lord. When, thanks to Barrow's tutoring, his pupil's grades improved dramatically, the lord recommended Barrow to Lord George Macartney, who had just been appointed England's first ambassador to China. On his own, Barrow had learned Chinese, and when Macartney left for his new post he took Barrow with him as his interpreter. Later, when Macartney was given a new post in Africa, Barrow accompanied him as his aide.

Serving with Macartney in Africa soon provided Barrow with yet another opportunity to further what was rapidly becoming a meteoric career. While there, he met and impressed General Francis Dundas, a member of one of England's most powerful and influential families.

Dundas's uncle was Lord Henry Melville. And, when Melville was appointed First Lord of the Admiralty, both Macartney and Dundas convinced him to name Barrow the Admiralty's Second Secretary.

It was unprecedented in British class-dominated politics. This son of an itinerant village farmer had, before he was forty, risen to one of the most prestigious positions in the nation, an office which, in fact, was far more powerful than the name implied. Under the English naval system, the Admiralty was overseen by a board made up of seven lords and two secretaries. None of the lords had any true knowledge of or interest in naval affairs. It was the secretaries who made the decisions, which they then recommended to the board. Like the members of the board, the First Secretary was a member of Parliament whose main responsibility was to deal with all political matters that concerned the navy. It was the Second Secretary who was responsible for day-to-day operations and, if he was so inclined, was in the position to initiate key policy decisions. And John Barrow was more than willing, able, and ambitious enough to take on this responsibility.

Barrow officially became Second Secretary in 1804. Except for a one-year period, he would serve in that post for more than forty years. He brought to the position not only his intelligence and his skills, but also his extraordinary devotion to work (some historians have estimated that he read and answered some forty thousand letters a year) and his unflagging dedication to any cause about which he was passionate. During his first thirty-five years in office, the British navy waged five wars in which, among other victories, the last remains of French naval power were eliminated, the Algerian pirates were finally overcome, the Chinese fleet was destroyed during the Opium Wars, and the Egyptians were driven out of Syria. But, despite these triumphs, military victory was not his main interest. His consuming passion was exploration, particularly that which would lead to the discovery of the Northwest Passage.

Most of this passion was motivated by pure national pride. He was convinced that the search for the passage (and for the exploration of other areas of the world) would immeasurably enhance England's contribution to scientific knowledge. "To what purpose could a portion of our naval force be, . . . more honorably or more usefully employed," he would write, "than in completing those details of geographical and hydrographical science of which the grand outlines have been boldly and broadly sketched by Cook, Vancouver, and Flinders, and others of our countrymen?"

Barrow was, of course, also motivated by the commercial advantages that a Northwest Passage would bring. But perhaps more compelling than anything else—even greater than his obsession with exploring the unknown—was his almost obsessive desire to make certain that no other country such as the United States or Russia be the first to find the passage. For him nothing less than national honor was at stake. "It would be somewhat mortifying," he stated, "if a naval power but of yesterday should complete a discovery in the nineteenth century, which was so happily commenced by Englishmen in the sixteenth."

Fortunately for Barrow the time had never been so propitious to launch his passage quest. English ships were more powerful than ever, the fruits of the Industrial Revolution were making more money available to the Admiralty than ever before, and there were, he believed, officers in the British navy bold and skilled enough to make it happen. "From the zeal and abilities of the persons [to be] employed in the arduous enterprise," he predicted, "everything may be expected to be done within the scope of possibility."

Not only was it possible, but it could be accomplished, he believed, in a single season. It was an optimism without foundation. For, in truth, Barrow, like almost everyone else of his time—except the whalers—knew very little about the Arctic. He was convinced that the North Pole was surrounded by an Open Polar Sea, a warm, ice-free ocean, entry into which was blocked by a barrier of ice. Break through this barrier, enter the Open Polar Sea, he told the first seekers he sent out, and you'll find the passage.

He could not have been more wrong. There was no Open Polar Sea and, as his explorers quickly discovered, the Arctic was unlike any place they could ever have imagined—enormous (more than one million square miles), confusing, foreboding, and immensely dangerous. It was, as later commentators would characterize it, an "Otherworld" marked by extraordinary extremes. For two months in the summer the sun never set. For more than two months in the winter it was never seen. "I long for the sunlight," American polar explorer Elisha Kent Kane wrote poetically in his journal during his first voyage to the Arctic in 1850. "Dear sun, no wonder you are worshipped." From January to July in particular, temperatures could range from forty degrees below zero to fourteen above. The logs of various passage-seekers recorded temperatures as low as sixty degrees below zero. Yet, on one of four expeditions led by Edward Parry, the British rear admiral, there was a period during which temperatures rose to sixty-six. The sun was so hot that tar oozed out of the seams of Parry's ships. To his astonishment, it actually rained for thirty consecutive hours.

But mostly the Arctic was unbelievably cold. On an Arctic expedition in 1848, one of the sailors aboard the HMS *Enterprise* foolishly attempted to carry out some work without wearing gloves. When one of his hands froze, he tried to thaw it out by putting it in a basin of water. His hand was so cold that it froze the water solid, and the poor sailor had to have it amputated.

It was frigid; it was unpredictable—but above all else it was a region dominated by ice. "Lagoons are largely closed by the end of [September]," whaling historian Everett S. Allen noted in his 1973 book, *Children of the Light*:

> Ice in the freshwater ponds is already ten inches to a foot thick, and the weather very likely may be no better . . . until spring. By sometime in November, ice begins to form in the ocean. This is the beginning of the sea's closing, the freezing of the pack that may remain unbroken, not only until the early summer following, but even later, if there is no offshore wind to help the rising temperature dissipate it. Sometimes in the fall, the gales drive the main pack of ice in toward the land. But if this does not happen, the sea alongshore freezes over comparatively smoothly except for the small floes that always drift back and forth. . . . This shore

*ice may remain unbroken until midwinter when the heavy,
continuing winds from the west drive in the old pack ice that lies
parallel to the coast and about one and a half miles from it. Inside
this bar, the ice often forms to a thickness of more than five feet,
with four fathoms of water below that. One might consider this a
possible winter anchorage for a ship . . . except that periodically, the
bar is not enough to hold off the wind-driven pack coming in from
the sea. And when the old ice drives in on the land, it comes with
terrible force, and nothing can survive its crushing."*

Those who sought the passage left home knowing that the journey
would inevitably include at least one winter, if not more, locked in the
ice, unable to move until a hoped-for spring thaw, always aware of
the deadly unpredictability of the ice that imprisoned them. They also
knew that, even under the best of circumstances, wintering in the ice
would be a supreme test of their courage and resolve. "When the cabin
door was opened," recalled one Arctic adventurer, "a blast of cold air
rushed in, causing condensation which made the walls damp. At night-
time the condensation froze, and we slept in a miniature ice palace,
crystals sparkling in the light, gleaming icicles hanging from the deck
above, some several inches long. All along the outer side of my bunk
was a sheet of ice which melted when I got into bed, so that during the
night the upper part of my blanket was sodden while the bottom half
was like a small ice floe."

Not that the Arctic was without its unique beauty. Even the most
articulate of the explorers found themselves lacking the words to adequately describe the magnificence of the aurora borealis, a sight made
even more unforgettable by the fact that it appeared most often during
the calmest, coldest nights when the frozen world around them was
eerily silent. The crusty polar veteran John Ross was moved to wax
poetic about the icebergs that never failed to amaze him. "It is hardly
possible to imagine anything more exquisite," he wrote. "By night as
well as by day they glitter with a vividness of color beyond the power
of art to represent."

There was one Arctic phenomenon, however, that was as disturbing as it was often beautiful. At one time or another, almost every venturer into the frozen North experienced dramatic mirages caused both by the refraction of the pale Arctic light and the seemingly endless snow- and ice-covered flat landscape. Seeing things that weren't really there was, at best, disturbing. At worst, it led to claims of discoveries of mountains or bodies of water that existed only in the "discoverer's" imagination. Elisha Kane found himself particularly prone to these mirages. "There is a black globe floating in the air about three [degrees] north of the sun," he noted in his journal. "Is it a bird or a balloon? . . . On a sudden, it changes shape . . . It is a grand piano . . . You had hardly named it before it was an anvil . . . *Presto* it has made itself duplicate—a pair of colossal dumbbells. A moment! and it is the black globe again."

A ship floats past a glacier in an illustration from Elisha Kent Kane's best-selling book *Arctic Explorations* (1857). Like most of his fellow northern explorers, Kane never stopped marveling at the ever-threatening yet sublime Arctic landscape, particularly the icebergs he encountered.

A volatile land of bitter uncertainties, the Arctic was indeed a place like no other. The thousands who sought the passage and the thousands of others who went searching for those who disappeared in the quest quickly learned that, above all else, it was the most humbling experience of their lives. On his first exedition to the Arctic, Elisha Kane was fascinated with the icebergs he encountered. In his journal he wrote: "An iceberg is one of God's own buildings, preaching its lessons of humility to the miniature structures of man."

So why did they do it? Why did they sail off into the most hostile environment imaginable, into uncharted waters, never knowing what lay ahead or whether they would ever return? Some, no doubt, were lured by the financial rewards that Barrow, in 1818, had persuaded Parliament to offer to whoever could penetrate furthest into the Arctic. The first passage-seeker to reach longitude 110 degrees west would receive £5,000. Whoever first reached 130 degrees west would get twice that amount. At 150 degrees west, the prize soared to £15,000. The jackpot would go to the explorer who first reached the Pacific, making the Northwest Passage a reality: £20,000, or almost a million and a half U.S. dollars in today's currency.

It was a strong enticement, but one that would benefit only the few who achieved these goals. A much larger motivation lay in the state of British naval affairs. By 1817, England's long war with France was over, Napoleon was in exile, Europe was at peace, and there were no wars left to occupy the British navy. Of the 140,000 seamen who had fought in the Napoleonic Wars, more than 120,000 had been discharged. Six thousand officers had been retained, but now there was little meaning-ful work for them to do. Without the challenges and dangers of war, there was little chance for heroism, little chance for public acclaim, and thus little chance for advancing their careers, which was the consuming ambition of all British naval officers. The opportunity for recognition suddenly presented by the renewed search for the Northwest Passage offered a way to excel. Three hundred years after he uttered them, the words of early British passage-seeker Martin Frobisher still rang true.

The discovery of the Northwest Passage, he had declared, "is still the only thing left undone, whereby a notable mind might be made famous and remarkable."

There were other motivations as well. An anonymous thirteenth-century Viking explorer explained his reasons for undertaking a voyage to Greenland and Vinland, in a treatise entitled *The King's Mirror*: "As you are anxious to know what one looks for in that land, or why one goes there at such peril, it is that one is moved to do so by the character of human nature, . . . the thirst for knowledge: for in man's nature lies that inclination to explore and see things of which he has been told, in order to know whether it is as he has been told or not." After four hundred years, only the periphery of the Arctic had been explored. For those brave enough to sail in to the unknown, the search for the Northwest Passage presented the greatest chance they would ever have to attain immortality by, as Alfred Lord Tennyson put it, "inscribing themselves on the Arctic chart."

All of these men also brought something else with them, something that transcended the desire for promotion and fame. Almost to a man, they saw themselves as knights of old, off on a romantic, quasi-religious crusade. Like John Barrow, they were determined that the passage be found by Englishmen, not Americans or Russians, and that the landmarks of the Arctic, once discovered, be marked with English names. At the same time, they were imbued with the unshakable belief that the English way of doing things was the only way.

Almost all the naval officers were from the British upper class. Their inbred Victorian snobbery would not permit them to listen to the advice of English or American whalers, men who had spent years coping with the Arctic environment. Once in the Arctic, most of the officers did not seek the help or advice of the natives, insisting instead on having their heavy, equipment-laden sledges pulled by their men— rather than by dogs, in the fashion of those who lived in the frozen North. And they remained in the Arctic dressed in full dress British wool uniforms rather than in the practical furs worn by the Inuit. It was an arrogance that went beyond national pride. It would lead to extraordinary heroics and accomplishments. But it would also lead to colossal failures and tragedies.

They were a special breed, these men who sought the passage. They wanted to be heroes, and, for the most part, they were. Driven by a noble obsession, they were willing to leave homes, wives, and families behind for the credit of finding something new. Most had no choice. " They cannot help it," England's former Lord Chancellor, Lord Henry Brougham explained. "It is in the blood."

CHAPTER 2

First Attempts

"Thus vanished our golden dreams, our brilliant hopes,
our high expectations."
—WILLIAM HOOPER, purser, HMS *Alexander*

WHATEVER THEIR MOTIVATION, the would-be explorers' chances for fame, fortune, or promotion depended upon being selected by John Barrow to take part in his crusade. Early in 1818, a royal decree announced that the crusade was about to begin:

His Royal Highness the Prince Regent having signified his pleasure to Viscount Melville, that an attempt should be made to discover a Northern Passage, by sea, from the Atlantic to the Pacific Ocean; We have in consequence thereof, caused four ships or vessels to be fitted out and appropriated for that purpose; two of which, the Isabella *and the* Alexander, *are intended to proceed together by the north-westward through Davis' Strait; and two, the* Dorothea *and the* Trent, *in a direction as due north as may be found practicable through the Spitsbergen sea.*

Actually, the decree was misleading. Barrow was not sending all four ships out to find the Northwest Passage. That was the mission of the *Isabella* and the *Alexander*. The task of the *Dorothea* and the *Trent* was to reach the North Pole. Although it was never as much of a priority for Barrow as finding the passage, the discovery of the North Pole, he knew, would be a great feather in England's cap. Heaven forbid that the first person to step out on the Pole hail from another nation. And, in Barrow's mind, reaching the Pole should not be any more difficult than discovering the route to the Orient.

Although none of the officers who Barrow chose to lead the two expeditions had ever been anywhere near the Arctic, he was certain that they would succeed. His belief in them and his confidence that they would accomplish their missions with relative ease were evident in the orders he gave them. After David Buchan, leader of the North Pole expedition and commander of the *Dorothea,* and Lieutenant John Franklin, commander of the *Trent,* crossed the Pole, they were to rendezvous with John Ross and Edward Parry, who had been selected to find the passage.

Buchan's main claim to fame as a naval officer had been his 1811 penetration some 160 miles into the interior of Newfoundland. Franklin had been at sea since he was twelve and had taken part in the historic naval battles of Copenhagen, Trafalgar, and New Orleans. Barrow had, in all probability, chosen Buchan because of his reputation for physical toughness—particularly the hardiness he had demonstrated during an 1811 expedition to Newfoundland where, despite horrendous weather and constant icy conditions, he had penetrated some 160 miles into the interior. John Franklin had been born in 1786 in the small eastern town of Spilsby, in Lincolnshire County. His father had wanted him to enter the church, but the youngster was determined to become a sailor. When he was fourteen, Franklin joined the British navy. Although he had seen action at the battles of Copenhagen, Trafalgar, and New Orleans, he was, unlike Buchan, anything but tough; he was regarded as a person who, if he could possibly avoid it, would not harm a fly. An officer who served with him remembered how Franklin's hands had trembled when he had been compelled to have one of his sailors flogged. It was his greatest trait, and ultimately, his final undoing.

In 1818, as John Barrow was about to send Buchan, Franklin, Ross, and Parry off on their quests, whaler William Scoresby was putting the finishing touches on a book titled *An Account of the Arctic Regions with a History and Description of the Northern Whale Fishery*. No other person was as qualified to write such a book, for its contents were the result of the more than sixty thousand miles Scoresby had traveled on and through the ice during the seventeen voyages he had made to the frozen North. When, in 1820, the book was published, it was hailed

An etching from William Scoresby's seminal book on Arctic whaling illustrates the dangers of the job. Long before John Barrow launched his first passage search, whalemen like Scoresby braved the Arctic waters hunting the world's greatest creatures. The story of the quest for the passage would probably have been much different if the Admiralty had taken advantage of Scoresby's knowledge and advice.

as "one of the most remarkable books in the English language." Today it is widely regarded as nothing less than "the foundation stone of Arctic science."

Born in 1789 in Cropton, Yorkshire, Scoresby was the son of a highly successful whaling captain. He was only eleven years old when he made his first whaling voyage with his father, and was still only sixteen when, as the elder Scoresby's first mate, they reached a latitude of 82°30', the northernmost point that had ever been attained at sea.

Scoresby was twenty-one when he was given command of his own whaling vessel, and during the next two decades he became the greatest of all English whalemen. Even more successful than his father had been, he brought back larger hauls of whale oil and bone, made more money, and probed deeper into ice-filled waters than any of his competitors.

But his interests went well beyond catching whales. From an early age he was fascinated with science, particularly physical geography, magnetism, and the natural history of the polar regions. Every winter, between whaling voyages, he devoted himself to studying science and philosophy. When he returned to sea he found time, when not pursuing whales, to add to his scientific knowledge. On one of his first voyages, he made important observations on the nature of snow and ice crystals. On another, employing a brass water-sampling bottle that he had invented (dubbed a "marine diver"), Scoresby established, for the first time, that the water on the ocean floor was warmer than at the surface. Another of his inventions was a contraption that looked very much like a pair of skis (which he had never seen) that made it much easier to walk across the Arctic ice pack.

As early as 1810, Scoresby became fascinated with the prospect of a Northwest Passage. He was, in fact, one of the first to urge key members of the Admiralty to launch a renewed search. But the letters he wrote them also contained cautions based on what he had learned from his northern whaling voyages. "I firmly believe," he wrote, "that if . . . a passage does exist, it will be found only at intervals of some years." This was, he said, because conditions in the Arctic were almost never the same in successive years. The same strait, sound, or other water-way that was free of ice one season might well be completely frozen over the next. Because of this, he stated, even if the passage was found, "it might not again be practical in ten or twenty years." As even today's mariners have learned, he was absolutely right.

In his letters suggesting that the time was now propitious to seek the Passage, Scoresby left no doubt that he believed that he was the man to head one of the earliest expeditions. But he was never chosen. One of the reasons was that he and John Barrow never saw eye to eye on many things regarding both the nature of the Arctic and how an Arctic search should be conducted. This was particularly true of Barrow's belief in the existence of an Open Polar Sea. Scoresby had seen the barriers of ice that lay in the Arctic. How could Barrow believe that to the north, beyond the barriers—where temperatures actually were lower—there could be a warmer, ice-free sea?

However, the main reason that Scoresby was never chosen to lead a search had nothing to do with his disagreement with Barrow's theories. It was simply because he was a whaling captain, not a British naval officer. In the class-conscious English naval system, it was proper for experienced whalemen to be employed as "ice masters" upon royal ships, but certainly not as captains of naval vessels.

Not only was Scoresby not selected, but the advice that he con-tinually offered as others searched the Arctic was also most often dis-regarded. He was ignored when he said that the polar ice cap drifted, causing continual changes in the flow and location of the ice pack. He was ignored when he suggested that rather than pulling their heavy sledges across the frozen landscape themselves, the explorers should, like the Inuit, use lighter sledges pulled by dogs. And he was ignored when he warned that sledging parties needed to conduct their searches early in the season when the ice cap was still frozen solid and thus relatively flat, rather than later when the ice became so uneven and bumpy that it was it was often almost impossible to traverse. One of the biggest mistakes the Admiralty made was not taking advantage of the participation and advice of William Scoresby.

Buchan and Franklin sailed from England in April 1818. At first, things could not have gone better. Arriving at Spitsbergen's Magdalena Bay around June 1, they were astounded by what they first encountered—icebergs whose size and shapes were unlike anything they ever could have imagined, a sun that never set. But abruptly it all changed. On June 7, just as they were entering a vast ice field, enormous winds blew in, coating both the *Dorothea* and the *Trent* with tons of ice. The crews of both vessels were forced to hack away at the ice on their bows and ropes in order to keep the ships under control.

By June 12, they could move no further. "The brig, cutting her way through the light ice, came in violent contact with the [now hardening] pack," recounted Lieutenant Frederick William Beechey, a geologist aboard the *Trent*. "In an instant, we all lost our footing, the masts bent with the impetus, and the cracking timbers below bespoke [enormous] pressure. The channels by degrees disappeared, and the ice, with its accustomed rapidity, soon became packed, encircled the vessels and pressed so closely upon them that one boundless plain of rugged snow extended in every direction."

For more than three weeks the ships remained trapped. At one point, a party tried to walk to the shore but got lost in dense fog. Fortunately, a rescue party found them and led them back to the ship. Then, on July 6, temperatures rose and the ice that surrounded the ships suddenly began to break apart. Immediately, they began sailing up what Buchan believed to be a promising open stretch of water. But that night the ice returned, locking in the vessels even more tightly than before.

Desperate to escape the icy prison, Buchan ordered that both ships be warped forward. This meant attaching anchors to far-off blocks of ice and then winching the vessels towards them. For three days, the backbreaking warping continued, with frustrating results. At one point the vessels actually slipped back two miles. In the process, both ships were damaged by the ice, and the *Trent* began to spring leaks.

To his credit, Buchan refused to give in. He knew that open sea was some thirty miles away, and for the next three weeks, day and night, the warping continued. Initially, it took five hours to move the vessels forward just one mile, but he urged the men on and finally the open waters were reached. At this point, despite the weariness of his crews and the battered condition of his ships, he headed west for Greenland, still hoping to find a passage that would lead to the Pole. But within twenty-four hours, a sudden, unrelenting storm drove the ships back to the very edge of the ice pack from which they had so laboriously escaped. When the storm abated, the *Dorothea* and the *Trent* were found to be in even worse condition than before. Buchan was, at last, forced to admit that his search for the Pole had to be abandoned.

After putting into Spitsbergen Harbor, where both vessels were repaired, the expedition headed for home. But even then, Buchan was not ready to totally abandon hope. Four times during the return voyage he tried to penetrate the ice pack, only to find no opening. Finally, when severe weather threatened once more he had to admit defeat. In the third week of October the *Dorothea* and the *Trent* arrived back in England. They had not found the Pole. Despite their heroics, they had not, in fact, even reached the northernmost recorded point of 80°48'.

Meantime, nothing had been heard from the two ships that Barrow had sent in search of the bigger prize. The *Isabella*, commanded by the expedition's leader John Ross, and the *Alexander*, with Edward Parry in command, had set sail just three days after Buchan and Franklin had departed on their ill-fated voyage. Both officers had been carefully chosen. The son of a Protestant minister, John Ross had entered the Royal Navy when he was only nine years old and was a veteran of the Napoleonic Wars. Short, red-haired, and both stubborn and vain, he was known for his quick temper. Yet, when he needed to, he could be disarmingly charming. Edward Parry had also seen action in these wars and in the British-American War of 1812, during which, in 1814, he took part in the destruction of twenty-seven American vessels on the Connecticut River. The physical opposite of Ross, the dashing Parry was tall, slender, and among the most handsome of all the naval officers.

The first of Barrow's passage-seekers, John Ross was still searching the Arctic when he was seventy-three years old.

The intrepid Edward Parry led three searches for the passage; he also commanded an expedition seeking the North Pole.

He was also one of the most ambitious. The son of a prosperous doctor, he moved easily through the highest levels of British society.

Barrow had given specific orders to the two explorers. Among other objectives, they were to attempt to solve Arctic riddles that were the result of much earlier explorations. Did the bay that William Baffin claimed to have discovered, one that Barrow felt was key to finding the passage, really exist? And what about Greenland? Was it an island, or was it connected to North America? They were also to make navigational recordings, including currents and tides, and were to collect whatever specimens they could find. Barrow's orders, however, made it very clear that their main objective, by far, was "to endeavor to ascertain the practicability of a passage from the Atlantic to the Pacific Ocean along the Northern Coast of America."

By the middle of June, the pair had entered Davis Strait, and, like Buchan and Franklin had been, Ross and Parry were dazzled by the colors, shapes, and colossal size of the icebergs and frozen mountains they drifted past. Some of the bergs, with their tall columns supporting icy slabs, reminded Parry of the mysterious structure at Stonehenge. A deeply religious man, he would later write that the magnificence of the landscape around him immediately caused him to ponder "upon the immensity of the creator who could call these enormous masses of ice into being." To th explorers' amazement, they discovered that they were not alone. After sailing a few miles up the strait, they encountered a fleet of thirty-six British whaleships whose crew cheered their arrival. But the whalers also had dire warnings for the explorers: The ice, they told them, was building up faster and earlier than in previous winters.

Sobered by the warnings, Ross and Perry moved on along the Greenland coast, picking their way through steadily mounting ice floes, constantly surrounded by dense fog. Then, near-disaster struck. Without warning a vicious gale erupted, causing the ships to collide, tearing apart spars, rigging, and lifeboats. When the storm abated the pair resumed their search, aware that a similar event could take place at any time.

Two days later, they made their first discovery—the Netsilik people, an Inuit culture that was completely unknown to the outside world. The Netsilik had never seen a white man. They had no knowledge of ships or boats and, in fact, thought that the vessels were alive. When one of the British officers showed the Inuits his watch, they thought that it, too, was a living being. They were particularly astounded at the sight of John Sacheuse, the native interpreter from South Greenland whom Ross had brought along on the voyage. They had no idea that other people like them existed.

The Englishmen were just as ignorant about the natives. When Parry's landing boat touched shore he had one of his officers carry a white flag with an olive branch painted on it—the universal sign of peace. The natives had no idea of what it meant. Not only had they never seen a flag; they had never seen a tree. But, thanks to Sacheuse's interpreting skills and Ross's desire to make friends with whatever natives he encountered, a rapport with the Inuit was established. Later, Ross described how this was accomplished in his 1819 published journal, descriptively titled *A Voyage of Discovery, Made Under the Orders of the Admiralty, in His Majesty's Ships* Isabella *and* Alexander, *for the*

Purpose of Exploring Baffin's Bay, and Inquiring into the Probability of a North-West Passage:

> *[The Eskimos] now began to ask many questions; for, by this time, they found the language spoken by themselves and Sacheuse, had sufficient resemblance to enable them to hold some communication. They first pointed to the ships, eagerly asking, 'What great creatures [are] those?' 'Do they come from the sun or the moon?' 'Do they give us light by night or by day?' Sacheuse replied, 'They are houses made of wood.' This they seemed to discredit, answering, 'No, they are alive, we have seen them move their wings,'... Our arrival produced a visible alarm, causing them to retreat a few steps towards their sledges; on this Sacheuse called to us to pull our noses, as he had discovered this to be the mode of friendly salutation with them. This ceremony was accordingly performed by each of us, the natives, during their retreat, making use of the same gesture, the nature of which we had not before understood. In the same way we imitated their shouts as well as we could, using the same interjection, heigh, yaw! which we afterwards found to be an expression of surprise and pleasure. We then advanced towards them while they halted, and presented the foremost with a looking glass and a knife, repeating the same presents to the whole, as they came up in succession. On seeing their faces in the glasses, their astonishment appeared extreme, and they looked round in silence, for a moment, at each other and at us; immediately afterwards they set up a general shout, succeeded by a loud laugh, expressive of extreme delight, as well as surprise, in which we joined, partly from inability to avoid it, and willing also to show that we were pleased with our new acquaintances.*

It was an extraordinary encounter. But it would prove to be a fateful missed opportunity as well. For now that they had established rapport with the natives, it never entered any of the white men's minds to ask the Inuit to explain how they managed to survive in such a hostile environment. It would not be the last time that such an opportunity was ignored—a lapse that would lead to tragic consequences in the future.

Leaving the natives, Ross and Parry sailed on and in mid-August made an even more important discovery, or more accurately, rediscovery. In finding what Ross's charts told him was undisputedly Baffin Bay, he realized that he was entering what Barrow believed was one of the gateways to discovering the passage. And after two centuries, he was confirming the fact that William Baffin had indeed discovered this important body of water. Baffin had long been one of Ross's heroes and later he would write of the satisfaction he derived in proving wrong those who, for so long, had doubted Baffin's accomplishment. (The existence of Baffin Bay had the subject of controversy since the early seventeenth century; see note, page 270.)

"In re-discovering Baffin's Bay," he wrote, "I have derived great additional pleasure from the reflection I have placed in a fair light before the Public, the merits of a worthy and able Navigator [William Baffin]; whose fate, like that of many others, it has not only been to have lost, by a combination of untoward circumstances, the opportunity of acquiring during his life-time the fame he deserved; but could he have lived to this period to have seen his discoveries expunged from the records of geography, and the bay with which his name is so fairly associated, treated as a phantom of the imagination."

After sailing through Baffin Bay without incident, Ross and Parry then followed the west coast of Greenland northward until, on August 19, they entered Smith Sound, distinguished by the two capes that lay on either side—which Ross named for his two ships. Two weeks later, they found the entrance to Lancaster Sound, another water-way that Barrow and others believed might be a vital link in the passage.

Shortly before entering Lancaster Sound, Ross had mistakenly thought that he had spotted a large body of land, one of several mirages that he had experienced during the voyage. But Lancaster Sound was not a mirage. Parry, in particular, was now convinced that the great prize was before them. Noting in his journal that the current in the sound flowed exactly as it did in the open ocean, he wrote: "It is impossible to remark this circumstance without feeling a hope that it may be caused by this inlet being a passage into a sea to the westward of it."

Ross however was not sure. Thirty miles up the sound, with Parry sailing some leagues behind him, his doubts, he believed, were confirmed. Peering off into the distance through a break in the fog he spotted a long range of connected, formidable mountains that completely blocked any further passage. Later in his published account of the voyage, Ross would recall what he saw:

> At half past two, (when I went off to dinner), there were some hopes of its clearing, and I left orders to be called on the appearance of land or ice ahead. At three, the officer of the watch, who was relieved to his dinner by Mr. Lewis, reported, on his coming into the cabin, that there was some appearance of its clearing at the bottom of the bay; I immediately, therefore, went on deck, and soon after it completely cleared for about ten minutes, and I distinctly saw the land, round the bottom of the bay, forming a connected chain of mountains with those which extended along the north and south sides. This land appeared to be at the distance of eight leagues; and Mr. Lewis, the master, and James Haig, leading man, being sent for, they took its bearings which were inserted in the log; the water on the surface was at temperature of 34. At this moment I also saw a continuity of ice, at the distance of seven miles, extending from one side of the bay to the other, between the nearest cape to the north, which I named after Sir George Warrender, and that to the south, which was named after Viscount Castlereagh. The mountains, which occupied the center, in a north and south direction, were named Croker's Mountains, after the Secretary of the Admiralty.

Immediately upon spotting what he believed to be an impenetrable barrier, Ross ordered his crew to halt the *Isabella*. Declaring that to continue would be fruitless, he not only ordered that the ship be turned around and sailed back through the sound, but commanded that it should continue on directly back to England. If there were indeed mountains blocking his way, and if Ross had continued sailing toward them only to find that they were impassable, his decision to abort the voyage through Lancaster Sound would seem justified. But to abandon the search for the passage altogether? As Parry would later point out, there were enough provisions on both ships to permit the explorers to winter down and then resume the search after the spring thaw.

Even more inexplicable was the fact that not only had Ross decided not to sail further to determine if the mountains were indeed impenetrable, but no one else on either ship had seen the mountains. The answer was quite simple. They were not there. The Croker Mountains existed only in Ross's imagination. He had suffered his most serious mirage.

As the *Isabella* sailed back past him, the astonished Parry had no choice but to follow his commander. He, and most of the other men, were angry and disappointed. Their feelings were dramatically expressed by the *Alexander*'s purser, William Hooper. "Thus vanished our golden dreams, our brilliant hopes, our high expectations," he wrote in his journal, "and without the satisfaction of proving these dreams to be visionary, these hopes to be fallacious, those expectations to be delusive! To describe our mortification and disappointment would be impossible, at thus having our increasing hopes annihilated in a moment, without the shadow of reasoning appearing."

Why did John Ross turn tail and head for home? Perhaps, as was the case with so many others who would follow him, his struggles through the Arctic, although relatively brief, simply proved too much for him. Perhaps he never really believed that there was Northwest Passage, and despite Barrow's orders, felt that his real objective was to rediscover Baffin Bay. It remains a puzzle, one of the first of many mysteries that would be so much a part of nineteenth-century polar exploration.

Ross and Parry arrived back in England on November 11, 1818, and within a few days made their reports to the Admiralty. Barrow had been deeply disappointed with Buchan and Franklin's failure to reach the North Pole, but his feelings had been tempered by his understanding that they had encountered conditions beyond their control. He was absolutely furious with Ross. He would never forgive him for not checking to see that the so-called Croker Mountains really existed and particularly for abandoning the entire expedition so prematurely.

He was not alone in his criticism. Ross was lampooned throughout Great Britain, especially in the press. How, the newspapers decried, could such an opportunity be missed because of what so many of the officers and men on the *Isabella* and *Alexander* felt certain was a mirage? Try as he did to justify his actions, John Ross would never regain the confidence of Barrow and the Admiralty.

CHAPTER 3

The

Man Who Ate His Boots

Here it is
The ragged coast—the coast that no one knows.
How far the lands march inland?
No one knows.
—STEVEN VINCENT BENÉT, *Western Star*, 1943

THE POLE had not been reached; the passage had not been found. But John Barrow was not to be deterred. If anything, he was more determined than ever that England stake its claim to the Arctic. Every day lost meant another day when a Russian or an American might claim the prize. It was May 1819, little more than six months after Buchan and Ross had returned home, and Barrow had already organized two more expeditions and was ready to send them out.

One of these ventures, Barrow believed, was practically risk-free. It involved no ships, a small contingent of men, and minimum expense. It was to be an overland surveying expedition, aimed at exploring and mapping an area of the Arctic Coast that, once known, might well lead to more important discoveries. Perhaps most important to Barrow, the expedition would further establish the British presence in the Arctic.

Barrow's choice to lead the surveying party was, to many in the navy and the Admiralty, most surprising. He chose John Franklin, a man who had never participated in, let alone led, an overland trek through the wilderness. He had absolutely no knowledge of hiking, canoeing, or hunting. Moreover, at the age of twenty-three, he was overweight and had a circulation problem that affected his fingers and toes even in the warmest weather.

On the other hand, Franklin had an admirable war record, had taken part in the first circumnavigation and charting of Australia, and had, Barrow hoped, gained valuable Arctic experience the previous year during the search for the Pole. Probably the most important reasons that he was chosen were that he was brave, charming, totally committed to whatever orders he was given, and came from a well-known and highly respected family—all qualities that ranked high with Barrow.

The men selected to accompany Franklin included Dr. John Richardson, a multitalented Scotsman who was both a physician and a naturalist. Richardson had been a surgeon in the Royal Marines and had been cited for bravery while taking part in several campaigns. A mild-mannered man whose most striking physical characteristics were his broad and high cheekbones, Richardson was endowed with an enormous amount of energy. He could read both Greek and Latin, and aside from medicine, his scientific interests included botany, geology, and natural history. In signing on as the expedition's naturalist, he left no doubt as to why he was happy to accept the assignment: "If I succeed in making a good collection," he stated, "I have no doubt of promotion on my return." As events would unfold, Richardson would not only earn his promotion, but would eventually become known for having conducted more reliable surveys of the Canadian Arctic than any other explorer.

Midshipman George Back, who had served as artist on Franklin's search for the Pole, was named to fill that post on this new expedition. Back had joined the Royal Navy at thirteen and only a year later, while participating in a raid on French shore batteries, had been captured and marched across France to a prison camp at Verdun where he remained for almost five years. Finally released, he rejoined the fleet and received his first assignment to serve with Franklin. Back was a highly talented artist, and like Richardson, was possessed of unusual physical stamina. But he was also vain and loved to brag, particularly in the company of women—and was, as one of his companions claimed, "charming to those from who he hopes to gain something."

As this early daguerreotype reveals, John Franklin was hardly the picture of the robust Arctic explorer. Yet he would become the most famous of all the adventurers who sought the passage.

Rounding out the expedition's naval contingent were midshipman Richard Hood, who was to be the party's mapmaker, and sailors John Hepburn and Samuel Wilkes. Later they were all to be accompanied by boatmen from the Orkney Islands, by Indian guides and hunters, and by French-Canadian *voyageurs* (porters), all of whom were to be recruited in the Arctic.

Specifically, Franklin's orders called for the party to book passage on a Hudson's Bay Company ship to York Factory on the western shore of the island sea. From there he was to follow the route taken by fur traders and proceed overland, first to Fort Chipewyan and Lake Athabasca and then to Great Slave Lake. He was then to trek north to the headwaters of the Coppermine River and proceed down it in canoes to map the unexplored Arctic Coast. (John Franklin was not the first to make an overland journey through the Canadian arctic; see note, page 271.) Altogether it would be a five thousand mile journey by foot and canoe. There was an implied agenda as well: If, while exploring the Arctic Coast, Franklin should discover any possible link that might lead to the ultimate discovery of the passage, that would, of course, be regarded as one of the expedition's greatest accomplishments.

The Franklin expedition left England in May 1819, and arrived at York Factory on the Manitoba side of Hudson Bay on August 30. Almost immediately, problems arose. Franklin's orders called for him to recruit a large number of Orkney boatmen as soon as he landed at York Factory. But despite the fact that this recruitment had been prearranged, most of the Orkneys were not there. They had decided that the long hike across the wilderness would be both dangerous and fruitless. To his dismay, Franklin was able to hire just four of the boatmen—and only under the condition that they would accompany him no farther than Fort Chipewyan.

The expedition also could not have arrived at a more unfortunate time. The Hudson's Bay Company, from whom Franklin was to buy most of his food, had become engaged in a bitter conflict with its competitor, the North West Company. Because of this struggle he was able to buy only a small portion of the provisions he was planning to initially acquire. It was a bad omen. The lack of food and other supplies would hound the expedition to the end, with tragic consequences.

On September 9, determined to put these setbacks aside, the Franklin party left York Factory and began their overland journey to Fort Chipewyan some 1,350 miles away. Franklin was totally unprepared for the long trek. Even with the problems he had encountered at York Factory he was certain that he had enough provisions to reach Fort Chipewyan. He was wrong. The weather was colder than he thought possible and he was shocked when his thermometers actually froze. He had not thought to arrange for tents and at night all in the party found that sleeping on the open ground was almost unbearable. Franklin himself had never been on snowshoes and on several occasions his men found themselves having to slow down to allow their leader to catch up. He had expected to reach Fort Chipewyan in one uninterrupted journey, but he had underestimated how quickly the dead of winter would set in. About halfway to the fort, conditions got so bad that he had to put into Cumberland House, a depot on the Saskatchewan River, where the party was forced to spend the remainder of the winter.

It was not until late March 1820 that the expedition reached Fort Chipewyan, and it was July before they reached Fort Providence, the last outpost of civilization. There it took him more than a month to recruit the voyageurs and Indian hunters he needed for the last leg of the journey—the long trek across the frozen tundra to the Coppermine River and then the trip down it to the coast.

The expedition left Fort Providence during the final week of July, accompanied by a party of Yellowknife Indians and their chief. Franklin later recounted their first meeting in his 1823 memoir of the expedition, *Journey to the Polar Sea*:

> *The chief whose name is Akaitcho or Big-foot, replied by a renewal of his assurances, that he and his party would attend us to the end of our journey, and that they would do their utmost to provide us with the means of subsistence. He admitted that his tribe had made war*

upon the Esquimaux, but said they were now desirous of peace, and unanimous in their opinion as to the necessity of all who accompanied us abstaining from every act of enmity against that nation.

This time Franklin was certain there would be no serious interruption. Once again he was wrong. Less than three weeks out, just as the party reached a lake above the headwaters of the Snake River, it was brought to an abrupt halt. Akaitcho suddenly informed Franklin that winter was near and that by the time the expedition was halfway across the barren tundra it would find itself with no wood for fires and no means of acquiring food to sustain itself during the fast-approaching bitter season. If Franklin insisted on going on, Akaitcho declared, he and his men would never return home.

Franklin was dumbfounded. It was only August 19 and his instruments told him that winter was still a long way off. But Akaitcho would not be moved. Franklin had no choice. He had to have the food that only the Indian hunters could provide. And he needed them to help paddle the canoes once they were in the ocean exploring the coastline. Reluctantly he ordered the voyageurs and the Indians (the British officers performed absolutely no manual labor during the entire expedition) to build a large cabin for the naval men. He then allowed them to build a smaller cabin for themselves. When the buildings were completed, the encampment was named Fort Enterprise.

It was fortuitous that the cabins were built. Even before they were completed, temperatures dropped below freezing and the skies threatened snow. Akaitcho had been right. It would have been folly to go on. The winter that descended upon them was so severe and so prolonged that it was the better part of a year before the journey could be resumed. By this time they were running out of supplies. Desperate to procure them, Franklin decided to send George Back, who had proven to be particularly adept at snowshoeing, off to Fort Resolution, a well-equipped installation they had passed by over a year ago.

Sending off Back for supplies was, Franklin knew, absolutely essential. And, he felt, it would serve another purpose as well. The last thing

Franklin needed was rancor between his officers. The problem he was having with both the voyageurs and the Indians was hardship enough. But he also found himself dealing with a situation involving Back and Richard Hood. Both had well-earned reputations as ladies' men. Hood, in fact, had fathered at least one child with a Yellowknife woman since they had left York Factory. Now both he and Back were focusing their attentions on the same young woman, the sixteen-year-old daughter of one of the Indian hunters. The situation became so contentious that the two men were about to fight a duel, and only the fact that the sailor John Hepburn had secretly removed the charges from their pistols prevented what could only have been a disaster from happening. Now, Back was about to leave. Hopefully things would have cooled down by the time he returned.

Accompanied by John Wenzel, a clerk with the North West Company, two voyageurs, and two Yellowknife hunters and their wives, Back set out for Fort Resolution on October 18. Franklin had little food to give them. They would have to live off what they could capture and kill.

George Back's journey in search of provisions was one of the most harrowing of the entire expedition. Haze and fog continually threatened to make his small party lose their way. All along their route, fallen trees impeded their progress. Heavy snow constantly slowed them down. Worse of all, most of the lakes they encountered were not completely frozen over and they were forced to trudge over high hills to get around them. Only the Indians' hunting skills kept them from starving—and just barely.

Miraculously they made it. Finally arriving at Fort Resolution late in December 1820, Back and his party procured the needed supplies from the North West Company employees who manned the trading post. Ahead of them lay the equally difficult return trip. During the trek, Back and Wenzel became separated, but Wenzel, accompanied by two Inuit interpreters he had recruited, arrived safely back at Fort Providence on January 27. Back appeared on March 17. He had been gone for five months. A simple entry in his journal sums up his ordeal. "I had traveled 1,104 miles on snow shoes," it states, "and had no other covering at night, in the woods, than a blanket and deer skin, with the thermometer frequently at -40 deg. and once at -57 deg.; and sometimes passing two or three days without tasting food." It had been an extraordinary ordeal, but Back and his companions had succeeded in keeping the expedition alive.

In mid-June, fortified by the new supplies, the Franklin party set off for the Coppermine River, and its ultimate goal, the uncharted Arctic coast. It was not until July that the ice melted sufficiently to allow them to use their canoes. For the first 117 miles, the voyageurs had to haul the canoes on sleds over the unmelted snow and ice. But Franklin soon encountered an even bigger problem. As the expedition crossed into Inuit territory, the Indian hunters, frightened of the natives, became increasingly terrified. When, upon reaching Bloody Falls (rapids located about nine miles above the mouth of the Coppermine), they came upon an Inuit encampment, the Indians abruptly turned and left for home. Franklin was left with only two men who had the ability to hunt—his French-Canadian interpreters—and they, too, soon indicated that they wanted to leave. Realizing that he could not afford to lose them, Franklin refused and ordered his officers to watch them closely for the rest of the journey, lest they escape. As if this was not problem enough, Franklin was aware that the voyageurs, who had never seen the ocean, were terrified of what they feared it held in store. Keeping them in line once they reached the coast would be yet another challenge. Though he kept it to himself, Franklin had to admit that what had once promised to be a risk-free adventure had turned into a journey fraught with peril. Painfully, he would note in his journal that the expedition had engendered "a great intermixture of agreeable and disagreeable circumstances. Could the amount be balanced, I suspect the latter would much preponderate." He had no idea what a gigantic understatement that would turn out to be.

By July 14, they had managed to paddle far enough down the rock-and rapids-filled Coppermine for Dr. Richardson to climb a hill where he spotted the Arctic Ocean. A few days later, they reached the river's mouth and the coast. Franklin was determined to begin exploring the coastline immediately, but dense fog and a stormy northeastern gale delayed his departure until July 21. Then, with his party now numbering twenty, including eleven frightened voyageurs, he began his exploration of the Arctic Ocean. The men knew that it would not be easy, and they were right. As they hung to the coastline, exploring every inlet and creek, they were assailed by heavy storms. The canoes took a terrible battering and began to splinter apart, striking even further terror into the hearts of the voyageurs. The several landings they made in search of food were almost totally unsuccessful. Yet somehow they managed to explore and chart 555 miles.

It was now August 15. Even the determined Franklin began to realize that it was time to call a halt to the journey. "In the evening," he would later write in his memoir, "we were exposed to much inconvenience and danger from a heavy rolling sea, the canoes received many severe blows, and shipped a good deal of water, which induced us to

The Franklin party's arrival at the Arctic Sea was a major accomplishment, one of the few triumphs of Franklin's otherwise disastrous first overland expedition. George Back, who proved vital to the survival of most of the party, drew this scene of Franklin's hastily erected camp on the bank of the Coppermine River, overlooking the sea.

encamp . . . Mr. Back reported that both canoes had sustained material injury. Distressing as were these circumstances they gave me less pain than the discovery that our people, who had hitherto displayed a courage beyond our expectation, now felt serious apprehensions for their safety. The strong breezes we had encountered led me to fear that the season was breaking up, and severe weather would soon ensue, which we could not sustain in a country devoid of fuel. I announced my intention of returning at the end of four days unless we should previously meet the Eskimos, and be enabled to make some arrangement for passing the winter with them."

On the eighteenth, even the ever-optimistic Richardson concluded that to continue would be pure lunacy. On that day, he and Franklin walked overland to a spit of land aptly named Point Turnagain (in an area originally discovered by Captain James Cook in 1778 and later named Turnagain by explorer George Vancouver). They agreed that it was the appropriate spot from which to turn back. But even though he knew that winter was rapidly closing in on them, that the winds were rising, and that the sea was becoming increasingly turbulent, Franklin dallied for another five days. He had accomplished the goal of mapping a significant portion of the coastline. But perhaps, he thought, a few more days would allow him to spot a link to the Northwest Passage. It was a tragic blunder. Finally, on August 23, he gave the orders for the party to head back. Although he had placed his expedition in further jeopardy by delaying his return for so long, Franklin felt compelled to defend his indecision to turn back. In his published journal, he wrote:

> When the many perplexing incidents which occurred during the survey of the coast are considered in connection with the shortness of the period during which operations of the kind can be carried on, and the distance we had to travel before we could gain a place of shelter for the winter, I trust it will be judged that we prosecuted the enterprise as far as was prudent and abandoned it only under a well-founded conviction that a farther advance would endanger the lives of the whole party and prevent the knowledge of what

*had been done from reaching England. The active assistance I
received from the officers in contending with the fears of the men
demands my warmest gratitude.*

His disappointment at not finding a trace of the passage was
shared by the other officers, including Back—who nonetheless was
convinced that the expedition had shown that it could be done, and
wrote in his diary: "Thus ended the progress of our Expedition which
we had fondly expected would have set at rest all future discussion on
the subject of a passage . . . It was now the season, not more particularly
the want of food that stopped us. . . . Be this as it may it must be obvious that we had incontestably proved the practicality of succeeding."

It was Franklin's intention to canoe back up the Coppermine as far as
conditions would allow, but after struggling through the storm-tossed
waves, he realized that the water route would have to be abandoned.
They would have to make the return journey on foot and their first
destination, the base camp at Fort Enterprise, was 325 miles away.

Winter was dead upon them by September 5. Three feet of snow
fell, and temperatures plummeted to twenty degrees below. Franklin
described their dire situation: "As we . . . were destitute of the means
of making a fire, we remained in our beds all the day; but our blankets
were insufficient to prevent us from feeling the severity of the frost,
and suffering inconvenience from the drifting of the snow into our
tents. There was no abatement of the storm next day and; our tents
were completely frozen, and the snow had drifted around them to a
depth of three feet; even in the inside there was a covering of several
inches on our blankets." The men were so frozen and debilitated that
they were barely able to pack after Franklin made the decision to
move camp: "The morning of the 7th cleared up a little bit . . . from
the unusual continuance of the storm we feared that the winter had
set in with all its vigour and that by longer delay we should only be
exposed to an accumulation of difficulties; we therefore prepared for
our journey, although we were in a very unfit condition for starting,

being weak from fasting, and our garments stiffened from the frost. A considerable time was consumed in packing up the frozen tents and bed-clothes, the winds blowing so strong that no one could keep his hands long out of his mittens."

They had now run completely out of food and were reduced to eating the lichen that grew on rocks and the boiled leather upper parts of their shoes. Their only chance for survival, Franklin decided, was to split up. On October 4, he sent Back and others off to see if he could find the Indians who had earlier abandoned them, hoping that if found, they would come to their rescue with food and supplies. Soon after Back departed, one of the voyageurs in his party, weakened by hunger and scurvy, dropped dead in his tracks. He was not the only one to have become desperately afflicted. Hood was so weak that he found it impossible to continue. To their credit, Richardson and Hepburn chose to risk their own lives by setting up camp, staying with him until help arrived.

In the meantime, Franklin and the remaining members of the expedition moved on. They had not gone far when four of the group decided that they would never be able to make it all the way to Fort Enterprise, still 350 miles away. Their only hope, they decided, was to head back to Richardson's camp. An Indian named Michel was the only one to reach the encampment. One by one, the others had died en route. For those in the camp, Michel appeared just in time, for he brought with him meat that he claimed he "had found from a wolf which had been killed by the stroke of a deer's horn." Although the meat tasted unlike anything they had ever eaten, Richardson, Hood, and Hepburn were literally starving and devoured it greedily. But from Michel's questionable explanation of where it had come from and from the Indian's demeanor, Richardson began to have a sickening suspicion of what they had just eaten. To his horror, he became convinced that the meat must have come from the bodies of the voyageurs, who had died en route to his camp.

In the days that followed, Michel's behavior became increasingly disturbing to the others. At times the Indian, who was armed with both pistol and knife, became openly hostile. Then, on a day when Richardson was off seeking lichen, they were suddenly alarmed at the sound of a gunshot coming from their camp. Racing back they discovered Hood lying dead on the ground from, as Richardson described it, "a shot that had entered the back part of his head and passed out of the forehead." Michel immediately claimed that Hood had taken his own life. But Richardson and Hepburn knew otherwise. They were certain that Michel had not only murdered Hood, but that when the opportunity arose he was determined to kill and cannibalize both of them.

With Hood dead, Richardson, Hepburn, and Michel broke camp and set out hoping to find either Franklin, or Back and the Indians he had gone seeking. Richardson had no doubt as to what he had to do as soon as possible. The first time he caught Michel off guard, the doctor acted. "I determined," he stated in his journal, "as I was thoroughly convinced of the necessity of such a dreadful act, to take the whole responsibility upon myself; immediately upon Michel coming up, I put an end to his life by shooting him through the head with a pistol."

Calling upon every ounce of strength they had left, Richardson and Hepburn were able, on October 29, to reach Fort Enterprise. And there were Franklin and three voyageurs. They had made it. But their joy was immediately tempered by the sight before them. "No language that I can use," wrote Richardson, "[was] adequate to convey a just idea of the wretchedness of the abode in which we found our commanding officer [and the others]. The hollow and sepulchral sound of their voices, produced nearly as great horror in us, as our emaciated appearance did on them." Franklin and the others were indeed close to death. Two days later one of the voyageurs passed away. But on November 7, just as all hope was fading, an advance party of Indians sent ahead by Back arrived with lifesaving supplies. Back had once again saved the day.

"Lieut. Back, Dr. Richardson, John Hepburn . . . and I returned to York Factory on the 14 July," Franklin wrote. "Thus terminated our long fatiguing and disastrous travels in North America, having journeyed by water and land (including our navigation of the Polar Sea) 5,550 miles."

It had been a journey without precedent. And there had been some significant achievements. More than five thousand miles of uncharted wilderness had been crossed. Five hundred miles of unexplored Arctic Coast had been mapped. Back, at least, believed that the expedition had proved that finding the passage was possible. But Ross and Parry had already done that. What had been proven was that it was possible to survive in even the Arctic's most harrowing conditions.

Yet it had also been an unmitigated disaster. Eleven men had died. Two had been murdered. Although it would never be discussed in Victorian England, there had unquestionably been cannibalism. Ironically, Franklin, the architect of many of these disasters, returned home to fame and promotion. His published journal became an instant best-seller. The problems that his leadership had caused were almost completely ignored. He had become a hero simply by surviving. He was, after all, the man who had eaten his boots.

CHAPTER 4

The

Indomitable Parry

"How I long to be among the ice."
—EDWARD PARRY

OHN BARROW had spent sleepless nights deciding who should lead the overland expedition into the Canadian Arctic. He had no such problem choosing the man who would make the next attempt at finding the Northwest Passage. Barrow was convinced that if Edward Parry rather than John Ross had been in charge of the passage-seeking expedition they had conducted just one year earlier, there would have been no turning back because of imaginary mountains, and the prize would have been gained. While Parry had been as circumspect as he could in criticizing John Ross's behavior during their aborted search, he and Barrow were in total agreement that, as Parry would state, "Attempts at Polar discovery had been hitherto relinquished at a time when there was the greatest chance of succeeding."

Parry set out just days after Franklin had left on his expedition, reached the Davis Strait on June 28, 1819, and proceeded on to Lancaster Sound. Ahead of him lay open water. There were no Croker

Mountains. This time there would be no turning back. The same William Hooper—the *Alexander's* purser—who had expressed such dismay a year earlier over Ross's actions, now exclaimed, "There was something particularly animating in the joy which lighted every countenance. We had arrived in a sea which had never before been navigated, we were gazing on land that European eyes had never beheld . . . and before us was the prospect of realizing all our wishes, and of exalting the honour of our country."

From Lancaster Sound, Parry sailed on to Prince Regent Inlet, hoping that that waterway was the next link to the passage. But he found it blocked by ice. His two ships, the *Hecla* and the *Griper*, then pushed on, entered Barrow Strait, and explored the south shore of a previously unknown group of islands that Parry named the North Georgian Islands. The vessels had now reached the Arctic Archipelago, the first European ships ever to do so. On September 4, they were off the south shore of Melville Island when Parry's instruments told

Edward Parry was the first of the British naval officers to deliberately spend the winter in the ice so that his search for the passage could be extended a second season. Here, with the ice beginning to thaw, the crews of the *Hecla* and the *Griper* undertake the arduous task of cutting a channel to free the vessels from their entrapment.

him that they were crossing latitude 110 degrees west. They had earned the five-thousand pound prize that Parliament had offered for reaching this point.

Aware that winter was pressing in on him, Parry tried to keep moving west but his path was increasingly being blocked by building ice. Rather than risk disaster, he decided to put into what he named Winter Harbor on Melville Island. He had planned well. He was fully prepared to become the first to voluntarily "winter down" in the Arctic and wait for the ice thaw before resuming his journey.

Parry knew it would be a long and challenging winter. But his spirits had never been higher. He had confirmed that there were no Croker Mountains blocking Lancaster Sound. He had claimed the first of Parliament's rewards. And even better things, he believed, lay ahead. "Our prospects, indeed, were truly exhilarating," he wrote in his journal. "The ships had suffered no injury; we had plenty of provisions, the crew in high health and spirits; a sea, if not open at least navigable; and a zealous and unanimous determination in both officers and men to accomplish, by all possible means, the grand object on which we had the happiness to be employed."

But first they would have to get through the winter. He knew that the greatest challenge—greater even than the ice or snow—would be boredom. "I dreaded," he stated, "the want of employment as one of the worst evils that was likely to befall us." Long before he had left for the Arctic, Parry had carefully planned for a work regimen and an ongoing array of entertainments to keep everyone occupied should they have to spend the winter in the ice. Every day, from 5:45 A.M. until nightfall, the men on both ships were kept busy with activities ranging from scrubbing the decks to mending and checking the rigging and sails. Anticipating the need for evening entertainment, Parry had brought with him costumes, makeup, and scripts—even a barrel organ, so that classic and comic productions and musicals could be presented. A weekly newspaper, *The North Georgia Gazette and Winter Chronicle* was published. Cricket and other games were held on the ice that surrounded the vessels. Although he had no way of knowing it,

Parry had instituted a program for dealing with spirit-killing boredom that, in years to come, would be employed time and again by winter-bound Arctic ships.

The *Hecla* and the *Griper* remained in their frozen entrapment for almost a full year. It was not until the first of August that the ice finally began to break up and the ships could get underway. But as Parry resumed sailing westward he discovered that the waters ahead of him were still clogged with ice. Miles off in the distance he could see land, which he named Banks Land, but he knew he would never be able to reach it in that season. It was time to go home.

The passage had not been found, but Parry had accomplished more than any other seeker had ever achieved. He had proven that Lancaster Sound opened a passage to the west. He had verified the need to map the maze of islands through which any successful passage-seeker would have to travel, and he had demonstrated that wintering in the Arctic without disaster was possible.

Immediately upon returning, Parry was promoted to the rank of commander. He was elected unanimously as a fellow of the Royal Society and was publicly honored by various institutions and hailed wherever he went. Most important to his future prospects, he had justified the faith that Barrow and the Admiralty had placed in him. "No one," Barrow would write after reading Parry's report, "could rise from its perusal without the fullest conviction that Commander Parry's merits as an officer and scientific navigator are not confined to his professional duties; but that the resources of his mind are equal to the most arduous situations, and fertile in expedient under every circumstance, however difficult, dangerous, or unexpected."

High praise indeed. And in six months Barrow had sent his hero off again. Parry could not wait to return. "How I long to be among the ice," he had told his friends. Once again he was given two ships. He would command the 375-ton *Fury*. Command of his old ship, the *Hecla*, was given to George Francis Lyon, who had become a favorite of Barrow's by overcoming extreme hardships during an expedition that Barrow had sent to Africa to trace the course of the River Niger.

This time, instead of pursuing the path through Lancaster Sound, Parry had been instructed to sail westward through Hudson Strait toward Repulse Bay. Again, any scientific observations he might make were secondary. He was to finish the job; he was to find the passage.

The *Fury* and the *Hecla* set sail on May 8, 1821, and by the end of July had entered Repulse Bay. But Parry soon found that, even this early in the season, his progress westward was blocked by ice. Turning from the bay, he and Lyon spent the next two months following the coast of Melville Peninsula, exploring every inlet, anxiously searching for a passage to the west. By October, ice was forming everywhere and the two ships were forced to put into a sheltered spot that Parry named Winter Island. There, for the next nine months, they would be frozen in position.

Immediately, masts and sails were stored and the work and entertainment regimen was begun. Parry, now a veteran of "wintering over," had added new features to occupy his men. Along with regular performances by the Royal Arctic Theater, now equipped with stage lights, Parry introduced a school aboard each of the vessels where crew members were taught both reading and writing. An observatory was built onshore where men of the *Fury* and *Hecla* took magnetic measurements and made other scientific observations.

Much of the inevitable boredom of the long winter was relieved by something for which Parry could not have planned. On February 1, 1822, a group of Inuit suddenly arrived and informed Parry that they had built a winter settlement just two miles away. For the next several months the Eskimos paid regular visits to the ships. Most important, they spoke of a strait that lay to the north of Winter Island, a passageway that provided access to open water to the west. Now the monotony of the wintering over was replaced by impatience. Could this passageway lead to success at last?

Impatient as he was, Parry was forced to wait until the first week of July before the ships were freed from the ice. Immediately he set sail for the strait that the Inuit assured him was there. And within two months he found it, naming it the Fury and Hecla Strait. But, to his dismay, he also discovered that huge ice floes made it impassable. Leaving the ship, he explored the area on foot, and from a high vantage point spotted the open body of water to the west.

But it was miles away, his passage was blocked, and winter was setting in. He had no choice but to put into a harbor at Igloolik Island and make preparations for another long stay in the ice. Even for the always-optimistic Parry it was almost too much. "It required but a single glance at the chart," he confided to his journal, "that whatever the last summer's navigation has added to our knowledge of the eastern coast of America, and its adjacent lands, very little had, in reality been effected in furtherance of the North-West Passage. Even the actual discovery of the outlet into the Polar Sea, had been of no benefit in the prosecution of our enterprise; for we had only discovered this channel to find it impassable, and to see the barriers of nature impenetrably closed against us to the utmost limit of the navigable season."

At this point, both ships were running short of supplies. And there was an even more serious problem. Nine of the *Fury*'s crewmen were suffering from scurvy. (Scurvy had plagued sailors since the 1500s; see note, page 272). One of the officers aboard the Hecla had died from the affliction. Parry ordered Lyon to sail his vessel back to England as soon as the ice broke up. Once he was free from the ice, Parry would make one last try at penetrating the Fury and Hecla Strait. But this final attempt proved as futile as the first. The strait was still blocked and a disappointed Parry headed for home.

His second voyage had not been without its accomplishments. He had learned much about the Inuit and their ways. And once again he had discovered a promising channel that might be a gateway to the passage. But once again, the hopes he shares with Barrow for a quick discovery had been dashed. He arrived back in England in the second week of October 1823, only to discover that Franklin had returned from his overland trek a year earlier to even greater acclaim than he himself had received after his first passage-seeking voyage. For the proud Parry, it was almost as big a disappointment as not having found the passage.

It did not take long for the disappointment to turn into renewed hope. While he had been away, Parry had been promoted to the rank of captain. He had also been appointed acting hydrographer of the Admiralty. But he had accepted this position only on the condition that it would not preclude his being given the opportunity to make yet another attempt to find the passage. He soon got his chance. In January 1824, he was again given command of the *Hecla* and the *Fury*. This time his orders were to sail through Lancaster Sound, proceed down Prince Regent Inlet, and then search for the pathway to the passage along the northern coast of North America.

But this time there would be no promising beginning to the voyage. Arriving at Baffin Bay on the way to Lancaster Sound, Parry found the ice so thick that he fell weeks behind schedule. Once in the sound, he was forced to battle winds so fierce that they actually drove his ships backwards at times. Through sheer determination and no small amount of navigational skill, the expedition was finally able to reach Port Bowen on the east coast of Prince Regent Inlet. But by this time Parry's old nemesis winter had once again set in. For the third time in less than five years he was forced to make his home in the ice.

Bigger troubles lay ahead. In July 1825, when they were once again able to get underway, Parry decided to sail across to the other side of the wide inlet, hoping to find yet another new passageway to the west. He was only ten days into this journey when he was once again battered by heavy winds. This time he did not escape. As both ships were being blown toward land, an iceberg struck the *Fury*, throwing it against the ice that lined the shore. The vessel was so badly damaged that even around-the-clock manning of the pumps could not prevent the vessel from continually taking on water. Parry knew that with no harbor in the vicinity, repairs, if possible, would have to be made on the spot. He ordered that the *Fury*'s supplies be unloaded on the beach and that the ship's crew be transferred to the *Hecla*. Then the men of both vessels attempted to secure the *Fury* in a position where repairs could be made. But just as they were beginning this effort, they were hit with a series of blizzards. When these were followed by yet another storm, Parry ordered that the *Hecla*, with both crews aboard, be sailed southward to avoid the same fate as had befallen its sister ship. Four days later, after the winds had abated, the sailors returned to the Fury, only to find the ship on the beach, lying on her side. Nothing could be done but abandon her.

Noting in his journal that "the only real cause for wonder is our long exception from such a catastrophe," Parry returned to England where Barrow was not so quick to gloss over the fact that, this time, nothing had been achieved. "Parry's third voyage," he wrote, "has added little or nothing to our stock of geographical knowledge." He meant the Northwest Passage.

Although he would never again be given the opportunity of seeking the prize, Parry's days in the Arctic were still not over. In 1827, accompanied by Lieutenant James Clark Ross (John Ross's nephew), Parry headed an expedition seeking to accomplish what David Buchan had failed to do—find the North Pole. Sailing to Spitsbergen, Parry and his party of fourteen men attempted, beginning on June 21, to sledge their way to the Pole. But instead of encountering the flat, unbroken plain of ice that he had expected to find, Parry once again was confronted with rapidly moving packs of ice. By July 26, conditions had so deteriorated that the quest had to be abandoned. Parry, however, had reached latitude 82°45' north, a record that would stand for the next forty-nine years.

CHAPTER 5

Ross Tries Again

"It was the first vessel I had ever been forced to abandon . . .
It was like the parting of an old friend."
—JOHN ROSS

THEY HAD BECOME HEROES—yet neither Franklin nor Parry had found the passage. But there was another man determined to capitalize on what, despite their failure, Franklin and Parry had managed to discover, and gain the glory for himself. For almost ten years John Ross had waited for his chance to regain his lost honor, to redeem himself for aborting the *Isabella's* mission because of a mirage. And he was sure that he knew how to do it. If only he was given the opportunity, he would sail down Prince Regent Inlet past where Parry had made his last discovery, and find the passage by continuing on to where Franklin had tuned back at Point Turnagain.

He knew, however, that given the Croker Mountains fiasco, the Admiralty, and particularly Barrow, would never give him the chance. The only answer was to mount an expedition financed by private funds. He found them in the person of Felix Booth, the nation's largest gin distiller and a man known for his philanthropic pursuits, a man who was willing to fund Ross's expedition in return for the prospect of having a significant yet undiscovered Arctic landmark named in his honor.

Ross had definite ideas about how he would succeed where the others had failed. Despite the ridicule he had endured, Ross had lost none of his confidence in himself or his ability to find the passage. He was convinced that both Franklin and Parry had taken too many men along with them. Keeping an expedition supplied with food—especially when it was now obvious that spending at least one winter in the ice was to be expected—was, he believed, perhaps the greatest challenge. The fewer men to feed, the better the chance of success. Ross was also convinced that the ships that Buchan and Parry had sailed in were too large for Arctic waters. A smaller ship would be far more capable of maneuvering through the ice-filled waters, particularly if that vessel was powered by steam.

On May 23, 1829, with a crew less than a fifth the size of the 117-man contingent that Parry had taken on his third voyage, Ross sailed from England in the 164-ton steam picket *Victory*, towing a sixteen-ton tender behind him. On July 28, he reached Disko Island on the west coast of Greenland.

Fortune smiled down upon him. He had entered the Arctic during one of the mildest seasons that even the oldest Greenlanders could remember. Entering Baffin Bay, he found it incredibly free of ice and steamed across it in nine days. On his second voyage, it had taken Parry two months to get through. On August 6, Ross was at the entrance to Lancaster Sound. This time he saw no mountains and in thirty-six hours he was into Prince Regent Inlet. His one frustration was with the steam engine, which had been giving him trouble since he had departed. Finally tired of having his men spend so much time repairing the faulty boiler and the pumps, he had the engine turned off and raised his sails.

On August 12, the *Victory* was off Fury Beach, the site where Parry had previously abandoned the *Fury*. An important part of Ross's plan was to assure himself of having enough supplies by taking on some of the huge amount of stores that Parry had been forced to leave behind. But he found that both the current and the tide prevented him from anchoring close enough to the beach. Disappointed, he sailed on and found Cresswell Bay, which at first appeared as though it might be a passageway to the west. When he discovered that it was a dead end, he turned back north for another try at Fury Beach. This time the tide and currents were in his favor and he was able to put in close enough to get at the supplies.

Again, he was in luck. Parry's abandoned stores were not only still in good condition; there were more of them than Ross had hoped for. Before his men were finished loading whatever they could onto the *Victory*, they had replenished their supplies with ten tons of coal, new sails, masts, and anchors, and found enough food to last them for at least three years. No wonder that as they rowed back to their ships, the Arctic air was filled with the cry "God save Fury Beach."

Underway again, Ross sailed south down Prince Regent Inlet. By August 16, he had traveled further down the inlet than anyone had ever done. By the end of September he had penetrated three hundred miles further than Parry. He was only some 289 miles from where Franklin had first seen the Polar Sea. Success was at hand. Although he was reluctant to give Barrow any credit, perhaps he was right. Perhaps the passage could be found in a single season.

Then his luck abandoned him. The first week of October brought with it enormous winds, mountainous seas, and towering icebergs. He had reached the huge gulf that lay at the bottom of Prince Regent Inlet but he was being assailed by ice that threatened to destroy him. Later he would write in his *Narrative of a Second Voyage in Search of a North-West Passage*, published in 1835, that his readers should remember that "ice is stone—a rock floating in a stream ... [and] imagine if they can, these mountains of crystal hurled through a narrow strait by a rapid tide; meeting, as mountains might meet, with a huge noise of thunder, breaking from each other's precipices huge fragments, or rending each other asunder, till, losing their former equilibrium, they fall over head long, lifting the sea around in breakers, and whirling it into eddies while flatter fields of ice, formed against these masses . . . by the wind and the steam, rise out of them until they fall back on themselves, adding to the indescribable commotion and noise."

He had no option. He had to find a suitable place to winter down. Fortunately, he found it, naming the land adjacent to where he put in (which he mistakenly thought was an island, but was actually a peninsula), Boothia Felix. He then named the water, which he had barely managed to get through, the Gulf of Boothia. Felix Booth and the gin he bottled had received their measure of immortality.

Like Parry before him, Ross now turned his attention to preparing for the long winter ahead. Like Parry, he had his men build an observatory on shore. He set up a daily schedule that kept the men busy at work throughout each long day. He initiated an afternoon regimen of exercise. He set up a school in which reading, writing, and the principles of navigation were taught.

But Ross was no Parry. He was not interested in providing entertainment for his crew. To Ross, who believed that expeditions should be run like military operations, plays, pageants, and shipboard news-papers were frivolities that got in the way of needed discipline. And unlike Parry, Ross did not believe in mingling with his men in order to boost their spirits during their winter imprisonment. He spent most of his time in his cabin and refused to listen to any advice or suggestions given to him by either his men or his officers—among them his nephew James Clark Ross, who he had taken along as second in command. Ross's aloofness, at times, made the challenge of maintaining morale even more difficult.

Fortunately, as had been the case during Perry's second expedition, the monotony of the long winter was broken periodically by visits from groups of Inuit who came from a nearby village. Ross's men taught the natives how to play leapfrog and football, and entertained them with dances aboard ship. In turn, the crew paid regular visits to the native village where, with the consent of their husbands, they slept with the Inuit women.

Ross did not engage in any of the social interaction with the natives. But he did accept their help. The Inuit showed him where salmon could be caught, and where game such as musk oxen could be found. They gave Ross and his nephew sledges and dog teams, along with mushing lessons. And, when Ross showed them his primitive map, they obligingly sketched in rivers and coastline. When, however, they told the commander that there was no way out of where he was to the south and that his only hope was in finding a way to the north, he told them that this was something he needed to determine for himself.

For eleven months, the *Victory* and the tiny tender remained frozen in the ice. Then, on June 20, 1830, the temperature amazingly rose to sixty-two degrees. Within three weeks the ice was breaking up around the ships. They were free! (Or so they thought.) But in choosing his winter refuge, Ross had unwittingly made a major error. He had anchored down during a period of high tides. Now the tides were so low that he was unable to get the *Victory* over a sandbar that stretched across Felix Harbor. The crew's only option was to unload almost everything off both the ship and its tender and haul them over the bar. This accomplished, they reloaded both vessels, a process that, in all, took them more than two weeks.

Now, at last, they could be off. But they were wrong again. To their horror, they found that the seas ahead of them were still frozen over despite the warming trend. Determined to break through, the crew struggled for two months but managed to move forward only three miles. Once again, Ross had no choice. It was October, and they would have to spend yet another winter marooned in the pack.

Naming the spot where he dropped anchor Sheriff Harbor (Booth had once been sheriff of London), Ross grimly faced the reality of an additional winter in the ice. His only consolation was the hope that this second winter would be shorter that the last. It would not only fail to be shorter; it would last for two more years. Even when the calendar told him that the summer of 1831 had arrived, the *Victory* remained trapped.

As the months in the ice had turned first into one year, then two, and then three, tensions aboard the ship became extreme. The men blamed Ross for having chosen the wrong harbor for their first wintering. There was concern that the food they had taken on at Fury Beach would run out. There was talk of mutiny.

Throughout the unprecedented ordeal, the one calming influence was James Clark Ross. Taller and swarthier than his uncle, he nevertheless had the same vanity and the same quick temper. Unlike his relative, however, he truly cared what people thought about him and openly courted popularity. It was he to whom the men turned when they had a complaint. It was he who committed himself to boosting morale whenever he could. And it was James Clark Ross who made the most meaningful discovery of the ice-plagued expedition.

During the first two winters that the *Victory* was frozen in the ice, the younger Ross left the ship and explored the coastline both by boat and in the dogsleds that the Inuit had donated. By the time he was finished with his roving, he had accounted for two-thirds of the charting of the more than six hundred miles of new territory that the expedition had encountered. Among his discoveries was the fact that Boothia Felix was not an island, as his uncle believed, but a peninsula. Even if the expedition had not been imprisoned, John Ross had been headed for a dead end, not the glory he sought. On the same long sledging excursion, James Clark Ross reached a desolate area that he named King William Land. It was really an island and, although of course he had no way of knowing it, it would be a place that would have enormous significance in the years to come.

The younger Ross's greatest achievement came in the still ice-bound spring of 1831. His ambition, in fact the reason that he had signed on for the voyage, was to find the Magnetic North Pole. A year earlier on one of his sledging trips, he had come to within a few miles of what he was sure was the long sought-after spot. But he didn't have the equipment with him to confirm it. Now, a year later—June 1, 1831—he stood on another desolate spot, which he named Victory Point. There the needle on his compass pointed straight downward and stopped moving. After another day's readings, he knew he had made the discovery. Later, stating that this was the spot (70°5'17" north and 96°46'45" west) that "Nature . . . had chosen as the centre of one of her great and dark powers," he planted the Union Jack and "took possession of the North Magnetic Pole and its adjoining territory in the name of Great Britain and King William the Fourth."

His nephew's accomplishments notwithstanding, John Ross was becoming increasingly disconsolate. The winter of 1832 was proving to be as unrelenting as the previous dark season had been, with no relief in sight. He doubted that he and the men could survive a fourth winter trapped in the ice. There was only one decision to be made—the most difficult of his life. The crew would have to abandon the *Victory* and trek overland to Fury Beach, where they could live off the food that still remained there. Then, hopefully, in the spring they could take to the boats they would drag with them and make their way into Lancaster Sound. If they were lucky, the whaling fleet would find and rescue them. (Franklin expedition member George Back organized a search

James Clark Ross and his men celebrate their discovery of the Magnetic North Pole. For Ross, it would be the realization of his greatest ambition, to him greater even than finding the passage. "It almost seemed," he would state, "as if our voyage and all its labours were at an end and nothing now remained but to venture home and be happy for the rest of our days."

party for Ross; in the end he was not Ross's rescuer, but instead had several harrowing adventures of his own over the course of two separate expeditions; see note, page 274).

Fury Beach was three hundred miles away. To make sure that there would be enough food to sustain them on their life-or-death march, Ross decided to set up a series of supply depots along the way. Crew members would drag a boat full of provisions to a certain point along the route to the beach and drop them off. They would then return with the empty boat, fill it up again, and hike to a spot beyond where they had deposited the previous cache. It was a long process that proved as arduous as the trip to Fury Beach itself. The route twisted and turned so much that at one point it took a supply party a month to progress just eighteen miles though they had traveled over one hundred.

Finally, on May 29, they were ready to leave the *Victory* and the tender and move out. "The colours were hoisted and nailed to the mast," he would write. "We drank a parting glass to our poor ship and having seen every man out, in the evening, I took my own adieu of the *Victory*, which deserved a better fate. It was the first vessel that I had ever been obliged to abandon, after having served in thirty-six, during a period of forty-two years. It was like the last parting of an old friend."

It was now a race against time. Traveling on two-thirds rations, the crew slept at night in trenches dug into the snow. Ross had made many mistakes, but one of his earliest decisions was being proven correct. The small party was barely surviving. A larger one would surely have perished.

By June 10, 1832, they had passed their last cache of food and were halfway to Fury Beach. Ahead of them lay ice so rugged that to continue carrying the boats seemed a hopeless task. Some of the men demanded that the boats be abandoned and that a final dash for Fury Beach be made. Ross refused, stating that if they abandoned the boats, they would have no chance of ever leaving the beach once they reached it. Instead, he sent James Clark Ross ahead with two men to see if the supplies that had still remained on Fury Beach when the *Victory* sailed on three years earlier were still there. Two weeks later his nephew returned. The food was still there and in good condition. And he had more good news: The younger Ross and his party had found three of the *Fury*'s whaleboat-type vessels, all in seaworthy condition, scattered along the coast. No longer needing to drag the two boats they had lugged for more than 150 miles, Ross and his men reached Fury Beach in six days. Immediately the half-starved crew fell upon the food, but Ross, knowing the effects that too much food would have on their empty stomachs, rationed it out. That night, however, when the commander was asleep, the men ate their fill, and, as Ross wrote in his journal, "suffered severely from eating too much."

It would be another month before the waters cleared sufficiently for them to leave the beach. As they made their way down the channel, most of the men, for the first time in as long as they could remember, felt a glimmer of hope. Maybe, once they reached the sound, there would be whalers there. Maybe they would be rescued.

On September 1, they had progressed far enough for Ross to stand on a high point on the northern tip of Somerset Island on Batty Bay and determine what lay ahead of them. As he looked out on Prince Regent Inlet, Barrow Strait, and Lancaster Sound, all he could see was an unbroken mass of ice. They were stymied again. There was nothing for them to do but abandon the boats and return on foot to Fury Beach.

It was too much. A fourth winter in the Arctic. And this time without a ship to shelter them. Even the always-cheerful James Clark Ross became despondent. "[My] nephew seemed to have more than hesitated respecting our escape," Ross wrote, "and I began myself to question whether we should succeed in passing the barrier of ice this season; in which case there would be no resource for us but another winter, another year . . . if indeed, it should be the fortune of any one to survive after another such year as the three last."

To his credit, Ross would not give up. The day after they arrived back at Fury Beach, he put everyone to work building a shelter that was nothing more than a framework of spars and canvas surrounded by a nine-foot wall of snow. Ross named it Somerset House.

The weather during the early months of 1835 was so severe that there was no game to be hunted. Spirits dropped to a new low when the expedition's carpenter fell ill and died. Several other crew members became sick and terribly weak. Remarkably, whenever the weather temporarily moderated, Ross was able to marshal his strength and lead the remaining thirteen healthy men back and forth to Batty Bay, where they sheltered provisions and prepared the boats they had left behind should they ever be fortunate enough to get underway again.

By July 1833, they had eaten the last of their meat; they were almost completely out of food. Once again, Ross found himself with no options. Spending another winter on Fury Beach meant certain death. Their only chance was to get back to the boats in the hope that the ice would clear in time for them to sail into Lancaster Sound before they perished.

They left Somerset House on July 8 and six days later reached the boats. For what had to be the worst month in the entire four-year ordeal, the crew waited for the ice to break up enough for them to

SOMERSET HOUSE.

Perhaps the greatest accomplishment of John Ross's five-year passage-seeking expedition was that it demonstrated how it was possible to survive in the Arctic even under the most threatening circumstances. Key to the expedition's near-disastrous frozen season of 1833 was the erection of the snow-insulated winter shelter named Somerset House.

escape their latest imprisonment. And their prayers were answered. On August 14, a single channel to the north became clear. Within four hours the tide came in and they launched the boats. Ross could hardly believe it. "It was a change like that of magic," he recalled, "to find that solid mass of ocean . . . suddenly converted into water; navigable and navigable to us, who had almost forgotten what it was to float at freedom on the seas."

With renewed strength, they sailed their three boats until, on August 17, they had finally departed Prince Regent Inlet. The next day they passed by the mouth of the fifteen-mile-long Admiralty Inlet, the longest fjord in the world. When the wind died down, they furled their small sails and rowed—for as long as twenty hours at a time. Finally, on August 25 their strength gave out. They were now at the east side of Navy Board Inlet and Ross decided that they had to put ashore. At four in the morning the next day, a lookout that Ross had posted awoke him with a shout. He had seen a sail. Instantly the men began sending off smoke signals. Then they took to the boats, rowing desperately towards where the lookout believed the ship to be. But it had vanished over the horizon. Devastated, they were about to return to shore when another sail was spotted. Feverishly they rowed towards it and this time the ship turned about and headed back towards them. They were saved. When the rescue vessel came close enough, it lowered one of its boats, which pulled alongside Ross's haggard crew. When one of Ross's men asked the name of the ship that had saved them, the vessel's mate replied that his ship was the "*Isabella of Hull*, once commanded by Captain Ross." Immediately Ross stood up and identified himself. That could not be, the startled mate responded, Ross had been given up for dead two years ago. Calmly the commander stated that he was very much alive.

It had been an extraordinary journey. Despite four years of entrapment, despite prolonged periods of near starvation, despite being battered by almost everything the Arctic could present, Ross was returning with all but one of his twenty-three-man contingent still alive. They had

The whaling vessel *Isabella of Hull* rescues John Ross and his men. That Ross was saved by the very same vessel that he had commanded during his first Arctic adventure was but one of a number of ironic incidents and developments that characterized the entire saga of the long search for the Northwest Passage and the dramatic events that followed.

penetrated the Arctic further south than any other explorers. They had come tantalizingly close to linking up with the Polar Sea. And John Clark Ross had discovered the Magnetic North Pole.

Although it was a private expedition, Ross felt that there were important lessons that the navy could learn from his experiences. Chief among them, Ross believed more than ever, was the necessity of seeking the passage with as small a contingent as was necessary. Would the Inuit have been able to hunt for enough food to supply a much larger party than Ross's during his first winter in the ice? Would a larger party have been able to make its way back and forth to Fury Beach and then survive for so long on such a short supply of rations? And would a larger number of boats than Ross's three small vessels have been able to make their way to rescue? Ross thought not.

But the navy did not listen. The next great passage-seeking expedition would be larger than ever. And, to the dismay of all England, its members would not be as fortunate as Ross.

CHAPTER 6

All Hopes

Rest on Franklin

"There appears to be but one wish among the whole of
the inhabitants of this country, that the enterprise in which
the officers and crew are about to be engaged may be
attended with success."
—RODERICK MURCHISON, president of the
Royal Geographical Society

B Y THE MID-1840s, Barrow, despite all the setbacks his explorers had experienced, was more confident of success than ever. He still believed that there was an Open Polar Sea. Much of the Arctic coastline had been mapped. Straits, inlets, bays, and islands had been discovered. Possible links to the prized route had been spotted. The discovery of the passage was at hand. It had to be. He was now eighty-two and he knew that the next search he launched would be his last.

British technological advances would allow Barrow to send out ships that would be marvels of their age. All of the new expedition's officers and crew would be handpicked. But—and it was a vital concern—whom should he trust to command his largest and most important expedition?

Parry, who was still Barrow's favorite, was his first choice. But after three expeditions, Parry had had enough of the Arctic, and he politely refused. The next choice was James Clark Ross, who had recently returned from a South Pole–seeking expedition. Although he had not made the Pole, he had had planted the English flag further south than any explorer had previously traveled. But Ross had recently married and had promised his new wife that his days in the Arctic were over. Because Barrow was planning to rely on steam power to assure the expedition's success, his third choice was Commander James Fitzjames who, while lacking any Arctic experience, had worked successfully with steam engines. But the Admiralty turned Fitzjames's appointment down. He was, they told Barrow, simply too young to command so vital an enterprise. George Back was also a contender, but despite the heroics he had displayed during John Franklin's first overland expedition, Barrow felt Back was too argumentative to lead such an important expedition. Captain Francis Crozier also seemed a logical choice. He had made five successful Arctic voyages and had served James Clark Ross well as second-in-command on his Antarctic achievement. But once again naval upper-class snobbery held sway: Crozier was not only common-born, but Irish. He would never do.

Barrow was stuck. His final and most ambitious search—and he had no one to lead it. He knew that he had to have a recognizable figure, someone who would engender support from both the public and the press. Reluctantly, he had to admit that he had only one choice left, a person he didn't really want. It was John Franklin.

Franklin had led a varied career since returning from the overland expedition that had almost killed him. In 1823, he had married poet Eleanor Porden, who had given him a daughter, Eleanor. Two years after the marriage, when Franklin was offered a second overland search, his wife lay dying of tuberculosis. Despite her illness, she urged Franklin to accept the opportunity, and off he went. She died six days after his departure.

The second overland journey was far better organized than the first had been. With Dr. John Richardson (who had served as the naturalist on Franklin's first overland expedition) as second-in-command, the party traveled overland more than two thousand miles and successfully charted an area comprising half the Arctic coast of Canada and a large portion of the Alaskan seaboard. Under Richardson's guidance, the expedition recorded important meteorological and geological information and made notes of more than 663 plants.

Franklin returned to England in 1827 and a year later he married a friend of Eleanor's, thirty-six-year-old Jane Griffin. Together they spent the next six years in the Mediterranean, where Franklin had been assigned to oversee Greece's transition to an independent nation. For Franklin, it was a matter of biding his time, waiting for the next Arctic assignment. Surely it would come. His second Canadian venture had been an unqualified success. And he was now *Sir* John Franklin, knighted by George IV for his accomplishments.

But he did not get the call. Returning to England in 1834, he had petitioned for the next passage-seeking assignment. It went to George Back. Two years later, he was appointed Governor of Van Diemen's Land (present-day Tasmania). It would be a horrendous experience. Van Diemen's Land was a prison colony, the home of eighteen thousand of England's most hardened criminals. It had been long controlled by upper-class colonial officers who lived a life of luxury by profiting handsomely from the convicts' labor.

Determined to make the best of the situation, Franklin, at the strong urging of his wife, attempted to institute a series of reforms, chiefly aimed at providing more humane treatment for prisoners. He was opposed every step of the way by the colonial officials, who were accustomed to having their governor join in on the profit-taking. True to his character, Franklin spent seven agonizing years attempting to overcome the opposition. But the man who had repeatedly faced death in pitched naval engagements and the Arctic wilderness was no match for the political machinations of those whose way of life he threatened. In 1843, they succeeded in having Franklin recalled.

It was the lowest point in his life. He was almost sixty years old; he had been removed from the search for the passage for almost twenty years, and he had returned to England an administrative failure. What he didn't know was that, largely by default, he was about to be given the most prized assignment of them all.

As he approached the painful conclusion that Franklin was emerging as his only option, Barrow was deeply torn. No one was more aware of Sir John's strengths and weaknesses. It was Barrow, after all, who had entrusted the man with three of his earliest missions. On the downside, Franklin had taken part in the Buchan failure. He had lost eleven men on the Coppermine search. His experience in Van Diemen's Land had been a disaster. Physically, he was still plump and out of shape. Moreover, he was old for such an assignment. And he had not been in the Arctic for more than sixteen years.

It was not that Franklin was without considerable strengths. In both combat and his previous Arctic experiences he had demonstrated remarkable courage. He was an excellent seaman. He was genuinely liked, even admired, by those who served under him. He was unflaggingly loyal and he had again proved in both his overland expeditions that he was dogged, particularly in his determination to follow whatever orders he was given.

In the end, however, it was none of these qualities that got Franklin his command—aside from the default factor, it was his petite, elegant, and highly intelligent wife who was the catalyst. Lady Jane Franklin was one of the most remarkable females of her era. She would eventually become the most influential woman in all of Arctic exploration.

Born in London in 1791, Jane Franklin defied every taboo of her day. Rather than devote herself to the genteel domestic life dictated by society, she became a social activist who took a backseat to no one in expressing her opinions on any matter. Endowed with boundless energy, she visited prisons, sat in on lectures at the Royal Institution, and attended meetings of the British and Foreign School Society. Before marrying Franklin, she had traveled widely with her father to a number of foreign countries where she meticulously recorded her impressions of every landmark she visited. Those who knew her well were particularly impressed with her thirst for knowledge—during one three-year period she had read 295 books, delving into issues ranging from social problems to education and religion.

Most of all, Jane Franklin was a woman determined to get what she wanted, and more than anything else, she wanted to get for her husband what she believed he deserved. And ultimately, that meant helping him to gain the greatest honor of all—to be forever known as the discover of the Northwest Passage. She would simply not sit idly by while he, the naval hero, the man who had eaten his boots, the man who had charted much of the Arctic coast, was being denied his moment of glory.

She loved her husband dearly, but she felt that—lacking her own aggressive nature—he needed to be reminded of what, despite his setbacks, had elevated him to the esteem in which he was held by the British public. "The character and position you possess in society," she confided to him, "and the interest—I may say celebrity—attached to your name, belong to the expeditions and would never have been acquired in the ordinary line of your [naval] profession . . . You must not think I undervalue your military career. I feel it is not that, but the other, which has made you what you are."

But for Jane Franklin, simply reminding her husband of his destiny was not enough. Action had to be taken. While Barrow debated with himself over Franklin's selection, Lady Jane began to campaign relentlessly on his behalf. No influential body escaped her lobbying— the navy's Arctic Council, the Lords Commissioners of the Admiralty, members of Parliament, the officers of the Royal and Geographical Societies. Aware that James Clark Ross had been one of Barrow's prime candidates, and concerned that he might change his mind and accept the command, she even wrote to him, stating, "If you do not go, I should wish Sir John to have it . . . and not be put aside by his age. . . . I think he will be deeply sensitive if his own department should neglect him. . . . I dread exceedingly the effect on his mind."

By the time her petitioning was through, each of these bodies was convinced that John Franklin was their man. Given the absence of other notable candidates, Sir John would have received the command in any case. But any lingering doubt was effectively removed by what Lady Franklin had managed to accomplish. It would not be the last time that her indomitability and will would influence naval events.

Now that he had decided, Barrow was equally determined. The choice was Franklin, weaknesses and all. But everything possible would be done to make certain that he succeeded. Above all, that meant sending him out in the strongest, most technologically advanced, and best supplied ships that had ever entered the Arctic.

They were the *Erebus* and the *Terror*, the two most famous and celebrated vessels in Great Britain. Only two years earlier they had returned from successfully carrying James Clark Ross and his men to the Antarctic. The *Terror* was particularly renowned. Stories still circulated throughout the country of how, after being tossed and battered among the ice floes for the better part of 1836, it had held together long enough for George Back to escape with his life. Two decades earlier, it had been the *Terror* that had fired the shots on Fort McHenry, which had led to that irritating song the Americans had adopted as their national anthem.

The *Erebus* and the *Terror* were what the navy called bomb ships, designed to bombard enemy shore batteries. Constructed of English oak, they were built to be strong enough to accommodate the weight and recoil of multi-ton mortars, and hundreds of pounds of shells and explosives. The *Erebus*, the largest vessel Barrow had sent to the Arctic, weighed 372 tons, was 105 feet long, and had a 29-foot beam. The *Terror* weighed 326 tons, was 102 feet long, and had a 27-foot beam.

Both ships had been extensively refitted to make certain they could withstand the pressure of even the thickest ice packs. Their bows were reinforced inside with a maze of beams, eight feet thick in all, and outside with inch-thick plates of iron. Five layers of African oak, English oak, and Canadian elm were added to the vessel's sides, which were also raised to keep ice from cascading over them. The decks and the bottoms of the ships were also heavily reinforced—an additional three inches of fir planking laid on the decks and seven layers of solid oak added to the bottoms.

Unlike any ships before them, the *Erebus* and the *Terror* were each also fitted with an internal heating system to protect against the cold. Huge pipes installed around the lower deck of each vessel carried steam provided by tubular boilers and supplied heat to the officers' cabins and the crew's living quarters. As a further precaution against subzero temperatures, double doors were added to all hatches and ladderways.

The most dramatic improvements, however, were in the way the ships were to be powered and propelled. Determined that they were to be independent of the wind and able to force their way through any conditions the ice might present, Barrow had the *Erebus* fitted with a fifteen-ton, twenty-five-horsepower locomotive engine. The *Terror* was equipped with a slightly smaller engine. Then he went a step further. Rather than paddle wheels, which, although they were the standard means of propulsion on steam vessels, were particularly vulnerable to ice, the *Erebus* and the *Terror* were equipped with screw propellers, which promised to be far better able to handle the batterings of ice and storm. Still not content, Barrow had engineers design the propellers in such a way that they, like the ships' rudders, were retractable, capable of being hoisted out of harm's way if their destruction by ice seemed imminent.

Finally, in case of the unlikely event of a calamity, Barrow saw to the lifeboats. Each vessel would be supplied with enough boats to carry all of its crew if the ship was destroyed or had to be abandoned. When his improvements were completed, Barrow was convinced that he had done what he had to do. Franklin's one task would be to find the passage. His ships would carry him through.

Barrow also made sure that the *Erebus* and the *Terror* were the most extravagantly provisioned vessels that had ever headed for the Arctic, carrying enough food and other supplies to last for a minimum of three years, and as many five if conditions demanded it. The supplies included 7 tons of flour, 4,500 gallons of alcohol, and almost 4 tons of tobacco. And, like the technological improvements, the nature of the food provisions was revolutionary as well. Barrow had also decided to take advantage of another recent invention—the tin container. Packed

RESOLUTE

This front page of the *Illustrated London News* depicts Franklin and thirteen of his men. All were aboard the Erebus, except Crozier. Left right by row: Lieut. Couch (mate), Lieut. Fairholme, C. H. Osmer (Purser), Lieut. Des Voeux (mate), Capt. Crozier (Terror), Capt. Sir John Franklin, Cmdr. Fitzjames, Lieut. Gore, S. Stanley (Surgeon), Lieut. H.T.D. Le Vesconte, Lieut. R. O. Sergeant (mate), James Reid (ice-master), H. D. S. Goodsir (assistant-surgeon).

aboard the *Erebus* and *Terror* were over 8,000 cans containing 15 tons of a variety of meats, 9 tons of canned vegetables, and 12 tons of different kinds of canned soups. To protect against scurvy, more than 30 barrels of lemon juice were loaded aboard. In addition to all these essentials, the ships were equipped with hand organs, mahogany writing desks, and libraries totaling some 3,000 books.

As the day of Franklin's departure drew near, the names Franklin, *Erebus*, and *Terror* echoed throughout England. Surely this was the search that would bring the long-awaited glorious result. (The air of confidence that surrounded Franklin was partially due to the fact that in 1839 two Hudson's Bay Company explorers had completed an expedition that many believed had already charted the way to the Northwest Passage; see note, page 275). The toasts of all London, Sir John and Lady Franklin were honored at dozens of social events. The newspapers seemed to write of nothing else but the impending voyage. "There appears to be but one wish amongst the whole of the inhabitants of this country," exclaimed the normally staid London *Times*, "that the enterprise in which the officers and crew are about to be engaged may be attended with success." In another article, the *Times* stated reasons for its obvious optimism: "The Lords Commissioners of the Admiralty," it proclaimed, "have, in every respect, provided most liberally for the comforts of the officers and men of an expedition which may, with the facilities of the screw-propeller, and other advantages of modern science, be attended with great results." One observer, awed by the acclaim the expedition was receiving even before leaving the dock put it simply: "One would fancy," he stated in wonderment, "England celebrating Franklin's return rather that his departure."

He was right. It was indeed a celebration, one that continued to grow right up to the point of departure and included exultations from the most respected officials—including the president of the Geographical Society. "I have the fullest confidence," stated Roderick Murchison, "that everything will be done for the promotion of science, and for the honor of the British name and navy, that human efforts can accomplish. The name of Franklin alone is, indeed, a national guarantee." Lady Franklin had done her job well.

On May 19, 1845, more than ten thousand people crammed the docks to see the expedition off and wish it good fortune. Just before boarding, the officers and crew had taken the last opportunity to send their letters to loved ones. Twenty-four-year old James Walter Fairholme, who had been promoted to the rank of lieutenant two years before being assigned to the *Erebus*, had made a point of describing the feelings for Franklin he had already developed: "He has such experience and judgment," he wrote, "that we all look on his decisions with the greatest respect. I have never felt that the Captain was so much my companion with anyoneI have sailed with before."

It appeared to be a good sign, and perhaps an even better one took place just as the ships left the dock. "Just as they were setting sail," Franklin's daughter, Eleanor, wrote that "a dove settled on one of the masts, and remained there for some time. Every one was pleased with the good omen." It was certainly that. But, at the same time, no one throughout the entire expedition's preparation or departure seemed to have attached any significance to the names of the two vessels charged with carrying Franklin to glory: *Erebus*—the word for the dark region below the earth where the dead must pass to reach Hades, and *Terror*, meaning intense, overpowering fear.

CHAPTER 7

Vanished

"Expectation darkened into anxiety—anxiety into dread."
—*Dollar Magazine*

N 1912, NORWEGIAN EXPLORER ROALD AMUNDSEN, who a year earlier had led the first group to reach the South Pole, reflected upon all of the nineteenth-century Arctic explorers who had gone before him. "Few people of the present day," he wrote, "are capable of appreciating this heroic deed, this brilliant proof of human courage and energy. These men sailed into the heart of the pack, which all previous explorers had regarded as certain death . . . These men were heroes—heroes in the highest sense."

The men of the *Erebus* and the *Terror* may or may not have regarded themselves in such heroic terms, but as they cleared the harbor, the cheers of the well-wishers still resounding in their ears, they were, almost to a man, aware that the hopes of all England sailed with them and that theirs was a mission of destiny. "Never, no never shall I forget the emotions called forth by the deafening cheering," Charles Osmer, the *Erebus*'s purser would write. "The suffocating sob of delight

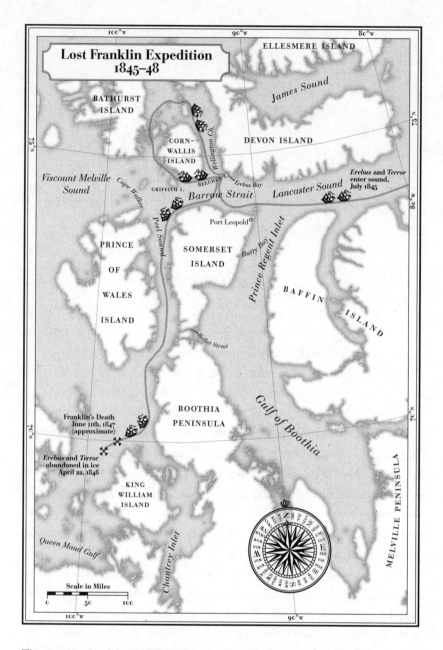

Lost Franklin Expedition
1845–48

ELLESMERE ISLAND

James Sound

BATHURST
ISLAND

CORN-
WALLIS
ISLAND

DEVON ISLAND

Viscount Melville
Sound

Wellington Ch.

GRIFFITH I.

BEECHEY I.

Erebus Bay

Barrow Strait

Lancaster Sound

Erebus and *Terror*
enter sound,
July 1845

Cape Walker

Port Leopold

Batty Bay

Peel Sound

PRINCE

OF

WALES

ISLAND

SOMERSET

ISLAND

BAFFIN

ISLAND

Prince Regent Inlet

Bellot Strait

Franklin's Death
June 11th, 1847
(approximate)

BOOTHIA

PENINSULA

Gulf of Boothia

Erebus and *Terror*
abandoned in ice
April 22, 1848

KING

WILLIAM

ISLAND

MELVILLE PENINSULA

Queen Maud Gulf

Chantrey Inlet

Scale in Miles

0   50   100

This map, based on John Franklin's directive and Inuit testimony gathered in the years
following his disappearance, shows the route that the *Erebus* and the *Terror* were assumed
to have taken—through Lancaster Sound, around Cornwallis Island, through Barrow Strait
to the area north and west of King William Island.

mingled with the fearful anticipation of dreary void . . . could not but impress on every mind the importance and magnitude of the voyage we have entered upon. There is something so thrilling in the true British cheer."

The orders that Franklin carried with him—the last that Barrow would ever issue to a passage-seeker—were, like all the instructions given to those previously sent out, clear and optimistic. Franklin was to sail to Greenland, proceed on to Baffin Bay, and once having crossed it, move through Lancaster Sound to Barrow Strait. At the Strait's westernmost end he was to steer south—he would now be in uncharted territory—following any open waters he could find until he reached the North American mainland. He was then to proceed west along the coastline that Franklin himself had mapped on his Canadian expeditions until he entered Bering Strait, which would lead him to the Pacific—and victory.

To Barrow, his orders were more than instructions. Given how much of the Arctic had already been explored and the capabilities of Franklin's two ships, they were nothing less than a road map that he simply had to follow. He did, however, provide a contingency plan. If, after passing through Barrow Strait, Franklin found his way south blocked by ice or unknown land, he was to seek an alternative route north that Barrow still felt might lead to the Open Polar Sea. It would be these alternative instructions that would play a larger role in the events of the better part of the next fifteen years than anyone could ever have imagined.

By the end of July, Franklin was right on target. He had been able to follow his orders to the letter. Having reached Baffin Bay, he was waiting for conditions to clear before crossing the bay and heading for Lancaster Sound. While waiting, the *Erebus* and the *Terror* were unexpectedly joined by two whaleships, the *Prince of Wales* and the *Enterprise*, and Franklin and his officers were invited to come aboard the *Prince of Wales* for a visit. "Both ships' crews are well, and in remarkable spirits, expecting to finish the operation in good time," the captain of the *Prince of Wales* noted in his log. "They are made fast to an iceberg

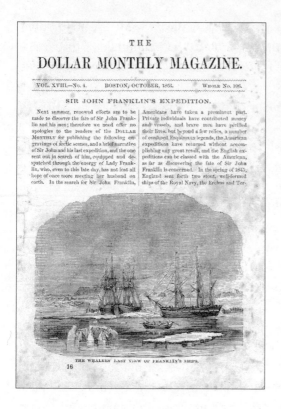

As anxiety over Franklin and his men began to grow, publications throughout Great Britain and in the United States began to express their concern. Boston's *Dollar Magazine* adorned the cover of one of its issues with this illustration titled *The Whalers' Last View of Franklin's Ships.* The accompanying story emphasized Lady Franklin's early pleadings that a rescue effort be launched.

with a temporary observatory fixed upon it." The *Enterprise's* skipper made his own notations, commenting on the fact that Franklin had told him that he had provisions enough for five years and, if he had to, could "make them spin out for seven years."

It was a welcome encounter, and before leaving the whaleship, Franklin reciprocated by asking the two captains to join him on the *Erebus* the next evening. But in the morning, conditions suddenly improved and the *Erebus* and *Terror* weighed anchor. They would never be seen again.

Two years elapsed, years in which Franklin was expected to return any day in triumph. Given the difficulty in communicating over such a long distance from such a remote region, there was no real concern—yet. But by the end of 1847, there was still no news. Public concern began to grow. Where was he? Where were the two greatest ships on the planet? The following spring the first official mention of a rescue mission was made in the House of Commons. Not surprisingly, it was instigated by Jane Franklin. Increasingly, the newspapers and other journals joined in commenting on the national mood. As *Dollar Magazine* proclaimed, "Expectation darkened into anxiety—anxiety into dread."

By this time the Lords had, to a large degree, turned over affairs dealing with northern exploration to the Arctic Council, an exclusive fraternity of naval officers whose deeds had already made them legendary, men whose names now appeared on capes and straits and other waterways throughout the Arctic. More than anyone else, they could imagine what Franklin, if he was still alive, had to be going through. Each of them—Edward Parry, George Back, John Clark Ross, John Richardson, Frederick Beechey—had risked his life to help England triumph in the Arctic. There was no question in their minds: Franklin had to be found. Everything possible had to be done to find him.

The one thing the Admiralty had done was to offer rewards— £20,000 to anyone who "might render efficient assistance in saving the lives of Sir John Franklin and his squadron," and £10,000 for anyone who simply found his ships. But it was not enough. Simply by having disappeared, Franklin had risen in status from hero to godlike figure. Something had to be done; the public and English national pride demanded it.

One man was more than willing to do something. It was John Ross, now nearly seventy years old. From the beginning, he had been the one critic of the Franklin venture. Why, he had asked, was the expedition so large? Repeatedly he had pointed out that in his 1829–33 voyage he had brought only twenty-three men, and they were barely able to sustain themselves. Why, he wanted to know, was Franklin taking such huge vessels? Admittedly they were technological wonders, but as far as Ross was concerned they drew far too much water for Arctic conditions.

In 1845, Ross had supposedly promised Franklin that if the *Erebus* and the *Terror* went missing in the ice, he would return to the Arctic

£20,000
REWARD

WILL BE GIVEN BY

Her Majesty's Government

TO ANY PARTY OR PARTIES, OF ANY COUNTRY, WHO SHALL RENDER EFFICIENT
ASSISTANCE TO THE CREWS OF THE

DISCOVERY SHIPS

UNDER THE COMMAND OF

SIR JOHN FRANKLIN,

1.—To any Party or Parties who, in the judgment of the
Board of Admiralty, shall discover and effectually relieve the
Crews of Her Majesty's Ships "Erebus" and "Terror," the

£20,000.

OR

2.—To any Party or Parties who, in the judgment of the
Board of Admiralty, shall discover and effectually relieve *any*
of the Crews of Her Majesty's Ships "Erebus" and "Terror,"
or shall convey such intelligence as shall lead to the relief of
such Crews or *any* of them, the Sum of

£10,000.

OR

3.—To any Party or Parties who, in the judgment of the
Board of Admiralty, shall by virtue of his or their efforts first
succeed in ascertaining their fate,

£10,000.

W. A. B. HAMILTON,

Admiralty, March 8th, 1850.

Secretary of the Admiralty.

This reward poster revealed both the Admiralty's and the Arctic Council's growing
concern about Franklin's disappearance. Eventually the £10,000 reward for ascertaining
the expedition's fate would engender bitter controversy.

to lead the search-and-rescue mission. Ross was now ready to keep his promise. But the Council turned him down. He was too old, they told him. Instead, plans for a three-pronged rescue effortwere adopted. First, an overland expedition would be mounted to the Canadian northwest. Its mission would be to try to find Franklin by following the MacKenzie River north to the Arctic coast before proceeding eastward along the rim of Wollaston Land and Victoria Land. Franklin's friend and two-time Arctic companion John Richardson was chosen to lead the expedition, a decision applauded by Jane Franklin. She was now spending all of her working hours lobbying for rescue efforts. When Richardson's selection had been announced, she had actually volunteered to join the search, an offer that Richardson diplomatically declined. In one of the many letters she wrote to her husband and placed in the hands of search parties, she explained, "It would have been a less trial to me to come after you . . . but I thought it my duty and my interest to remain . . . yet if I thought you to be ill, nothing should have stopped me." Like every other letter she would dispatch, it was brought back unopened.

At the same time that Richardson searched for Franklin by land, two ships would be sent out to trace the route that Franklin had been instructed to follow. This meant sailing through Lancaster Sound and Barrow Strait to Melville Island and Banks Land before turning south. Command of this search was given to James Clark Ross, who had been one of John Barrow's prime choices to lead the expedition that was now the object of the search. With all of England clamoring for news of Franklin's whereabouts, Ross's wife had released him from his promise of never returning to the Arctic.

Finally, a third rescue party was to be sent out, two ships commanded by Lieutenant W. J. S. Pullen and Captain Henry Kellett. Their orders were to proceed directly to the Bering Strait in the hope that Franklin had made it that far. Their main objective was to serve as supply depots for both Richardson's and Ross's expeditions.

The Richardson rescue party, made up of five English seamen and fifteen British soldiers, left for the Arctic in late March 1848. After having screened hundreds of requests from men who wished to be named second-in-command, Richardson felt blessed to have secured the services of Dr. John Rae, a skilled surgeon and a man whose inquisitiveness about nature rivaled Richardson's. Lean, bewhiskered, and seemingly inexhaustible, Rae had been described by one of his contemporaries as "muscular and active and full of animal spirit." At thirty-four, he was already a veteran of fourteen years in the Arctic where, in the employ of the Hudson's Bay Company, he had become something of a legend within the fur-trading company. (At the time company's governor was George Simpson, a key player in the search for the passage and Franklin, see note, page 277.) In 1846, while engaged in a survey of Melville Island, he had found himself beset by winter. With no ship in which to gain shelter, Rae and his party had become the first Europeans ever to winter on the Arctic coast, and the first to survive without any provisions except what he and his Inuit guide were able to provide by hunting caribou, musk oxen, and birds, and by fishing.

The following summer the Rae legend continued to grow as, in the process of charting 625 miles of hitherto unexplored Arctic coastline, he snowshoed 1,200 miles, living entirely off the land. Regarded by the Inuit as the most skilled snowshoe walker of his time (George Back might have argued the point), Rae prided himself on the name the natives had given him—*Alooka* ("he who takes long strides").

It was Rae's relationship with the Inuit that would ultimately best define him. His participation in the Richardson party would be but a prelude to his involvement in the search for John Franklin. Before it was over, Rae, more than anyone else, would have learned the natives' ways and dedicated himself to dressing like them, living like them, hunting like them, and traveling as they did. Eventually he would be the center of a controversy that would rock all of England.

But in 1848, with the Richardson party, the search for Franklin was just starting. And it was not a successful beginning. By August the expedition had reached the estuary of the MacKenzie River. It then traveled in four small boats to Wollaston Land (which, along with Victoria Land, made up a massive 135,000 square-mile island, but no one knew this at the time). After abandoning their boats, Richardson, Rae, and the others trudged overland to Fort Confidence on Great Bear Lake where they hunkered down for the winter, all without finding a single clue.

In the spring, Richardson, worn out from the journey, returned to England, leaving Rae in command. But when Rae tried to scout Wollaston Land and Victoria Land he found his way completely blocked by ice. Like Richardson, he would return home without having shed a bit of light on the Franklin mystery.

For John Rae, there would be other expeditions. But as James Clark Ross set out on *his* rescue effort he knew that this would be his last trip to the Arctic. Franklin had to be found. But there were 128 others out there as well, something Ross felt that the public sometimes tended to forget. And included among them was his closest friend, Francis Crozier, who had been given command of the *Terror*.

The Admiralty sent Ross's expedition off in two large vessels, the *Enterprise* (450 tons) and the *Investigator* (400 tons). Together they carried enough supplies for a three-year search plus a full year's provisions for Franklin and his men once they were found. Aboard the vessels were two senior officers destined to become leaders in the next generation of Arctic explorers. Forty-one-year-old Robert McClure, who had been born in Wexford, Ireland, had been in the navy for twenty- four years, and had shared George Back's traumatic year aboard the *Terror* in 1836. Leopold M'Clintock had been born to Scottish parents in Dundalk, Ireland. Now twenty-nine and a seventeen-year navy veteran, he was making his first northern voyage. Neither had any idea of the momentous roles each would eventually play in the saga that was just beginning to unfold.

For whatever reasons, Ross, although one of the most experienced of the Arctic adventurers, left England later in the season than he should have, some two months after Richardson had departed. After following Franklin's path by sailing through Barrow Strait and attempting to proceed through Wellington Channel, he found his way blocked by ice. Concerned that winter was already setting in, he made his way to Port Leopold on the northeastern tip of Somerset Island in Lancaster Sound. He had no choice. He would have to spend his ninth winter in the ice.

But he would not be idle. The search for Franklin would go on even when the ships were imprisoned. After securing the vessels for the long, dark months ahead, Ross had his men begin shooting off rockets every morning and evening. If the Franklin expedition was anywhere in the area, surely they would see them. Ross also sent out members of his party to capture foxes that roamed through the vicinity where the ships lay. The animals were then fitted with metal collars upon which were punched the names of the rescue vessels, their position, and the date, "in the hopes," as Ross would write, "that Sir John Franklin, or some of his people, might in [this] ingenious manner be appraised of assistance."

Ross's greatest hope of finding some trace of Franklin or his whereabouts, however, was to leave his immobile ships and search as wide an area as he could by sledge. Surprisingly, he had not brought dogs with him, and the backbreaking labor of hauling the heavy, equipment-loaded sledges over the hummocks and crushed ice fell to his men.

On May 15, Ross himself took charge of the first of the sledging searches. It would be a forty-day journey that would take him first along the north side of Somerset Island and then down the island's western perimeter. His goal was to travel as far as the Magnetic Pole, the site of the discovery that had made him forever famous. But by the time he reached a point some 170 miles short of the Pole, some of his men were showing signs of snow blindness; others had sprained ankles and other injuries, and he was forced to return to the ships. By the time they got back, they had covered 539 miles.

Before making the long return journey, Ross had had his men construct a large cairn into which was placed a copper cylinder containing a lengthy note:

> *The cylinder which contains this paper was left here by a party detached from Her Majesty's ships* Enterprise *and* Investigator

under the command of Captain Sir James C. Ross, Royal Navy in
search of the expedition of Sir John Franklin; and to inform any
of his party that might find it that these ships, having wintered
at Port Leopold in long. 90°W, lat. 73°52'N have formed there
a depot with provisions for the use of Sir John Franklin's party
sufficient for six months; also two very small depots about fifteen
miles south of Cape Clarence and twelve miles south of Cape
Seppings. The party are now about to return to the ships, which, as
early as possible in the spring, will push forward to Melville Strait,
and search the north coast of Barrow Strait; and, failing to meet
the party they are seeking, will touch at Port Leopold on their way
back, and then return to England before the winter shall set in.

In the months that followed, other sledging trips were launched. On one of them, a foray down the west shore of Prince Regent Inlet, Fury Beach was reached. There they found, still intact, the structure known as Somerset House where, in the winter of 1832–33, Ross, his uncle, and twenty-one others had just barely managed to survive.

By August, the sledging trips had taken a serious toll. Many of the men had become ill, some seriously. Ross himself had to take to his bed for a time. Commenting on the consequences of long-range sledging, Leopold M'Clintock would later write: "One gradually becomes more of an *animal*, under this system of constant exposure and unremitting labor." Ironically it would be M'Clintock who, beginning with his experiences on this expedition, would become the most knowledgeable sledger of them all. It would be his expertise at coping with the difficulties of preparing the sleds properly, loading them with the proper amount of supplies, rationing the food, and providing medical care on long journeys over ice, that would enable him to facilitate the most important discoveries in the entire Franklin saga.

By the final week of August the ice around the *Enterprise* and the *Investigator* had loosened sufficiently for the crews to cut a two-mile channel to open water. The long winter ordeal was over—but not quite. On August 28, after erecting a small house filled with supplies for the sustenance of any members of the Franklin expedition that should find it, the party set sail. Only a few days later however, they were hit by ice flows and carried 250 miles west towards Baffin Bay. Somehow they were able to escape this trap and, by September 25, managed to fight their way into open waters. By this time, almost every member of both ships had become ill. The search was over. It was time to head home.

The Ross Expedition had hardly been a success. They had found absolutely no evidence of Franklin's whereabouts. They had seen no sign of the depot ships that were supposed to have aided them in their search. (Due to miscommunications, Pullen's and Kellett's vessels arrived in the Arctic a year late and did not return until October 1851.) And their voyage back to England was calamitous. Almost immediately, the *Investigator*'s cook died from scurvy. A week before England was reached, another crewman passed away. Days after their return, another seaman succumbed in the hospital. In all Ross had lost six of his sixty-man contingent and almost every other member had become alarmingly ill.

Yet Ross had come much closer to finding important evidence than he could have imagined. Although it was within his reach, he had not investigated Beechey Island where, it was later discovered, Franklin had spent his first winter. He knew that, according to his instructions, Sir John was supposed to sail southward through Peel Sound. But when Ross put into Port Leopold for the winter and looked out across the sound he concluded that that would have been impossible. "No vessel could have gone south through Peel Sound," he wrote in his final report. "All I could see for fifty miles was an unbroken sheet of ice." Incredibly, the searchers of the passage, and now the searchers *for* the searchers of the passage, had still not learned the basic Arctic tenet that William Scoresby had tried to teach them more than thirty years ago. Despite all his years in the North, James Clark Ross failed to understand that an Arctic channel could be open one year and completely frozen over the next.

CHAPTER 8

The

Prize at Last

"Can it be that so humble a creature as I am will be
permitted to perform what has baffled the talented and
wise for a few hundred years?"
—ROBERT MCCLURE

I
T HAD NOW BEEN more than five years since John Franklin had
sailed away. The national anxiety over his disappearance, combined
with the published reports of Richardson's and Ross's adventures in
seeking him, emblazoned the mysteries and romance of the Arctic
in the British national consciousness as never before. Newspapers
became filled with accounts of past expeditions, of northern discoveries
already made, of the ways in which the passage-seekers were bringing
greater glory to the nation than even the most honored military heroes,
all wrapped around the great burning question—where was Franklin?
The *Illustrated London News* led the charge:

> *Of all the expeditions which private enterprise and public policy
> has fitted out for the exploration of the still unknown regions of the*

*globe, the several expeditions for the discovery of the North-west
Passage are looked upon by the people of this country, and by the rest
of the world in general, with the greatest interest and anxiety. The
failure of one expedition is but the incentive to fit out another; and
the greater danger, the greater is the eagerness of enterprising and
resolute men, from the most able and experienced Commander to
the hardest-working common sailor, to share it, upon the chance
of imperishable renown which success will afford them. Captains
Parry, Ross, Back, Franklin and their brave companions, who
have been engaged at intervals for the last thirty years and
upwards in the endeavor to solve this deeply interesting problem
and to determine the configurations of the great North American
continent . . . have carried with them on their departure the cordial
good-wishes of their countrymen for their success.*

  *Their return in safety, after the manifold privations and
hardships of such a voyage has invariably been greeted with
fervent enthusiasm; and the long absence of Sir John Franklin,
the last gallant explorer of those seas, has excited in the public
mind an affectionate and deep interest, amounting at last to
a painful solicitude for his fate and that of the brave men who
share his perils and his glory.*

Actually, it was far more than "a painful solicitude." Finding
Franklin had become nothing less than a crusade. "Since the zealous
attempts to rescue the Holy Sepulcher in the Middle Ages," one
newspaper exclaimed, "the Christian world has not so unanimously
agreed on anything as the desire to recover Sir John Franklin, dead or
alive, from the dread solitude of death into which he has so fearlessly
ventured." (The search for Franklin became such a cause célèbre that it
was the subject of many songs and poems, see note, page 278.)

All England was now caught up in the great concern. In one
gigantic outpouring of emotion, prayers for the expedition's safe return
were said in sixty different churches. More than fifty thousand citizens
attended the services.

Not surprisingly, the most visible concern was that expressed by Lady Franklin. More than ever, she was doing all she could do to facilitate the search for her husband. Determined to try everything, she even visited a psychic, hoping to hear that Sir John was still alive and learn where in that vast, frozen wildness he might be found. She spoke with everyone she could, anyone who might suggest anything that might be done. Accompanied by her friend and advisor, William Scoresby, she traveled to various ports from which the Arctic whalemen departed and implored them to carry extra food and supplies in the event they came upon the missing expedition. And, as she had done when she had so successfully campaigned for her husband's selection as commander of the expedition, she devoted hours to letter writing. Putting national pride aside (John Barrow would have been appalled), she even wrote to the newly elected American president, Zachary Taylor, imploring him to launch an American search. The obsession that England or that even Sir John must be the first to find the passage was no longer her concern. All that mattered was that her husband be found. "I am not without hope," she wrote, "that you will deem it not unworthy of a great and kindred nation to take up the cause of humanity ... and thus generously make it your own ... I should rejoice that it was to America we owe our restored happiness."

Once again her efforts energized the press. Increasingly they adopted the theme that much more had to be done. Even Ross's and Richardson's efforts had been lacking, they intimated. The London *Times* spoke for them all when it dared ask why both expeditions had given up the search while their ships were still loaded with so many provisions. "We shall never attain our end," explained the newspaper, "by sailing up to the ice and then back again."

The public agreed. "Let 1850 be the year to redeem our tottering honour," a reader wrote to the *Times*. Obviously the writer was aware of the letter that Jane Franklin had written to the American president but, unlike Lady Jane, was not willing to surrender British pride: "Let not the United States snatch from us the glory of rescuing the lost expedition," the writer pleaded.

Together—press, public, Lady Franklin—it was pressure that even the most recalcitrant member of the Admiralty could not withstand. The result was the launching of the greatest activity the Arctic would ever witness. In the next twelve years, as many as forty ships and more than two thousand officers and men would join in the search for the Franklin expedition. It would be the longest and most expensive search and rescue mission ever undertaken.

It began on January 20, 1850, with an expedition commanded by Captain Richard Collinson aboard the hastily refitted *Enterprise*. Joining him as second-in-command was Lieutenant Robert McClure, in charge of the *Investigator*. Theirs would be the first of six expeditions that would head for the Arctic before the year was out.

Two more different leaders could probably not have been chosen. The painfully thin, often dour Collinson was a cautious man, averse to taking risks, while the muscular and animated McClure was known for his mercurial nature. He was also extremely ambitious. This was his first command and he was ready to do almost anything to gain the renown that came with finding Franklin, or maybe even the passage.

Because James Clark Ross had vividly described the impenetrable ice that blocked Barrow Strait, the expedition was given orders different from most of their predecessors. After sailing around Cape Horn to Honolulu for a supply stop, they were to enter the Arctic from the west and then make their way eastward. Whichever ship reached Honolulu first was to wait for the other so that they could conduct the search together. But when McClure, who had been separated from Collinson on the voyage over by fog, reached Honolulu, he discovered that the commander, having waited for four days, had left the island and had headed for the Arctic. To his even greater consternation McClure was given a message telling him that if he did not catch up with Collinson, the commander would replace the *Investigator* with the *Plover*, the ship that had originally been sent to assist James Clark Ross's expedition, and which was still in the Bering Strait.

McClure was beside himself. Was he to lose his big chance by being replaced by a supply ship? He most certainly would miss the glory he craved if Collinson were to find Franklin before he did. The next scheduled rendezvous point for the two ships was at a spot near Bering Strait. He knew that Collinson would travel to that point by sailing around the Aleutian Islands. Without hesitation, McClure made his decision. He would cut straight through the islands, chancing a route that would require him to navigate through dangerous, shallow, and uncharted waters.

It would not be the last time on the fateful voyage that McClure would risk his ship and the lives of his men to feed his ambition. But he made it. Negotiating the thick fog, the tumultuous tides, and the ever-present reefs and shoals that characterized the inner Aleutian waters, he entered Kotzebue Sound on July 29, days ahead of when Collinson could be expected to arrive.

Now McClure's actions turned into outright deception. Shortly after entering the sound, he surprisingly encountered another naval vessel. It was the *Herald*, one of the ships that had been originally sent in 1848 to supply James Clark Ross and John Richardon, but had stayed on in the Arctic to search for Franklin. The *Herald* was commanded by captain Henry Kellett, an officer superior in rank to McClure. When Kellett came aboard the *Investigator*, McClure brazenly told him that he was sailing behind Collinson and that he was racing to catch up. A veteran explorer, Kellett was not deceived. He knew that McClure was lying. Kellett had been receiving updates from the Admiralty from passing ships, but had been given no orders from the Admiralty as to what to do should the *Enterprise* and the *Investigator* fail to rendezvous in the Arctic. Convinced that his main duty was not to impede the search for Franklin, he "swallowed" McClure's false tale, decided not to pull rank by ordering that McClure wait for Collinson, and reluctantly allowed him to sail on.

Although he had no way of knowing it, McClure's true adventure was about to begin. Only a few days after leaving Kellett, he encountered solid ice but, refusing to stop, he plowed his way through the pack. Reaching Point Barrow and finding it completely icebound, he ordered forty of his men into five of the boats and had them haul the *Investigator* around the point. He was now in waters off northern Alaska into which no white men had ever entered. Seeking Banks Land, he tried to enter every channel he encountered, only to find his way totally blocked. All along the way he was surrounded by the tallest, most spectacular Arctic cliffs that any European had ever seen.

But McClure had little time to admire them. Suddenly the *Investigator* was stuck by a fierce gale, so strong that it completely took over control of the ship. Unable to do anything but struggle to keep the vessel upright, he was driven along by wind and ice until, on August 7, he reached a mountainous land dominated by two-thousand-foot peaks. Thankful to still be alive, he planted a flag and named it Baring Land, after the first lord of the Admiralty. (McClure didn't know it but it was actually Banks Land, the very region he had been looking for. Nor did he know that it was really an island).

The crew of the *Investigator* included Lieutenant Samuel Creswell, a gifted artist. His dramatic drawings illustrated the major events in the voyage that resulted in the discovery of the last link in the passage. Here, two members of the ship gaze out at the long sought-after final link—the frozen gap between Banks and Melville Islands.

He had been fortunate thus far and now he got even luckier. Once again the wind and the flowing ice picked up. Once again he had no control over where he was being taken. Unwittingly he was being driven northward up a narrow channel. What was this waterway? No other explorer, he was sure, had ever entered it. Was it yet another dead end? Or could it be a strait leading to—he hardly dared think of the possibility. "I cannot describe my anxious feeling," he would later write in his published account of the expedition. "Can it be possible that this water communicates with Barrow's Strait and shall be the long sought North West Passage? Can it be that so humble a creature as I am will be permitted to perform what had baffled the talented and wise for hundreds of years?"

Never in his life had McClure been so excited; he was eager to confirm that the waterway linked up with areas already discovered, making it the final connection between the West and the East. But then his luck turned against him. Ahead of him, he discovered, the channel was completely frozen over, much too thick to even attempt to try to plow through. Winter was definitely setting in. Should he head back south and find a safe shelter for the winter? Or should he remain where he was, risking the elements in this unprotected spot? For him, one thing was certain: Before making his decision he had to know that this epic discovery was real. The next day he sent his ice mate up to the crow's nest where he could see for twenty miles. And there in the distance was a vast expanse of open water.

For McClure, there was no choice. He had to winter in the pack so that in the spring he could complete the passage. Once more he would be risking the ship and the lives of all aboard. But he was too close to retreat now. Then, for the third time, the Arctic weather controlled his fate. As stronger winds than he had yet encountered blew in, the *Investigator* was torn from the ice and driven thirty miles back up the channel. For more than a week the vessel was pounded relentlessly until, on September 26, McClure was certain it was about to be blown apart. Calling all hands on deck, he was ready to give the orders to abandon ship when miraculously the winds abated. Yet again he had escaped disaster.

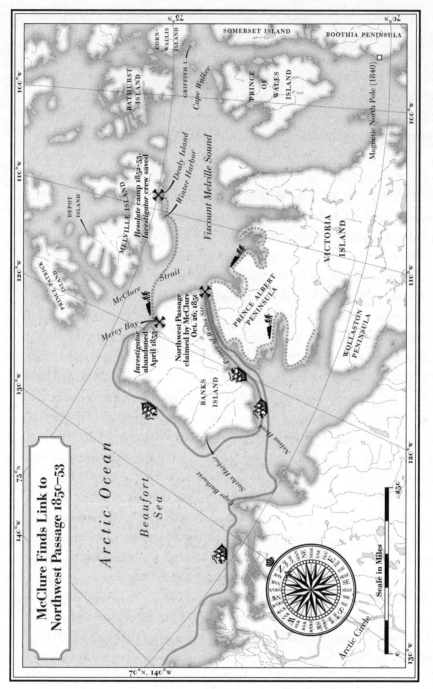

McClure Finds Link to Northwest Passage 1850–53

75°N

70°N

Arctic Ocean

Beaufort Sea

PRINCE PATRICK ISLAND

DEPOT ISLAND

MELVILLE ISLAND

Resolute camp 1852–53; Investigator crew saved

Dealy Island Winter Harbor

McClure Strait

Mercy Bay

Investigator abandoned April 1853

Northwest Passage claimed by McClure, Oct. 26, 1850

BANKS ISLAND

Steele Harbor

Cape Bathurst

Nelson Head

BATHURST ISLAND

CORN- WALLIS ISLAND

GRIFFITH I.

Cape Walker

SOMERSET ISLAND

Viscount Melville Sound

Prince of Wales Str.

PRINCE ALBERT PENINSULA

VICTORIA ISLAND

WOLLASTON PENINSULA

PRINCE OF WALES ISLAND

BOOTHIA PENINSULA

Magnetic North Pole (1840)

Arctic Circle

Scale in Miles

0   250

100°W   110°W   120°W   130°W   140°W

75°N

70°N, 140°W

100°W   110°W   120°W   130°W

NW N NE NNE ENE E ESE SE SSE S SSW SW WSW W WNW NNW

This map shows the major events in the dramatic voyage of the HMS *Investigator*: The route that Robert McClure took in finding the last link in the Northwest Passage, the site where his ship became entrapped, and the spot from which members of the *Resolute* launched the sledging party that resulted in the rescue of McClure and his crew.

The storm was over and the *Investigator* was totally covered and surrounded by ice. But McClure had only one thing on his mind: He had to be even more certain that what his lookout had spotted was correct. Leaving the *Investigator*, he led a sledge party across the ice to the land on the east side of the waterway. Then, with the ship's doctor, Alexander Armstrong, and a few of his men, he climbed a fifteen-hundred-foot mountain and from that height spied the end of the ice-filled channel (which he had earlier named Prince of Wales Strait) and the open water beyond. "The highway to England from ocean to ocean lay before us," Dr. Armstrong would later write.

It was still not good enough for McClure. Nothing would do but actually standing on the shore of the passage. Eleven days later he led another sledge party along the eastern shore of Banks Land to the end of the channel. There, on October 26, 1850, Robert McClure, standing on a six–hundred-foot hill, became the first man to ascertain that there was indeed a water route from the Atlantic to the Pacific. The more than four-hundred–year-old dream was real; the Northwest Passage existed—and it had been found. In words that would have gladdened the heart of John Barrow, Dr. Armstrong would later describe the emotions he felt as he realized that "the maritime greatness and glory of our country were still further elevated above all nations of the earth."

Returning to the *Investigator*, McClure informed the crew that, with the passage found, they could claim the £20,000 prize. Their joy was tempered, however, by the realization that they would have to spend the winter in the unprotected middle of Prince of Wales Strait. Yet again, luck was with them. Although the season was bitterly cold, no storms rivaling those they had experienced the year before struck the ship and in the early spring, before the ice released them, McClure sent out three long sledge expeditions in search of Franklin. All returned with nothing to report.

Six weeks later the ice broke up. At this point many in the crew were anxious to return home. They had had enough of cheating disaster. And although they had not found Franklin, they knew they would be returning to a heroes' welcome. But McClure had another agenda.

It was not enough to have proved the existence of the passage. He had to sail through it.

He almost made it. He was less than sixty miles from sailing through Prince of Wales Strait when once again he found the final stretch of the channel frozen over. He still wouldn't give up. Turning around, he made his way back up the strait and began looking around for another channel that might lead him into the open sea. He found one that looked promising and sailed three hundred miles down it before it became so narrow and icebound that he was forced to halt.

Once again McClure had led his men into a life-threatening situation. As the tide mounted, huge blocks of ice slammed against the *Investigator*, threatening to sink it. For the second time in the voyage, McClure was ready to abandon ship and, for the second time, just as he was about to do so, the weather changed and the ice became motionless. McClure had still not run out of miracles.

It was time to find another winter haven. Escaping the channel, he sailed south for the better part of a month looking for a protected spot. Finally he found one and named it Mercy Bay. Later, Dr. Armstrong remarked upon the name, stating that "some of us not inappropriately said it ought to have been so-called, from the fact that it would have been a mercy had we never entered it. He was right. McClure had unwittingly chosen a bay in which the tides were such that the waters leading out of it remained frozen all year long. McClure and his men would be trapped in Mercy Bay for two years. The *Investigator* would never be released, and the officers and crew that had finally found the Northwest Passage would come within days of starving to death.

CHAPTER 9

The

Arctic Traffic Jam

"Graves, Captain Penny, graves!"
—Sailor from the WILLIAM PENNY
RESCUE EXPEDITION, 1850

THE SELECTION OF RICHARD COLLINSON and Robert McClure to command the first of the many 1850 rescue expeditions had engendered little surprise. Both were respected, seasoned naval veterans, accustomed to navy discipline, traditions, and ways of doing things. The man who led the expedition sent out some four months after Collinson and McClure, however, was a most unlikely choice. The selection of William Penny was perhaps the greatest indication of how concerned both the Admiralty and the Arctic Council had become over Franklin's fate and how much these two bodies were being pressured to do everything that could be done to find him.

Penny was not a navy man. He was, of all things, a whaler, the very sort that the navy had assiduously refused to put in command of any of its ships. Not that the navy did not recognize Penny's skills and knowledge; now forty-one, Penny—who was regarded by those

who had sailed under him as both humorless and overly ambitious—
had been a master of whaling vessels for sixteen years and had been
sailing the Arctic waters since the age of eleven. It had, in fact, been he
who, guided by an Inuit whom he had all but adopted, had discovered
the whaling grounds at the mouth of Cumberland Sound, an area
that would prove to be one of the most fertile of all places in which to
hunt the baleen-rich bowhead whale. For years the navy had sought
Penny's advice about Arctic topography and conditions, but giving

He was a whaleman, not a British naval officer. But it would be William Penny who would
prove to be one of the most determined of all the Franklin seekers.

him command of two Royal Navy vessels? Only a year ago it would have been unthinkable.

What really changed the Admiralty's position? Again it was Jane Franklin. Even before the Collinson-McClure expedition had been organized, she had begun making plans to mount her own private rescue mission. And she had asked William Penny, described by one of his shipmates as "vigorous and full of energy and zeal in the Franklin cause," to command it. Penny not only accepted but stated that he expected no compensation for undertaking such a "humanitarian mission." Lady Franklin then launched yet another lobbying campaign aimed at persuading the Admiralty to finance the expedition. As always, she made sure that the press was well aware of both her petitions and the fact that, if the navy refused to underwrite the search, she was prepared to use her dwindling funds to do so herself. As she expected, editorials and letters from readers began appearing, decrying the fact that this "brave woman" (now nothing less than a national heroine) was about to risk poverty to save her husband and his noble companions. The Admiralty was forced to give in; it would supply Penny with two naval vessels and would finance the mission. Once again, Jane Franklin had shamed the navy into bending to her will.

Penny sailed from England on April 13, 1850, with two relatively small vessels appropriately named *Lady Franklin* and *Sophia* (Jane and Sir John's favorite niece). He carried with him a letter from Lady Franklin to be delivered to her husband, should Penny find him. "I desire nothing," she had written, "but to cherish the remainder of your days, however injured and broken your health may be . . . I live in you my dearest . . . I pray for you at all hours." Exactly one week after Penny departed, another rescue expedition left in its wake. Its commander was seventy-three years old, his ships were private yachts, and he had raised the money for the search largely through public subscription. It was none other than John Ross, determined to keep his promise that, if necessary, he would rescue his friend. As he once again headed for the Arctic, John Ross, the oldest commander in the British navy, was convinced he would do just that.

Given his past history, the navy did not share Ross's confidence in the success of his private search. But it had great hopes for the man chosen to lead the fourth expedition sent out in 1850. A veteran of the War of 1812, where he had demonstrated great courage during the attacks on Washington, Baltimore, and New Orleans, the crusty, opinionated Horatio Austin was, at forty-nine, regarded by both the Admiralty and the Arctic Council as one of the navy's shining stars. The son of a Chatham dockyard official, he had gained his first Arctic experience while serving as a lieutenant aboard the ill-fated *Fury* during Edward Parry's third search for the passage. Promoted to captain, he had commanded the HMS *Cyclops* during the Syrian War of 1839–40, during which he had again been cited for skill and bravery under fire. He had then spent more than two years conducting research on the development of naval steam vessels.

Now he'd been given command of the largest and most ambitious expedition ever sent to the Arctic. His flagship was the HMS *Resolute*, a massively built 424-ton vessel, 115 feet long with a 28½-foot beam. More than any of the other ships in Austin's fleet, the *Resolute* was constructed for Arctic duty. Its bow and decks were built up with three thicknesses of wood to withstand the pressure of the ice and all of its decks were double planked. The furnace-fed steam pipe, which passed under every sleeping berth and through every cabin, was designed to keep the vessel warm even when the outside temperature plummeted to as low as seventy degrees below zero. The rest of Austin's fleet consisted of the *Assistance*, commanded by Captain Erasmus Ommanney; the *Pioneer*, led by Lieutenant Sherard Osborn; and the *Intrepid*, commanded by John Bertie Cator.

Four great navy ships, led by four proven navy men. Nothing had yet been heard from either Collinson or McClure. Perhaps there would soon be encouraging news from them. If not, then surely, the Admiralty believed, it would be Austin who would finally find Franklin or at least evidence of what had happened to him.

Jane Franklin, on the other hand, was still not satisfied. Yes, the navy had, at last, truly committed itself to finding her husband. But now she had another concern: What if all these recently departed expeditions were looking in the wrong places? She had talked with every one of the commanders who had gone looking for the passage. She had met with John Richardson and James Clark Ross almost as soon as they had returned. She had pored through every report and published account that these seekers had written. And she had studied every new map of the North that had been drawn. At this point, no one knew more about the Arctic than she.

Now, as she read and reread the orders that Penny and Austin had been given and considered the areas in which John Ross intended to search, she became increasingly troubled. Based on the report they had been given that all the passageways leading south were blocked, they were all focusing their attention on the far north. No one was looking along the coast to the south. According to his orders, that was where Franklin was supposed to go. And, as Lady Franklin knew better than anyone else, if those were his orders, her husband would do everything in his power to carry them out.

As usual, Jane Franklin acted upon her concerns. Since the navy was not sending anyone to look to the south, she would take care of that herself. Convincing a friend to lend her his ninety-ton former pilot boat, the *Prince Albert*, she outfitted the vessel by contributing yet more of her own funds and by raising the remainder of what was needed from other friends. To command the mission she chose Lieutenant Charles Codrington Forsyth, a man whom she had met and befriended while living in Van Diemen's Land. Although Forsyth had never been to the Arctic, he shared Lady Jane's conviction that Sir John would be found by searching to the south.

In the end, the Forsyth expedition would be made most memorable by the man Lady Franklin selected to be Forsyth's second-in-command. Of all those who would be involved in the Franklin saga, W. Parker Snow was among the most colorful and certainly had the most checkered background. After spending four years at sea as a youth, the thirty-three-year-old eccentric, egotistical Snow had gone to live in the Australian outback, where he had openly associated with known criminals and had undoubtedly engaged in illegal activities himself. Rejoining the navy, he had been in and out of scrapes, but had saved his career through various heroics, including risking his own life to save a seaman who had been attacked by a shark. What may have persuaded Jane Franklin that he was the right man to assist Forsyth was her knowledge of a suggestion that Snow had made to the Admiralty. He had seriously proposed that convicts, because of their daring and their ability to work their way out of tight situations, should be used in the search for the lost expedition. Not surprisingly, the Admiralty had been offended by the suggestion, but not Lady Jane. In her opinion, anything that might possibly help find her husband should be tried.

With Forsyth's departure, there were now eleven British vessels engaged in the Franklin search. And they were not alone. Almost at the same time that Austin's fleet had left for the Arctic, two American vessels had joined in the hunt. Jane Franklin's pleadings with President Zachary Taylor had borne fruit.

In December 1849, Lady Franklin had followed up her first letter to the president by once again pleading with him for an American rescue effort. By this time, Matthew Maury, one of the United States' foremost scientists and a man who would come to be regarded by many as the father of modern oceanography, had published his paper "proving" the existence of a Northwest Passage. Motivated partially by a desire to have the passage be an American discovery and sincerely moved by Jane Franklin's latest entreaties, Taylor asked Congress to fund a rescue mission. When legislators balked at releasing the funds, New Bedford native Henry Grinnell, whose New York shipping firm had earned him a fortune, stepped in and offered to provide and provision two ships for the mission if Congress would place them under the control of the United States Navy.

The two American vessels, the 144-ton *Advance* and the 81-ton *Rescue* sailed under the command of Lieutenant Edwin De Haven. But the Grinnell Expedition would be made noteworthy not by De Haven, but by its chief medical officer, twenty-nine-year-old Elisha

Kent Kane. In all the annals of Arctic exploration, there would never be a more unlikely candidate for fame and adulation than Kane.

While attending the University of Pennsylvania Medical School, the slender and frail Kane had contracted rheumatic fever, a condition so serious that he literally never knew if each day would be his last. After briefly practicing medicine in Philadelphia, he had joined the United States Navy as a physician in the hope of traveling around the world. He got his wish; his first tour of duty took him to such diverse locales as Brazil, India, and the Philippines, where, on a miss on to obtain water samples, he descended into the crater of the active volcano Taal, only to be overcome by fumes. Kane narrowly escaped with his life.

After two additional tours of naval duty, and still craving more adventure, he received the dangerous assignment of carrying a message to General Winfield Scott, commander of the American forces in Mexico City during the Mexican-American War. On the way, Kane—and his mercenary escorts—had a run-in with a Mexican troop led by a General Gaona. Although Kane and his men prevailed, there were injuries on both sides; Kane had received a nasty lance wound and Gaona's son had been seriously injured. Despite his own injury, Kane saved the young man by stitching up his wounds using thread and the tine of a fork. As if the lance wound was not enough, Kane also contracted "congestive typhus" in Mexico, tick fever in Macao, and coast fever in Africa, all before his career was over. These were only a few of the many incredible happenings that Kane would experience in his all-too-brief life. His friends were convinced that the risks that he continually sought were the result of his knowing that his days were numbered. They were probably right.

Whatever the reason, he would become the most celebrated American explorer of his day. Organizations around the world would beg him to present lectures. His books would be enormous best sellers. Future giants of Arctic achievement Roald Amundsen and Robert Peary would credit Kane's descriptions of his northern adventures with having directly inspired their becoming explorers.

But that was all ahead of him. Now Kane stood aboard the *Advance* as she and the *Rescue* reached Smith Sound, one of the main targets of their search. It was only the middle of August but to Kane's amazement the sound was completely frozen over. A few days later another ship was sighted, heading for the sound. It was the *Lady Franklin*, commanded by William Penny, who had attempted to search Jones Sound only to find that it, too, was impassable. Two days later yet another sail hove to view. This time it was John Ross's schooner *Felix* towing the yacht *Mary* behind it. Despite all the orders the commanders had been given, despite the widespread search they had intended to make, the Arctic had once again dictated the movements of those who would challenge its waters.

Kane, for one, was delighted to encounter John Ross. He had read all of the accounts of the veteran's Arctic adventures. He was aware of the fact that all five of the vessels were anchored almost at the very spot where Ross had been saved by the *Isabella of Hull* more than seventeen years ago. And he was in awe of the man who, at the age of seventy-three, was braving the Arctic once more to keep a promise to a friend. "Here he is again," Kane would write in his journal, "in a flimsy cockle-shell, after contributing his purse and his influence, embarked himself in the crusade of search for a lost comrade."

All of the commanders knew they had to move on. Winter was obviously approaching and they needed to fan out as much as possible. The American, De Haven, decided to explore the harbor at Port Leopold, where James Clark Ross had been icebound during his search for Sir John. No sooner had De Haven found it icebound again than he was unexpectedly joined by another ship. It was the *Prince Albert*, whose two officers, Forsyth and Snow, made their way aboard the *Advance* for a visit.

For Kane and Snow, it was a most pleasant encounter. Immediately, they discovered that they were kindred spirits, both animated, both passionate, both delighting in each other's stories. "Dr. Kane," Snow later wrote in his account of the voyage, "turned his attention to me, and a congeniality of sentiment and feeling soon brought both of us deep into pleasant conversation. I found that he had been in many parts of the world, by sea and land, that I myself had visited. . . . Old scenes and delightful recollections were speedily revived. Our talk ran wild; and there in that cold, inhospitable, dreary region of everlasting ice and snow, did we again, in fancy, gallop over miles and miles of lands far distant and more joyous . . . with all these was he personally familiar, in all he had been a traveler, and in all I could join him."

The carefree discussions were soon tempered, however, by the news that Forsyth delivered. Having attempted to search Prince Regent Inlet, he and Snow had progressed as far as Fury Beach, where the ice prevented them from going any further. Worse yet, at least in Snow's eyes, it seemed that Forsyth had had enough of his first encounter with the Arctic. He told a disappointed Snow that in order to escape the coming winter they were heading for home.

De Haven and Kane, on the other hand, were determined to search on. Making their way across channels that were still open in Barrow Strait, they reached a limestone projection of land that had been named Cape Riley. There, from on deck, the men of the *Advance* and the *Rescue* spotted two cairns rising above the shoreline. Immediately a small party from each vessel went on shore where they found a note telling them that two of Horatio Austin's ships had been there two days before and had made the first discovery in the agonizing Franklin search. Written by Captain Erasmus Ommanney of the *Assistance*, the note stated: "I had the satisfaction of meeting with the first traces of Sir John Franklin's expedition, consisting of fragments of stores and tagged clothing and the remains of an encampment."

As the Americans searched the area, they saw that the encampment that Ommanney had discovered included a roughly constructed fireplace marking where the tents had been erected, the rusted top of a tin container, and scraps of canvas. Kane, having read all the accounts of the previous Arctic voyages, knew that no other nonnatives had been in that area since Edward Parry, and that Parry had not camped at Camp Riley. Who else could have been there but some of the members of the lost expedition?

At this point, Penny and Ross, having also been rebuffed in their attempts to find any unclogged passageways, once again joined up with De Haven's vessels. Across from Cape Riley lay Beechey Island, and it was there that the three commanders decided to meet on shore to decide what to do next. They had hardly begun their discussion when suddenly one of Penny's sailors came rushing down one of the island's ice-covered hills.

"Graves, Captain Penny," the man shouted, "graves!" Rushing up the hill, the commanders and officers, and the men they had taken ashore with them, encountered an agonizing sight. Before them lay three mounds of earth, each marked by a weather-beaten headboard containing a carved inscription:

Sacred to the memory	*Sacred to the memory*	*Sacred to the memory*
of John Torrington	*of John Hartnell*	*of W. Braine*
who departed this	*of HMS* Erebus	*of HMS* Erebus
life January 1846	*died 4 January 1846,*	*died 3 April 1846,*
on board HMS Terror	*aged 25 years.*	*aged 32 years.*
aged 20 years.		

Noting that the headboards marking the graves had been placed facing westward in the tradition of honoring all those who died in the cause of British exploration, the commanders and their men then searched the wide area surrounding the burial site. There they found the remains of a smith's forge, an enormous pile of some six hundred empty cans that had obviously held preserved meat, charred areas where fires had been built, blankets, fragments of rope, scraps of paper, and animal bones. Two days later, Austin's ships arrived and joined in the search of the island. One of his officers found a pair of gloves that had obviously been laid out to dry, weighted down with small stones to keep them from blowing away.

It had been a vital discovery, the first indisputable evidence of the lost expedition. But there was deep frustration as well. Early in the search, a party scouring the island's coastline had come across what promised to be the most rewarding find of all: It was a cairn, and surely it contained a message from Franklin stating where he was headed from Beechey Island. But instead of pointing the searchers in the right direction, the discovery of the cairn only deepened the Franklin mystery. For it was completely empty.

"The cairn," Kane wrote, "was mounted on a high and conspicuous portion of the shore, and evidently intended to attract observation; but though several parties examined it, digging around it in every direction, not a single particle of information could be gleaned. This is remarkable; and for so able and practiced an Arctic commander as Sir John Franklin, an incomprehensible omission."

As the search of the island was about to end, John Ross abruptly returned to his ship and then came back carrying a small box. Inside were two carrier pigeons, each bearing a note Ross had written informing those back home of what had been discovered. As the birds circled the island before beginning their more than two-thousand mile

The three graves found at Beechey Island in 1850 startled their discoverers. Later, the graves would reveal shocking information about the fate of the Franklin expedition. This haunting engraving of the scene is by the artist James Hamilton, based on a sketch by Elisha Kent Kane.

journey, each of those who watched them disappear into the Arctic sky was lost in his own thoughts. Where had Franklin gone? Why had he left no note? Would the ever-deepening mystery ever be solved?

For whatever reason, Franklin had left no message in the cairn. But there was one clue as to where he might have headed after leaving Beechey Island. Along with the graves and the remains of the encampment, the rescuers had found sledge tracks heading north up the east coast of Wellington Channel. Lieutenant Griffin of the *Rescue* had followed the tracks for some forty miles until deteriorating conditions forced him to turn back to his ship.

Winter, as Griffin had discovered, was now fast setting in, and what had become a flotilla of Austin's, Penny's, Ross's, and De Haven's ships had to move out and seek safe winter shelter before they became trapped in an unprotected spot. Penny and Ross, after difficult maneuvering, were able to find a haven in a small cove on the coast of Cornwallis Island. Austin managed to find a suitable spot for his four vessels some fifteen miles away, close to Griffith Island. Aware of the close proximity of the various rescue vessels, Austin named the area Union Harbor.

Never before had so many ships from various search expeditions spent the winter so near each other. Never had there been such an opportunity to relieve the boredom by exchanging visits and sharing in the usual plays and other entertainment. There was even the opportunity for pranks. It did not take the men of the icebound flotilla long to discover that Penny, skilled and knowledgeable as he was, was almost entirely without humor, totally focused on finding traces of Franklin. One of the highlights of the wintering down was the day on which John Ross and some fellow pranksters placed some weather-beaten planks on the ice near Penny's ships, knowing that the whaler would find them and believe that he had discovered remains of either the *Erebus* or the *Terror*. When exactly that scenario took place, the onlookers from the various vessels could not contain their merriment. Penny was not amused.

But it was not all pranks and entertainment. Far from it. For it would be the searches for Franklin by sledge during this winter that, in addition to the discoveries at Beechey Island, would be the highlight of the unprecedented Arctic activity that took place in 1850–51. After a meeting of commanders, it was decided that while Penny and members of his crew would search Wellington Channel, the major sledging effort would be made to the south and the west by crews from Austin's ships.

Austin put all of the planning for the sledging expeditions in the hands of one of his officers, Leopold M'Clintock, the Irishman who had demonstrated his unique sledging skills during James Clark Ross's 1848 search for Franklin. In the interim, M'Clintock had spent considerable time developing an improved sledge design and ways of equipping the sledges more efficiently. He had also come up with the idea of laying caches of provisions at regular distances as he went so that future parties could increase their range of travel.

Eight expeditions, each traveling in a different direction, would be sent out from the Austin fleet. M'Clintock himself would lead the most ambitious search. During James Ross's expedition, M'Clintock had set a new standard by completing a forty-day sledging exploration. Now he was intending to undertake a search that would keep him away from the ship for twice that long.

After a month of training, the various sledging expeditions set off. One party tried to make its way southeast from Cape Walker (as Franklin had been ordered to do) but found the way ahead completely blocked. Another party made its way down the western shores of Peel Sound. Encountering a fierce blizzard, they turned back, convinced, as other searchers before them had been, that Peel Sound was never free of ice. Their report would only intensify the belief that Franklin could never have gone south and that all subsequent searches should concentrate on the north.

Meantime, M'Clintock and his party were engaged in the longest journey of all. Traveling westward down Barrow Strait they arrived at a point seventy miles beyond that which Edward Parry had reached in 1819. Traveling on, they found the remains of a cart that Parry and his men had used more than thirty years before. Further ahead, at Winter Harbor, where Parry had been trapped, they made a more dramatic discovery—a huge sandstone boulder, on which was carved an inscription proclaiming the year that Parry had been there. Before leaving the spot, M'Clintock announced that he also had been there by carving the year "1851" on the boulder.

It was now time to turn back. When the men returned to the ship, they had been gone for the exact eighty days for which M'Clintock had planned and had traveled 875 miles. Altogether, the eight sledging parties had covered 7,025 miles on foot and had explored and entered into the map 1,225 miles of previously unknown land. A remarkable achievement—but they had not found a single trace of Franklin. After the hope engendered by the Beechey Island discoveries, it was becoming a winter of frustration. But it was nothing compared to what the Grinnell expedition had been going through.

After leaving Beechey Island, the *Advance* and the *Rescue* had encountered ice everywhere they had turned. Unlike their fellow British searchers, the Americans had absolutely no experience in wintering in the Arctic and De Haven had no intention of doing so; he was heading for home. But first he had to find the *Rescue*, which had become separated from the *Advance* in a storm. Forced to waste precious time, he finally found the sister ship miles away to the west, in Barrow Strait. Taking the *Rescue* in tow, he made a dash for open water. But he was too late. By the time he reached the mouth of Wellington Channel, he could go no further. He had long since lost sight of the British ships. For the men of the *Advance* and the *Rescue* there would be no congenial Union Harbor. They would have to go it alone.

None of the Americans could have even imagined what they would be forced to endure that winter. Even when they wore two pairs of mittens, their hand became frost bitten when they touched any piece of metal. Burning hot coffee froze in their mugs as soon as it was poured. When they tried sucking icicles, the skin peeled off their lips. The only way they could cut butter was with the use of a hammer and a chisel. Their tongues froze to their beards.

Even more seriously, many of the men, including Elisha Kane, had been stricken with scurvy. Several became so weak that any activity caused them to faint. Fortunately, Kane began forcing the crew to regularly eat potatoes and sauerkraut and to drink lemon juice, all rich in Vitamin C, and a major disaster was averted.

Fortunately, when summer arrived, all of the ships were released from the ice. No one was more relieved by the thaw than Austin. Two winters in the ice had been enough. He was ready to return. But not William Penny. He argued vehemently that Austin should lend him one of his steamships so that Penny could continue the search beyond Wellington Channel. "You say we have been acting in concert," he reminded Austin. "Let us prove the sincerity of that concert. Give me a steamer and with the little *Sophia* I will go miles further." Austin, who had never warmed to Penny's abrasive personality and who had probably never accepted the presence of a whaler as the captain of a British naval vessel, would not listen. He was taking his fleet home.

For the Americans, there would be one final surprise. Before leaving the Arctic, they suddenly encountered another ship. It was the *Prince Albert*, the vessel that they knew had sailed back to England before the winter had set in. When the captain and second-in-command of the small vessel came aboard the *Advance* it was obvious that they were neither Charles Forsyth nor W. Parker Snow. Instead they were a Canadian, William Kennedy, and a French naval lieutenant, Joseph René Bellot. (Kennedy and Bellot were strange bedfellows, but equally devoted to Lady Jane and the search, see note, page 280.) Lady Franklin, they told De Haven and Kane, bitterly disappointed at the *Prince Albert's* premature return to England, had immediately raised more money, refitted the vessel, and sent it out again to look for her husband. Kane could only shake his head. The noble woman would never give up.

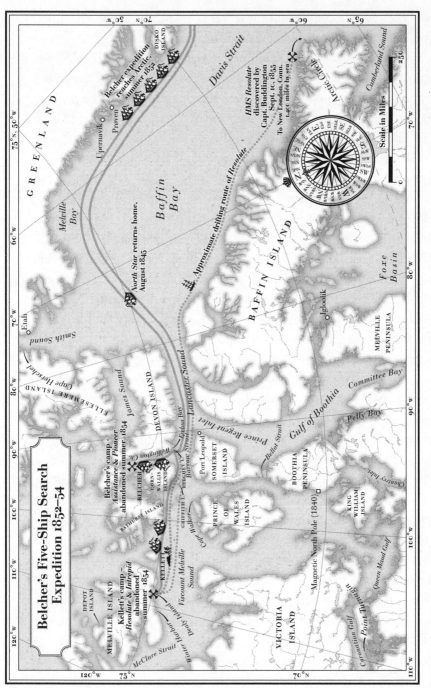

This map reveals various locations in the experiences of the Belcher rescue fleet in general, and of the *Resolute* in particular. It shows where the *Resolute* and *Intrepid* were abandoned and where the *Assistance* and the *Pioneer* were left behind. The map also indicates the route along which the *Resolute* drifted after being abandoned, and the spot where whaling master James Buddington discovered her.

CHAPTER 10

Rescue and Abandonment

"The announcement of relief being close at hand, when
none was supposed to be even within the Arctic Circle,
was too sudden, unexpected and joyous for our minds
to comprehend it all at once."
—ROBERT MCCLURE, on being found, 1853

WITH THE RETURN OF AUSTIN, Penny, and Ross to London in
the fall of 1851, only one ship was now left to search for the lost
expedition. It would never do. Even the Admiralty recognized
that. And now there was additional pressure. Nothing had been
heard from either McClure or Collinson. No longer was Jane Franklin
alone in her pleadings. Francis Cresswell—the wealthy and influential
father of Lieutenant Samuel Cresswell, second mate and artist aboard
the *Investigator*—launched a vigorous campaign aimed at reminding
everyone that it was not only Franklin and his men who were missing,
but that it had also been much too long since his son and his comrades,
as well as Richard Collinson and his crew, had been heard from.

The London *Times* summed up the nation's mood when, in an editorial written immediately after Austin's return, it called for an even larger rescue expedition to be sent out:

> *Though we do not think the geographical importance of these expeditions commensurable with the cost of exposure of a single sloop's crew, we unhesitatingly admit that our obligation to rescue those who have been dispatched on the enterprise of a very different magnitude. It signifies supremely little whether Boothia Felix is a peninsula, an island, or a gulf . . . but it does impinge most emphatically to our national honour that we should ascertain the fate of our missing countrymen, and redeem them, if living, from the dangers to which they have been consigned.*

This time, with far more alacrity than it had displayed when Franklin had first gone missing, the navy acted. It mounted a five-ship rescue expedition. Three of the vessels had been the core of Austin's fleet—the *Resolute*, now commanded by Captain Henry Kellett, the *Pioneer*, once again commanded by Captain Sherard Osborn, and the *Assistance*, with the expedition's overall commander Sir Edward Belcher aboard. The squadron also included the *Intrepid*, commanded by the recently promoted Leopold M'Clintock and the *North Star*, which would serve as the fleet's supply ship.

The selection of Sir Edward Belcher to head the expedition was based both on his seniority and his official record. On the surface, he seemed a logical choice. The son of a prominent Nova Scotia family, he had joined the navy in 1812, at the age of thirteen, and four years later had served in the campaign against the Barbary pirates. In 1818, as John Franklin was sailing in search of the North Pole, Belcher was promoted to lieutenant and seven years later he sailed with Captain Frederick Beechey in his attempt to link up with the Franklin and Parry passage-seeking expeditions.

Belcher had also distinguished himself as both an explorer and an inventor of a number of nautical devices, including a navigational protractor for fixing a ship's position in coastal water. As an explorer, his accomplishments included the discovery of a number of islands in Norwegian Bay and the first navigation of the Sacramento River. The highlight of his career had been his command of an 1836–42 around-the-world voyage during which he and his crew, in addition to making significant astronomical and meteorological observations, discovered several unknown rivers and a host of previously unknown tropical plants and animals.

On paper, he was certainly qualified to lead what the Admiralty now regarded as the most important rescue mission it had yet organized. But, as events would prove, Belcher was absolutely the·wrong man for the job. At fifty-three, he was extremely fit for his age, but he was pompous, quarrelsome, critical of everyone, and arguably the most narrow-minded commander that had ever been sent to the Arctic. Not only did he refuse to listen to the advice of those who had more Arctic experience than he, but he let it be known that he didn't want any officer with him who had served on more than one northern expedition. Fortunately, the Admiralty ignored that wish.

The Belcher rescue fleet makes its way through the crowded Royal Navy anchorage known as the Nore. The second ship from the left is the *Resolute*. To her left is the *Intrepid*. The fifth ship from the left is the *North Star*. At the center of the illustration is the *Assistance*. The vessel to the far right is the *Pioneer*.

Worst of all, unlike Parry, James Clark Ross, M'Clintock, Rae, or so many of the other northern venturers, Belcher had no enthusiasm for the mystique of the Arctic. "I shall proceed with our monotonous voyage," he wrote, "but really . . . I cannot flatter myself that bergs, floes, sailing ice, etc. will greatly interest anyone." More ominous yet, he had little faith in the effort he was about to lead. He was doing so only as a further advancement of his career.

Fortunately, that was not true of his captains and officers. Henry Kellett, the captain of the *Resolute*, was regarded as one of the navy's most capable senior officers. Respected by all who had served under him, he was passionate in his desire to find Franklin. And despite the fact that he had been the object of one of McClure's earliest deceptions, he was determined to rescue that missing passage-seeker as well. The ultimate story of this latest search for the lost explorers might have been very different if it had been Kellett rather than Belcher who had been chosen to lead it.

Kellett had been wise in his selection of the men who would serve under him on the *Resolute*. George Nares, the man he had chosen to be his second mate, would not only render valuable service but would go on to a career as one of the most distinguished of all Arctic explorers. Another of Kellett's mates, Émile-Frédéric de Bray, was an unlikely member of the *Resolute* crew. A sublieutenant in the French navy, he had volunteered to take part in the search for Franklin. It was ultimately Bray's journal that would provide a highly accurate account of the events that were soon to unfold.

The *Intrepid*'s captain was Leopold M'Clintock. During Austin's expedition, he had once again proved to be an invaluable member of the expedition, particularly through his sledging skills. From the beginning, he had looked upon the search for Franklin as the "Great Crusade." In the end, it would be M'Clintock who would become one of the greatest players of all in one of the greatest mysteries of his era.

According to the Admiralty's plans, the Belcher expedition was really two expeditions in one. As the ships set sail in the spring of 1852, two of the vessels—the *Resolute* and the *Intrepid*—headed directly for

Melville Island. Their job, along with searching for Franklin, was to try to find McClure and Collinson. The *Assistance* and the *Pioneer* set course for Wellington Channel, where they were to concentrate on the search for Sir John. The supply ship *North Star* was to remain at Beechey Island as a depot.

The huge sailing vessel *Resolute* and the much smaller steamer *Intrepid* were the first ships since those of Edward Parry to attempt to reach Melville Island. By September 1, 1852, they had made it, but not before the *Resolute* had been grounded in a narrow channel near ice-clogged Barrow Strait. Only the power supplied by the *Intrepid*'s steam engine in towing the *Resolute* back afloat had averted an early disaster. By now, winter was fast approaching. After briefly visiting Melville Island's Winter Harbor, Kellett found even better shelter thirty-five miles to the east at Dealy Island.

Belcher had also encountered building ice as soon as his squadron reached Lancaster Sound. After anchoring the *North Star* off at Beechey Island, the *Assistance* and the *Pioneer* made their way to Wellington Sound and sailed a few miles north before conditions made it apparent that they, too, needed to seek winter quarters—which they found in Northumberland Inlet on the northeastern point of Devon Island.

The *Resolute* and the *Intrepid* would be beset in the ice for the next eleven months. But that would not interrupt the search. As soon as all the preparations for wintering down were completed, Captain Kellett began to send out sledge parties to look for the missing expeditions. Several of these parties would be gone for as long as three months. All of their journeys would be extraordinarily difficult. To Kellett, a sledging expedition was even more demanding than combat. "I have been a long time at sea," he later wrote in an account of his Arctic experiences, "and seen varying trying services . . . but never have seen such labour, and such misery . . . Men require much more heart and stamina to undertake an extended traveling party than to go into action. The travelers have their enemy chilling them to the very heart and paralyzing their very limbs; the others the very contrary."

Still, it had to be done. Before Kellett's ships were finally released from Dealy Island, Leopold M'Clintock would sledge more than 1,325 miles in eighty days, while Lieutenant George Mecham of the *Resolute* would journey almost as far, traveling a record 1,150 miles in 71 days. And it would be Mecham who made the first significant discovery.

In early fall 1852, Mecham and his two-sledge party set out from the *Resolute* to search Melville Island. With his sledge flag bearing the motto *Per mare, per terram, per glatiem* (over mud, land, and ice) he reached the island, found no trace of either Franklin or McClure, and was headed back to the *Resolute* when, on October 12, he came upon a great sandstone boulder, about ten feet high and eight feet wide, and more than twenty feet long. Cut into the boulder was this inscription:

> *HIS BRITANNIC MAJESTY'S*
> *SHIPS* HECLA *AND* GRIPER
> *COMMANDED BY*
> *W. E. PARRY AND MR. LIDDON*
> *WINTERED IN THE ADJACENT*
> *HARBOR 1819–20*
> *A. FISHER, SCULPT.*

Careful not to disturb the small pile of stones that rested atop the boulder, Mecham started to carve his own inscription at the bottom of the rock to indicate that he, too, had been at the spot, when to his surprise a copper cylinder rolled out from beneath the stones.

"On opening it," Mecham recalled, "I drew out a roll folded in a bladder which, being frozen broke and crumbled. From its dilapidated appearance, I thought at the moment it must be some record of Sir Edward Parry, and fearing I might damage it, laid it down with the intention of lighting the fire to thaw it. My curiosity, however, overcame my prudence, and on opening it carefully with a knife, I came to a roll of cartridge paper with the impression fresh upon the seals. My astonishment may be conceived on finding it contained an account of the proceedings of 'H.M. ship 'Investigator' since parting company with the 'Herald' in August 1850, in Bering's Straits. Also a chart which disclosed to view not only the long-sought Northwest Passage, but the completion of the survey of Banks and Wollaston lands."

The "account" that Mecham had found was, in fact, a journal of Robert McClure's activities from the time he had encountered Kellett and the *Herald* in 1850 until he had found a winter refuge. It ended by stating:

> *My intention, if possible, is to return to England this year, calling at Melville Island and Port Leopold, but if we are not heard of again it is probably because we have been carried into the polar pack or west of Melville Island, and in either case no help should be sent for us, so as not to increase the losses, since any ship which enters the polar pack must inevitably be crushed; hence a depot of provisions or a ship at Winter Harbour would be the best and only guarantee of safety to save the rest of the crew.*
>
> *No trace has been encountered, and no information from the Eskimos, which might lead to the supposition that Sir John Franklin's expedition, or part of his crews, had visited the coasts we have covered; nor have we been any more fortunate as to the Enterprise which we have not seen since we separated in the Strait of Magellan on 20 April 1850.*
>
> *This document was deposited in April 1852 by the crew of a sledge consisting of Captain M'Clure, Mr. Court, second master John Calder, captain of the forecastle Sergeant Woon, Royal Marines, George Gibbs, A.B., George Bounsell, A.B., John Davis, A.B., and Peter Thompson, captain of the foretop.*
>
> *Whoever finds this paper, is asked to forward it to the Secretary of the Admiralty.*
>
> *Dated aboard HBM discovery ship* Investigator, *beset in the ice in Mercy Bay, latitude 74°N, longitude 117°54'W.*

> *—12 April 1852*
> *Robert M'Clure, Commander*

It was an astounding find. McClure and the crew of the *Investigator* had not been heard from in two years and here was news of them that was less than six months old. And, if the journal portion of the note was true, the Northwest Passage had been found. Most important, Mecham now knew where the *Investigator* in all probability still was. He had the exact location. And according to his quick calculations it was less than 170 miles from where the *Resolute* and the *Intrepid* were lying at Dealy Island.

Mecham could not wait to return to the *Resolute*. The exhilaration that greeted his news, however, was tempered by the fact that the ice in the strait leading between Dealy Island and Mercy Bay was so broken up that to attempt to cross it before the spring thaw—even in a small boat—would be disastrous. Even getting a message across to McClure was impossible.

It was frustrating; but it was nothing compared to what the men of the *Investigator* had been going through since they had put into Mercy Bay two years before. Long before the first winter's entrapment was over, most of the ship's crew was suffering from malnutrition and scurvy. An alarmed Dr. Armstrong pleaded with McClure to increase the men's rations. The commander, relying on hunting parties to bring back fresh meat, refused. But party after party returned empty-handed. The perpetual Arctic winter darkness made it impossible to spot any wildlife if, in fact, any animals even existed in the vicinity.

Adding to the misery was the incredible cold. As the first winter dragged on, the temperature fell to 99 degrees below the freezing point—the coldest temperature any passage-seeking expedition had been forced to endure. In order to conserve coal, McClure cut its consumption to eight pounds per day and drastically reduced the amount of oil that was to be used. Now the men were not only freezing; they were forced to live in the dark most of the time. Johann Miertsching, a Moravian missionary who accompanied the party as interpreter to the Inuit, confided in his journal that "as our stock of candles is very small, we therefore pass a great part of our time in darkness." He added: "Our principal occupations are walking and sleeping; reading and writing are out of the question, as we have hardly light enough for the most necessary duties. Wolves howl around the ship."

McClure's great hope was that all the problems would be solved when the ice broke up in the spring, or at least the summer, and the *Investigator* would be able to get underway once more. But in 1852, summer never came to Mercy Bay. The pack never thawed and it became clear that they would have to spend yet another winter in the ice. Faced with the real prospect of running out of food, McClure ordered that the food rations be further reduced. Now the men would be asked to survive on one meal a day—half a pound of meat and two ounces of vegetables. "Today the captain summoned the crew on deck, and told them he was now convinced the ice would not break up this year; therefore we must pass another winter here," Miertsching wrote. "He charged them not to let their spirits sink . . . In order to make the slender store last till next summer, it would be necessary now to reduce the allowance . . . but that would suffice for the period of total inactivity . . . One could see many dismal faces, yet there was nothing could be done but to yield to necessity."

Necessary it may have been, but by the time that Mecham had returned to the *Resolute* with McClure's note in hand, the situation aboard the *Investigator* had become desperate—so much so that two of the men had gone mad, and one them had tried to kill McClure. With the madmen howling throughout the night and his crew slowly starving to death, the commander knew that something drastic had to be done.

By the spring of 1853, he was ready to announce the plan he had devised. Two parties consisting of the weakest of the crew would be sent out by sledge—one east and the other south—in search of rescue. The twenty strongest crew members would remain on board in the hope that this coming summer would bring a breakup of the ice.

It was a most outrageous plan, even for the ever-devious Robert McClure. He knew full well that by sending his most weakened men— about two-thirds of his crew—out on such a journey he was condemn- ing them to their death. As far as anyone could guess, the nearest places where they had even the most remote possibility of finding rescue were more than five hundred miles away. There was no chance that, in their condition, the sledgers would survive the trip. Dr. Armstrong was absolutely appalled. He already disliked McClure, based in great measure on the fact that throughout the trip he had been the victim of rough horseplay at the hands of some of his fellow officers, and McClure had done nothing about it. Armstrong was also upset over the fact that while the sailors aboard the *Investigator* openly praised his medical work, McClure seemed to place no value upon it.

But all that was minor, Armstrong believed, compared to what McClure was about to do. Putting his feelings in writing on a paper that, should he survive, he intended to present to the Admiralty, Armstrong wrote: "Captain McClure has been fully informed by me on many occasions of the state of the men . . . Nevertheless I felt called upon again to represent their condition and to express my opinion of their unfitness for the performance of this service, without entailing great and inevitable loss of life. *It had no effect.*"

It had no effect because McClure knew just what he was doing. By removing the weakened crewmen from the ship he would be able to apportion their rations among the twenty he had selected to stay aboard. Once the hoped-for thaw came he and those he had spared would be able, he was convinced, to accomplish the only goal that now mattered to him. They would be able to sail the *Investigator* through the passage he had found.

It was now March, too early for the ice—if it was ever going to— to release the *Investigator*. But conditions had improved enough for the *Resolute* to risk sending out a sledge party to see if McClure was still at Mercy Bay. To lead the party, Kellett chose Lieutenant Bedford Pim, who had previously served with the captain aboard the *Herald*. Pim, like Kellett, was totally dedicated to finding both McClure and Franklin. He actually believed that there was a strong possibility that Sir John and his men might be in Russia, and had received permission from the Admiralty to walk across Siberia in an attempt to locate them. Hearing of the plan, Lady Franklin had contributed five

1.
Inuit interpreter John Sacheuse illustrated John Ross's first
encounter with the Inuit in 1818. His painting reveals how
the early passage-seekers refused to recognize the need to
dress adequately to cope with the Arctic's savage climate.

2.
While their ship, the *Victory*, was icebound during the winter
of 1829, the men of John Ross's second Arctic expedition paid
regular visits to the nearby igloo settlement. Ross named the Inuit
there "Boothians," after his sponsor, the distiller Felix Booth.

3.
The two ships of the Franklin expedition, below, the HMS *Erebus* and *Terror*, were the space capsules of their day. When they left harbor in May 1845, the hopes of all England sailed with them. Once they reached the Arctic, they were never heard from again.

SIR JOHN FRANKLIN, R.N.

4.
John Franklin was the most famous Arctic explorer of his time, revered throughout Great Britain. This tobacco trading card portraying the great hero, left, was based on a painting by Albert Jasper Ludwig Operti, who was renowned for his depictions of the Franklin saga.

5.
During its 1836–37 search for the Northwest Passage, George Back's ship, the HMS *Terror*, became trapped atop an ice floe for nine months. A short time after the below sketch was drawn, the *Terror* suddenly righted herself and would have crushed all the men working in the ice beneath her had they not, just minutes before, climbed back aboard the ship.

6.
The Arctic Council meets to plan its 1848 search for Sir John
Franklin. Shown (l. to r.): Sir George Back, Sir W. Edward Parry,
Edward Joseph Bird, Sir James Clark Ross, Sir Francis Beaufort,
John Barrow, Sir Edward Sabine, William Baillie Hamilton, Sir
John Richardson, and Frederick William Beechey.

7.
As illustrated by Samuel Cresswell, a naval officer on McClure's
1853 expedition, hauling sledges across the treacherous Arctic
terrain was arduous and often dangerous. But more discoveries
were made by sledge than by any other means.

8.
Lady Jane Franklin was the only woman directly involved in the John Franklin saga. Yet before the drama was over, no character would be more important than she.

9.
He deceived his fellow commander and constantly put the lives of his men aboard the HMS *Investigator* in jeopardy, but Robert McClure gained lasting fame by finding the last link in the Northwest Passage.

10.
Members of the HMS *Investigator*, trapped in the ice for more than two years, prepare to leave Mercy Bay in April 1853 by sledge.

11.
Sir Henry Kellett, captain of the HMS *Resolute*
during the *1852–54* Belcher expedition in
search of Franklin, was one of a select group
of highly respected British naval officers who,
after having distinguished themselves in battle,
sought even greater glory in the Arctic.

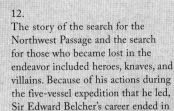

12.
The story of the search for the Northwest Passage and the search for those who became lost in the endeavor included heroes, knaves, and villains. Because of his actions during the five-vessel expedition that he led, Sir Edward Belcher's career ended in disgrace.

13.
A sledge party leaves the *Resolute* (left of the painting) and heads out for Mercy Bay hoping to find and rescue Robert McClure and his men who had been trapped aboard the HMS *Investigator* for more than two years. Led by Lieutenant Bedford Pim, the party accomplished its mission.

14.
Created to help reduce boredom during the long months of wintering down, the *Illustrated Arctic News* was published aboard the HMS *Resolute*, commanded by Captain Horatio Austin during the ship's 1850–51 search for John Franklin. The illustration in this 1850 New Year's Eve edition poked fun at the "Fashions for the Month."

15.
These relics of John Franklin's lost expedition were bought back from the Inuit by John Rae during his 1853–54 exploration of Pelly Bay and Repulse Bay. Included among the items that Rae brought back to England were spoons, knives, forks, medals, watches, pencil cases, and parts of navigational instruments—many clearly identifiable as belonging to members of the *Erebus* and the *Terror*. It was the discovery of these relics, the first of thousands that would eventually be found, that provided the first hard evidence of the fate of Franklin and his men.

hundred pounds to the cause. Pim's expedition, however, had never been launched.

Pim and his team left for Mercy Bay on March 10. Almost immediately they were forced to stop and wait out a four-day blizzard that made traveling impossible. When they were finally able to resume, Pim found that the going was more difficult than he could have imagined. "Hummocks after hummocks followed each other in apparently endless succession," he wrote in his diary on March 23. "Sometimes composed of very old, then young ice, on the former the surface was so glossy and uneven that the men could scarcely stand, on the latter the snow had filled up the interstices, into which men and sledges sank deeply at every step; in short after a hard day's work we only accomplished 2½ miles." (The art of sledging was a vital technique for Arctic explorers, yet it was one of the most demanding forms of transporation on earth, see note 1, page 281.)

Still he pushed on. On March 29 his sledge broke down completely and he decide to continue on by foot with just two of his men, ordering the others to take the damaged sled back to Cape Dundas and wait for his return.

Meantime, McClure was preparing to send his weakened crewmen out on their certain-to-be-disastrous journey. The party would probably have already left but for the sudden death of one of their companions. Now, on April 6, McClure and his first lieutenant were walking beside the *Investigator*, pondering the question of how they would be able to dig a grave in the frozen ground. They had no idea of how their fortunes were about to change.

Off in the distance, Pim—his face completely blackened from having sat huddled next to the campfire night after night—and his two men had found Mercy Bay and had spotted the ship. McClure later wrote of his encounter with the men in his journal:

> *We perceived a figure walking rapidly towards us from the rough ice at the entrance of the bay. From his pace and gestures we both naturally supposed that he was some of our party pursued by a bear,*

but as we approached him doubts arose as to who it could be. He was certainly unlike any of our men; but recollecting that it was possible someone might be trying a new traveling dress, preparatory to the departure of our sledges, and certain that no one else was near, we continued to advance. When within about two hundred yards of us, this strange figure threw up his arms, and made gesticulations resembling those used by the Eskimaux, besides shouting, at the top of his voice words which, from the wind and the intense excitement of the moment, sounded like a wild screech and this brought us both fairly to a stand-still.

The stranger came quietly on, and we saw that his face was a black as ebony, and really at that moment we might be pardoned for wondering if he was a denizen of this or the other world, and had he but given a glimpse of a tail or a cloven hoof, we should assuredly have taken to our legs; as it was, we gallantly stood our ground, and had the skies fallen upon us, we could hardly have been more astonished then when the dark-faced stranger called out;
"I'm Lieutenant Pim, late of the Herald *and now in the* Resolute. *Captain Kellett is in her at Dealy Island."*

"To rush at and seize him by the hand was the first impulse," McClure later recalled, "for the heart was too full for the tongue to speak." He went on:

The announcement of relief being close at hand, when none was sup-posed to be even within the Arctic Circle, was too sudden, unexpected, and joyous for our minds to comprehend it all at once. The news flew with lightning rapidity, the ship was all in commotion; the sick, forgetful of their maladies, left from their hammocks; the artificers dropped their tools, and the lower deck was cleared of men; for they all rushed for the hatchway to be assured that a stranger was actually amongst them, and that his tale was true. Despondency fled the ship, and Lieut. Pim received a welcome—pure, hearty and grateful—that he will assuredly remember and cherish to the end of his days."

But even in the hour of his greatest relief, McClure's deceptive nature came almost immediately to the front. Although it was probably the furthest thing from Bedford Pim's mind, McClure was aware that, according to the terms of the reward offered by Parliament, half of the £10,000 due to him for having discovered the Northwest Passage now rightfully belonged to the crew of the *Resolute*, who had rescued him. With a straight face, McClure informed Pim that, as grateful as he was to see him, he didn't really need his help. All of his men, he told Pim, were more than healthy enough to sail the *Investigator* out of the ice and would the lieutenant please take him to the *Resolute* so that he could inform Captain Kellett of that fact? Outranked by McClure, Pim had no choice but to grant the commander his wish.

Bedford Pim rescues the crew of the *Investigator*. This illustration appeared in the published diary of the ship's Inuit interpreter, Johann Miertsching. When the *Investigator* was abandoned, Robert McClure collected and purposely mislaid his officers' journals, knowing they contained negative accounts of his handling of the voyage. Somehow, Miertsching managed to keep his diary and publish his bitter account.

And so, about a week later, there on the deck of the *Resolute* they stood—the captain of the rescue ship and the man who earlier had so openly deceived him on his way to finding the passage. But this time Kellett would not be fooled. He ordered that the *Investigator*'s crew be examined by the *Resolute*'s surgeon and by Dr. Armstrong, who together would determine whether or not the *Investigator*'s crew, if circumstances allowed, were fit enough to sail the ship out of Mercy Bay and resume the search for Franklin. It did not take the doctors long to make their decision. Noting that a number of the men were either blind or lame and that even the healthiest ones were suffering from scurvy, they informed Kellett that they were in no shape to man a vessel. Immediately the captain ordered that the *Investigator* be left in the ice and that her officers and men be sledged to where they would be taken aboard the *Resolute* and the *Intrepid*.

Kellett had few qualms about ordering the abandonment of the *Investigator*. From what Pim had told him, not only was Mercy Bay so situated that the ice would perhaps never leave it, but the ship was so buried in the floes that even if the ice should one day happen to loosen its grip, the vessel was probably too damaged to be seaworthy. Any remaining doubts that Kellett might have had were quickly dispelled by the looks of gratitude on the faces of the rescued men.

The ordeals of the *Investigator*'s crew, however, were not over. On August 16, the *Resolute* and the *Intrepid* were rounding the point of a large, relatively unexplored bay, which Kellett hoped might hold some traces of Franklin. Suddenly and without warning, the *Resolute* was stuck by a huge ice floe, laying the ship dangerously to port and driving her close to the shore. Soon afterward, another huge floe hammered against the ship, placing the vessel in imminent danger of being torn apart. "There was nothing we could do against such a force," the French officer de Bray wrote, "we could only wait, counting on Providence which had protected us thus far. Fortunately the ship was not taking on water and withstood the pressures valiantly. Afteran hour of cruel anxiety we were delighted to see the ice sliding slowly past our stern; a few charges of powder were exploded underthe ice and helped the movement. Finally around 10 o'clock the floe which had threatened to overwhelm us had passed and the ship's stern was afloat."

It had been an extremely close call, and conditions did not improve. "30 August 1853," read de Bray's journal entry for that day. "The temperature is dropping rapidly, and sadly, we see that the ice is not disposed to allow passage. The prospect of second wintering, . . . is not a very pleasant one, and yet I believe that everyone is beginning to resign themselves to the inevitable. The ice which formed around the ship during the night is already 3 inches thick and we have been blasting it to free ourselves."

Barely making it back to the harbor at Dealy Island, the crews of the *Resolute* and the *Intrepid* prepared for their second winter in the ice. For the *Investigator's* refugees, it would be their fourth season of imprisonment. Once again Kellett would not allow the crews of the *Resolute* or the *Intrepid* to remain idle. It had been during the previous winter that they had found McClure. Now they would do whatever they could from where they lay to find traces of Franklin.

"At 7 o'clock," wrote de Bray, "we released our first balloon, which carries with it about a thousand squares of paper spaced along an iron wire with a slow match." It was an ingenious idea. Printed on each piece of paper was the *Resolute's* precise position. As the balloon was released, the match was lit so that the pieces of paper would fall at well-spaced distances: "Thus distributed at various points on the Arctic landscape they may fall in the hands of some travelers and thus give Franklin or his companions news of us," de Bray explained.

The winter of 1853–54 proved to be almost as bitterly cold as the previous record-breaking winter had been. In Wellington Channel where the *Assistance* and the *Pioneer* were hunkered down, Belcher's highly accurate instruments reported temperatures as low as 62 ½ degrees below zero, and for eighty-four consecutive hours, his thermometer never climbed higher than minus five degrees.

Cold as it was, Kellett's anchorage at Dealy Island was a good one and he was certain that the *Resolute* and the *Intrepid* would be released in the summer, along with Belcher's ships. But Kellett had no confidence in Belcher's commitment to search or in his ability to organize searching parties. From what he had learned, nothing had been accomplished by the Wellington Channel area explorations thus far. Once summer came, Kellett believed, things would be different. Despite its narrow escape from the floes, the *Resolute* was in excellent shape. So too was the *Intrepid*. M'Clintock and Mecham had proven themselves unrivaled as leaders of sledging parties. Bedford Pim had certainly shown what he could accomplish. With McClure found and safely aboard, the crew would be able to focus on Franklin. And Kellett hadn't forgotten the still-missing Collinson. They would search for him as well.

Edward Belcher, on the other hand, had no such optimism. He was having a miserable winter, most of it his own doing. He had taken to the bottle, and was now drunk much of the time. His relationship with his officers had fallen almost completely apart. When the *Pioneer's* capable captain Sherard Osborn had complained of his commander's lack of leadership, Belcher had had him arrested. And Belcher's penchant for pettiness had become worse than ever. One of his favorite targets had been the ship's artist, young Walter May. After being publicly humiliated by Belcher over such failings as having neglected to inform the commander of the shooting of a small rabbit or having written a report on the wrong-sized paper, May had argued back and had been relieved of his duties. None of it bothered Belcher. He had only one desire: He wanted to go home.

For his part, Kellett was determined to stay in the Arctic for as long as it took to accomplish the mission. When the first signs of spring appeared, he sent one of his officers by sledge to Belcher with a detailed report of his search plans once the ships were free to move about again. It is doubtful if Belcher even glanced at the report. Instead, he sent the officer back to the *Resolute* with an astounding reply. Beaten down by two winters in the ice and no longer in control of his officers, Belcher had had enough. He was ordering all of the ship's companies to make their way to the *North Star*, which had somehow gotten free of the ice off Beechey Island. The expedition was over. They were all sailing back to England.

Almost nothing in his life had ever as great an impact on Henry Kellett as Belcher's orders. At first he couldn't believe it. Then he was astonished. Finally, he became as angry as he had ever been. What was the man thinking? How could they possibly give up the search? Even more shocking—how could they even consider abandoning four seaworthy naval vessels to certain destruction? Anybody who had even the notion of doing so, Kellett stated, "would deserve to have their jackets taken off their backs."

He was not alone. Leopold M'Clintock had the same vehement reaction, as did all the officers of Kellett's two ships. "We still had enough provisions and spare parts for another year," de Bray wrote in his journal. "We were all in perfect health and filled with anticipation in thinking of our planned spring voyage . . . The order to abandon our ship was a distressing surprise to us." Surprise indeed! Kellett and M'Clintock were not about to accept the order without a fight. If nothing else, they decided they would keep the *Resolute* and the *Intrepid* in the Arctic and continue the search without the other vessels. There was also something else that was deeply troubling. As they reread Belcher's order it became increasingly clear to them that Belcher had deliberately

Sledging crews from the *Resolute* leave to search for John Franklin. Both the *Resolute*'s commander Henry Kellett, and Leopold M'Clintock, captain of the *Intrepid*, firmly believed that, given the courage and skill of their crews, traces of Franklin would have been found if Edward Belcher had not ordered the abandonment of their ships.

worded it in such a way as to make it appear that the decision to abandon the ships was as much Kellett's idea as his own. M'Clintock later wrote the details in his account of the incident:

> *I was sent for by Captain Kellett to read over . . . the orders from Sir E. Belcher . . . and to give my opinion of their meaning. I did so. Some paragraphs in these long orders contradict each other. . . . It is implied that we are to abandon [the ships]. By his orders Sir Ed. assumes that Capt. Kellett has determined upon abandoning the ships. Now this being exactly contrary to [Kellett's] intentions . . . [Captain Kellett] feels greatly puzzled.*

Henry Kellett had twice been lied to by McClure. He wasn't about to be hoodwinked by Belcher.

Preparing a strong reply to the order, Kellett then sent M'Clintock out on the more than 250-mile journey to Wellington Channel, where he was to deliver it in person to the senior commander. In the strongest language, Belcher was told that Kellett had plenty of provisions, and two sound ships that were in no danger and in excellent position to be free of the ice when summer arrived. But Belcher would not listen. This time the order he sent back with M'Clintock was crystal clear. The ships were to be abandoned.

Kellett was devastated. But, as a true navy man, he had no choice but to obey the chain of command. Robert McClure, on the other hand, had mixed feelings. He had now been trapped in the north for four years. Writing to John Ross, he stated that the Arctic was a region "which I hope to have done with forever." As for Belcher, he wrote: "Things are as bad as can be or as you might expect under B. Nothing but Courts Martial he, but as their Lordship will decide these matters, best to keep quiet until it becomes public which it must very speedily."

By the end of August, the Belcher expedition was gathered at Beechey Island, preparing to board the *North Star*. Among the late arrivals was the *Resolute*'s Lieutenant Mecham. On April 3, he had been sent out by Kellett to command a sledge party to Princess Royal

Islands in the Price of Wales Strait in hope of finding traces of Collinson. As he had when he had found McClure's note, Mecham was now returning with exciting news. At a depot at Princess Royal Island he had found a note left by Collinson stating that, in 1851, he had taken up winter quarters in Walker Bay. Immediately heading for the bay, Mecham had reached Ramsey Island where he found another note from Collinson stating that he was going to try to sail east through Dolphin and Union Strait. Mecham could hardly contain himself. He was on the track of the lost explorer.

Suddenly, however, his sledge team caught sight of an approaching stranger. It was a lieutenant from one of Kellett's ships sent out to inform Mecham that he was to proceed immediately to Beechey Island. Puzzled by the command, Mecham and his party accompanied the lieutenant to where the *North Star* was waiting. By the time he reached the ship he had traveled a distance of 1,157 geographical miles in seventy days—outdoing his own former record—and eight of those days had been spent in a tent while stormbound. It was a journey unparalleled in all of Arctic travel. Lieutenant Mecham had performed the last of the many of heroic acts accomplished by the men of the HMS *Resolute*, an achievement tempered by Mecham's discovery upon reaching the *North Star* that rather than looking for Collinson, the expedition was heading home.

On August 26, 1854, the *North Star*, dangerously overloaded with 263 men, headed for home. Only the fact that the *Phoenix* and *Talbot*—sent to the Arctic in 1854 by the Admiralty as supply ships for Belcher's expedition—fortunately appeared on the scene, enabling the crews to be divided between the three ships, prevented the expedition that had turned into a fiasco from becoming a probable full-blown tragedy.

Not that tragedy had been totally averted. A year earlier, as the *Phoenix*, commanded by Lieutenant Edward Inglefield (a polar explorer who disproved a troubling rumor about Franklin's disappearance; see note 2, page 282) was making one of its three attempts to reach Belcher's ships, a young officer had suddenly fallen through an opening between two broken masses of ice and died. It had been Joseph-René Bellot, Lady Franklin's "adopted" son who, after serving with William Kennedy, had volunteered to once again search for Franklin.

The *North Star*, the *Phoenix*, and the *Talbot* docked in England in September 1854. A year later Richard Collinson suddenly arrived. His had been a most unrewarding and acrimonious voyage. Tension aboard the *Enterprise* during its almost five-year wanderings had reached the point that, by the time of its unexpected but welcome return, Collinson had placed all three of his mates, as well as one of his ice masters, under arrest. When the ship docked, the vessel's surgeon and his assistant were the only officers on duty besides the commander. Already outraged at McClure for having gone off on his own, Collinson demanded that those whom he had placed under arrest be court-martialed. In turn, the officers claimed that Collinson should be brought to trial.

There were indeed courts-martial, but not for Collinson. Not only Belcher, but McClure and Kellett faced charges of abandoning their ships. It was a proceeding that all of England followed with an interest rivaling that which they had shown in the search for Franklin itself.

The observant de Bray recorded the proceedings:

> *Captain McClure appeared first and justified his action on the basis of written orders he had received from Captain Kellett for abandonment of his ship under exceptional circumstances. After withdrawing, the court martial declared that Captain McClure, his officers and crew deserved the highest commendations and they were all fully acquitted. Captain Kellett then appeared to give his account of the loss of* Resolute, *and produced the orders he had received from Sir Edward Belcher for the abandonment of* Resolute *and* Intrepid. *A large number of letters were read, some of them confidential; they proved that, despite the opinion of Captain Kellett and all his officers, who declared the ships would not suffer at all during the impending breakup, Captain*

*Sir Edward Belcher, by a letter dater 25 April, had peremptorily
ordered them to abandon the* Resolute *and* Intrepid *and proceed
to Beechey Island. Having thus been cleared of all responsibility,
Captain Kellett was honorably acquitted and in returning his
sword the president expressed his complete satisfaction with
the manner in which he had comported himself in the difficult
circumstances in which he had found himself.*

The courts-martial then turned to the actions of Sir Edward
Belcher. To the dismay and even outrage of many who hung on every
word of the proceedings, the court, after hearing a lengthy statement
from Belcher in which he based his case on the instructions he had
received from the Admiralty, decided that legally he had acted within
the discretionary powers that had been given to him.

Perhaps in acquitting Belcher, the members of the court truly felt
that legally there was nothing else they could do. There were many, both
in the public and the press, who would always believe that it was Sir
Edwards's high standing in society that had saved him from the punishment they felt he deserved. Whatever the case, the only action the court
took was the symbolic yet meaningful gesture of handing Belcher back
his sword in stony silence. He would never be given the command of a
British naval vessel again. Soon there would be other events that would
make him an even greater object of ridicule and disgrace.

CHAPTER 11

A
Devastating Report and a Remarkable Journey

"A fate as terrible as the imagination can conceive."
—from JOHN RAE's report to the Admiralty, 1854

EDWARD BELCHER's sudden return and the details of the inexplicable abandonment of four of his vessels threw all of Great Britain into shock. Its effect on the Admiralty was equally profound. The Lords had had enough. Too many men and too many ships had been lost in what had obviously become a fruitless endeavor. Even the *Times*, for so long a leading instigator of the Franklin rescue efforts, now changed its position. "Surely enough has been done in favour of a sentiment rather than of rational calculation," the paper exclaimed.

Soon there was another development. Late in October 1854, John Rae suddenly arrived in England. And the Hudson's Bay Company explorer and surgeon, the man who had conducted the first search for Franklin, had startling and, in his words, "melancholy tidings," news so important he had interrupted his latest Arctic undertaking and rushed across the Atlantic to present his report.

Rae, his report to the Admiralty stated, had launched yet another Hudson's Bay Company exploration, this one aimed at determining once and for all if Boothia Felix and King William Land were peninsulas or islands. With two boats and eleven men he had left York Factory (Hudson's Bay Company headquarters) in June 1953, and had headed for the Great Fish River that George Back had discovered and which had been renamed for him. On the way, Rae had discovered a river of his own, which he named Quoich ("cup" in Scottish) after a river in his homeland, and had spent more than ten days exploring it. After wintering in his old base camp at Repulse Bay, he and his party had set off for Boothia Felix. On April 21, while making his way there,

He knew more about the Inuit than any other explorer, had traveled more Arctic miles than any other Franklin seeker, and was highly respected by all those who served with him, but John Rae's controversial report made him a pariah among much of the English population.

he encountered the first group of Inuit he had seen since beginning his exploration. Immediately he noticed that a member of their party, a man named In-nook-poo-zhe-jook, was wearing a cap with a golden band, the same type of headgear often worn in the Arctic by English naval men.

Ever since the search for Franklin had begun, Rae had made a practice of asking every group of Inuit he met up with the same question. Had they heard any stories of white men or ships? When he posed this query to In-nook-poo-zhe-jook he got a startling reply.

"This man," Rae's report stated, "was very communicative and, on putting to him the usual question as to having seen 'white men' before, or any ships or boats—he replied in the negative; but he said, thata party of *Kabloonas* (white men) had died of starvation, a long distance to the west of where we then were, and beyond a large River. Hestated that, he did not know the exact place; that he had never been there; and that he could not accompany us so far." The substance of the information then and subsequently obtained from various sources was as follows:

In the spring, four winters past (i.e. 1850), whilst some Esquimaux [Inuit] families were killing Seals near the shore of a large Island named in Arrowsmith's Charts, King William's Land, about forty white men were seen traveling in company . . . southward over the ice and dragging a boat and sledges with them. None of the party could speak the Esquimaux language so well as to be understood, but by signs the Natives were led to believe that the Ship, or Ships, [that the white men came in] had been crushed by the ice, and that they were now heading south, where they expected to find deer to shoot. From the appearance of the Men (all of whom with the exception of a single officer, were hauling on the drag ropes of the sledge and were looking thin) the party seemed to be running out of provisions, and they purchased a small Seal or piece of Seal from the natives. The Officer was described as being a tall, stout, middle-aged man; when their day's journey terminated, the men pitched tents."

Rae's report then detailed more distressing news related by the natives:

> *At a later date the same season, but previous to the disruption of the ice, the bodies of some thirty persons and some Graves were discovered on the continent, and five dead bodies on an Island near it, about a long day's journey to the north-west of a large stream, which can be no other than Great Fish River (named by the Esquimaux Ool-koo-i-hi-ca-lik), as its description and that of the low shore in the neighborhood of Point Ogle and Montreal Island agree exactly with that of Sir George Back. Some of the bodies had been buried (probably those of the first victims of famine); some were in a tent or tents; others under the boat, which had been turned over to form a shelter, and several lay scattered about in different directions. Of those found on the Island one was supposed to have been an Officer, as he had a telescope strapped over his shoulders and his double-barrel gun lay beneath him.*

It was devastating news, and, as he had listened to the story, Rae had only one thought: If the tale was true, who else could these unfortunate souls have been but members of the lost expedition? And almost immediately he had proof. After relating his story, In-nook-poo-zhe-jook, along with other Inuit, had showed and then sold Rae items that, without question had belonged to the men of the *Erebus* and the *Terror.* Later, when Rae returned to Repulse Bay, preparing to rush to England with his news, other natives brought him even more items, which he also purchased. Included in the sad array were a silver tablespoon with the initials "F.R.M.C." (Francis Rawdon Moira Crozier, commander of the *Erebus*), a silver fork bearing the initials "H.D.S.G." (Henry Duncan Spens Goodsir, assistant surgeon of the *Erebus*), three other silver forks with the initials "A.M.D." (Alexander McDonald, assistant surgeon of the *Terror*), "G.A.M." (Giles Alexander McBean, second master of the *Terror*), and "J.S.P." (John Smart Peddie, the *Erebus*'s surgeon). There was also a round silver plate inscribed "Sir John Franklin, K.C.B."

and Franklin's cherished Royal Guelphic Order medal inscribed with the words "Difficulties do not terrify." Finally, there was a knife handle marked with the initials of the *Terror*'s caulker's mate, Cornelius Hickey, and many small items—coins, chains, and a silver pencil case.

Rae was well aware that the tragic story he had heard was second-hand. He also knew that Arctic conditions would not allow him to personally investigate the sites mentioned in the tale anytime soon, but he was convinced that the Franklin relics he now had in his possession would unquestionably support the Inuit's story. What he was unprepared for was the reaction that one of the final paragraphs he hadwritten in his report would elicit. In concluding his account of In-nook- poo-zhe-jook's story, Rae had written:

> *From the mutilated state of many of the corpses and the contents of the kettles, it is evident that our wretched countrymen had been driven to the last dread alternative resource—cannibalism—as a means of prolonging existence. A few of the unfortunate Men must have survived until the arrival of wildfowl, (say, until the end of May), as shots were heard, . . . and feathers of geese were noticed near the sad event. There appears to have been an abundant stock of ammunition, as the powder was emptied in a heap on the ground out of the case or cases containing it; and a quantity of ball and shot was found below the high-water mark having probably been left on the ice close to the beach.*

Cannibalism—with that one word John Rae would stir the greatest controversy since the quest for the Northwest Passage and the search for John Franklin had begun. The furor caused by John Ross's mirage fiasco or Edward Belcher's abandonment of four seaworthy ships would be nothing compared to the maelstrom caused by Rae's assertion that members of the Franklin party had suffered "a fate as terrible as the imagination can conceive."

Cannibalism? Among officers and men of the Royal Navy, members of the most awe-inspiring expedition that had ever set forth? The Victorian mind simply would not accept it. These men were Englishmen to the core. And was not England the most civilized nation the world had ever known? Only three years before, the Great Crystal Palace Exhibition—a monumental technology fair—had verified Great Britain's extraordinary industrial and scientific leadership. It was the home of Alfred Lord Tennyson, the Brontë sisters, Elizabeth Barrett Browning, Matthew Arnold, and John Ruskin. Cannibalism among Englishmen? It was impossible; it negated everything that the English believed themselves to be. (This would be the first documented case of cannibalism among Arctic explorers, but not the last; see note, page 284).

As would be expected, no one was more outraged by Rae's report than Lady Jane Franklin. It was one thing, she stated, for Rae to have recovered some relics, but to "embellish" them with accounts of cannibalism and starvation was inexcusable. Such things would never happen on her husband's watch. Immediately, she set out to discredit Rae, labeling him an opportunist, interested only in claiming the reward that had been posted for finding the first relics of the missing expedition. Once again she took her case to the highest authorities and the press.

This time, she felt even that was not enough. This time she needed a spokesperson, someone whose eloquence and position would remove any doubt that Rae's assertions were false. She found him in the person of one of the nation's—and the world's—most widely read and admired authors. At this point in his career, Charles Dickens had already written *Oliver Twist, A Christmas Carol,* and *David Copperfield.* His new book, *Bleak House,* was just appearing in the bookstores. As anyone who read his work knew, Charles Dickens was, above all, an Englishman. And as such, he had also been appalled by the report of cannibalism among Franklin's men. "It is in highest degree improbable," he had written, "that such men as the officers and crews of the two lost ships would or could, in any extremity of hunger, alleviate the pains of starvation by this horrible means."

Dickens chose *Household Words*—a weekly journal that he both edited and contributed to—as the vehicle in which to fully present his explanation of why he believed the assertions of cannibalism were false. Unlike Jane Franklin, Dickens was a great admirer of John Rae and actually began his lengthy, detailed article by applauding the explorer's motives in bringing the Inuit's story to the attention of the Admiralty. "Of the propriety of his immediate return to England with the intelligence he had got together, we are fully convinced. As a man of sense and humanity he perceived that the first and greatest account to which it could be turned, was, the prevention of the useless hazard of valuable lives; and no one could better know in how much hazard all lives are placed that follow Franklin's track, than he who has made eight visits to the Arctic shores."

After questioning the reliability of any secondhand accounts, particularly those gathered through an interpreter, Dickens got down to the business of challenging the whole idea that the reported cannibalism had really taken place:

> *If it be inferred that the officer who lay upon his double-barrelled gun, defended his life to the last against ravenous seamen, under the boat or elsewhere, and that he died in so doing, how came his body to be found? That was not eaten, or even mutilated, according to the description. Neither were the bodies, buried in the frozen earth, disturbed; and is it not likely that if any bodies were resorted to as food, those the most removed from recent life and companionship would have been the first? Was there any fuel in that desolate place for cooking "the contents of the kettles"? If none, would the little flame of the spirit-lamp the travellers may have had with them, have sufficed for such a purpose? If not, would the kettles been defiled for that purpose at all? "Some of the corpses," Dr. Rae adds, in a letter to the* Times, *"had been sadly mutilated." [Were there] no bears thereabout, to mutilate those bodies; no wolves, no foxes?"*

Not content with debunking the notion of cannibalism, Dickens, displaying the racist attitudes of his day, then presented his theories as to what might have actually taken place:

Most probably the scurvy, known to be the dreadfullest scourge of
Europeans in those latitudes, broke out among the party. Virulent
as it would inevitably be under such circumstances, it would of itself
cause dreadful disfigurement—woeful mutilation—but, more than
that, it would not only soon annihilate the desire to eat (especially
to eat flesh of any kind), but would annihilate the power. Lastly, no
man can, with any show of reason, undertake to affirm that this
sad remnant of Franklin's gallant band were not set upon and slain
by the Esquimaux themselves . . . We believe every savage to be in
his heart covetous, treacherous, and cruel; and we have yet to learn
what knowledge the white man—lost, houseless, shipless, apparently
forgotten by his race, plainly famine-stricken, weak, frozen, helpless,
and dying—has of the gentleness of Esquimaux nature.

Proclaiming that it was unimaginable that the "flower of the
trained adventurous spirit of the English Navy, raised by Parry, Franklin,
Richardson, and Back" could have resorted, even under the most dire
circumstances, to such a despicable act, Dickens concluded his article
by proclaiming how Franklin and his men should really be remembered.
"Because no Franklin can come back, to write the honest story of their
woes and resignation, read it tenderly and truly in the book he has
left us. Because they lie scattered on those wastes of snow, and are as
defenceless against the remembrance of coming generations, as against
the elements into which they are resolving, and the winter winds that
alone can waft them home . . . therefore cherish them gently, even in the
breasts of children. Therefore, teach no one to shudder without reason,
at the history of their end. [They are to be remembered for their] forti-
tude, their lofty sense of duty, their courage, and their religion."

In the end, Charles Dickens's article was one of the relatively few
outward signs of the turmoil that the report of cannibalism had engendered. For the most part, the angst would be hidden; few Victorians
would be able to face the issue openly.

As Dickens had acknowledged, John Rae had had no hidden
agenda in rushing back to England with his news. He truly was

motivated by a desire to prevent the launching of more life-threatening searches. But ultimately it would be he who would suffer most from the cannibalism report. Eventually he would receive the £10,000 reward that had been offered to the person who discovered Franklin's fate. But that too would engender controversy, particularly from Lady Jane Franklin and her supporters, who decried that granting the reward implied that some of Franklin's men had indeed resorted to the unthinkable.

Lady Franklin would never forgive John Rae. And although several Arctic authorities of the day privately believed his report, the Admiralty, by omission, inflicted its own not-too-subtle form of rejection. Among other major achievements, Rae had walked over twenty-three thousand miles and had surveyed close to ten thousand miles of Arctic coastline, all in the cause of English national honor. Yet he would go to his grave as the only major nineteenth-century British explorer never to receive a knighthood.

Ironically, even those authorities that doubted the veracity of Rae's report accepted his belief that it might well be time to end the searches. Much of the public agreed. The front pages of the newspapers were now dominated by news of a very different nature. The Crimean War had erupted. For the first time in years there were battles to be won, British military honor to be upheld. Steadily, cries for Franklin's rescue were literally being put on the back page.

However, the Americans, and especially Elisha Kane, were far from ready to give up. Kane had arrived back in the United States on September 7, 1851, to great acclaim, not because of anything he had done in particular but because of his writing skills. He had not made the discoveries at Beechey Island—that had been accomplished by Penny's men—but he had, in his own unique writing style, been the first to report the significant find. On September 24, 1851, six days before the *Advance* docked back in New York, both the *New York Daily Times* and the *New York Daily Tribune* ran articles Kane had written about what had been found—long before the first accounts of the discoveries had reached the English newspapers. Not by deed, but by association, Elisha Kane became a hero. He was quick to capitalize upon it. Immediately he began writing other articles and giving spirited lectures. At the same time, he wrote a long narrative titled *The U.S. Grinnell Expedition in Search of Sir John Franklin*, which became a huge success. Fortunately he had the field to himself. De Haven, the actual commander of the expedition, had little writing skill and even less inclination to seek publicity.

Kane could not have been more delighted with the spotlight that was now cast upon him. For he had a not-so-hidden goal. He was angling for his own expedition to search for Franklin. "I must seize the present occasion," he exclaimed in one of his many speeches, "to state that I hope the search is not yet ended. The drift by which the *Advance* and the *Rescue* were borne so far, conclusively proves that the same influence might have carried us into the same sea in which Franklin and many his companions are probably immured . . . I trust for the sake of the United States, for the sake of the noble-hearted woman who has been the animating soul of all the Expedition, for the sake of this flag which has so triumphantly borne the battle and the breeze, for the sake of the humanity that makes us all kin, I trust that [the] search is not yet ended, and the rescue of Sir John Franklin is yet reserved to this nation and the world."

Finding that his lectures were increasingly well received, Kane stepped up the pressure. He not only wanted the search to continue; he had a strong notion of where Franklin was to found. Like John Barrow years before him, Kane had become a firm believer in the existence of an Open Polar Sea. As the number of his speeches increased, so too did his emphasis on his conviction that Franklin and many of his men were still alive and were trapped in this sea, "unable to leave their hunting ground and cross the frozen Sahara which has intervened between them and the world from which they are shut out."

Typical of the expert persuader that Kane had become, he covered all his bases by publishing an article in the *Daily Pennsylvanian* stating that even if Franklin were no longer alive, it was imperative for the sake of humanity that the search be continued, and as soon as possible.

"Sir Franklin has now been absent about six years and eight months," he wrote. "More than a year beyond the longest period for which his provisions could hold out, according to the most favorable estimate of his friends . . . We are afraid that there is in prosecuting the search, but little hope for more than to put an end to uncertainty by bringing the fact and manner of their loss. Even for this purpose, however, with the remote probability of finding the adventurers sill alive, it is a high duty to humanity to persevere and hope to see . . . an early renewal of the search put into execution."

Once again, Henry Grinnell answered the call, this time with added support from American financier George Peabody, the United States Department of the Navy, and various scientific organizations. Kane would get his wish. He would be given a ship. Once again it would be the *Advance*. And this time, he would be in command.

On May 31, 1853, with a huge crowd of well-wishers cheering them on, the seventeen officers and men of the *Advance* left New York Harbor ready to fulfill their "high duty to humanity." It was a most unusual crew. As one Arctic historian would write, "Its captain was a physician in poor health, his chief officer a boatswain . . . and his principal navigator a landsman astronomer." But before the expedition was over, newspapers would call it "the ultimate romantic adventure."

Kane's goal was to sail to Baffin Bay and then proceed north to the shores of the Polar Sea. By July 20, he had reached Greenland and had put into the whaling port of Upernavik, where he enlisted the services of Johan Carl Christian Petersen, a Danish sledge driver and interpreter. He then made his way through Baffin Bay and, with ice building all around him, attempted to cross Smith Sound. He made it, but only after the crew had dragged the *Advance* through the ice much of the way. In early September he was completely icebound in Rensselaer Harbor.

It was to be a horrendous winter. Temperatures would drop to as low as seventy degrees below zero. Fifty-seven of the sixty dogs that Kane had purchased in Greenland for sledging purposes would die. Everyone aboard would, to one degree or another, feel the effects of both scurvy and malnutrition. The only positive note in the long, dark winter was

Kane's good fortune in being able to hire the nineteen-year-old Inuit Hans Christian Hendrik, who would prove invaluable to him.

When spring arrived and it became obvious that the ice was still a long way from breaking up, Kane decided to send out sledge parties to search the area. Surely, there must be some signs that Franklin had passed this way. They found not a trace, but their long explorations brought other results. Boatman William Godfrey and ship surgeon Dr. Isaac Hayes were able to map a large area of what became known as Kane Basin. Kane himself made two significant discoveries—an enormous ancient ice mass that he named Humboldt Glacier and a unique rock formation that he named Tennyson's Monument. To Kane, however, these discoveries paled in comparison to what Hans Hendrik and ship's steward William Morton had found. Late in July they had pushed on past Humboldt Glacier and eventually reached a

Elisha Kent Kane's second northern expedition was one of the most harrowing of all Arctic ventures. Here, in an illustration from Kane's bestselling book, the explorer (center) and his officers pose for the expedition's artist while spending yet another winter day trapped in the brig.

spot from which they spied open water. When they reported back to Kane, he could hardly contain himself. There *was* an Open Polar Sea, and along its shores maybe—just maybe—there was Franklin. He had to see it for himself. But even though it was now summer, conditions were becoming impossible. Ice formations blocked his way, and he and the other sledge parties were forced to return to the ship.

By mid-July, with the ice that surrounded the *Advance* for miles as thick as it had been when they had first become imprisoned, it became clear to all aboard that there would be no escape for at least another year. With several of his crew becoming increasingly desperate and difficult to manage, Kane decided upon a desperate measure of his own. Aware that Edward Belcher's fleet had its base of operations at Beechey Island, he took five of his men and, in a small boat, set out for help. But it was a futile attempt. Every passageway was blocked and they had no choice but to turn back.

Then, in early August, a group of the crewmen suddenly came to Kane with a decision they had made. They were convinced, they stated, that the only chance for survival was to leave the ship and attempt to gain rescue by journeying on foot to Upernavik. Kane was shocked. It was more than a thousand miles to Upernavik and they were still in the season of ice and blizzards. They would never make it.

After pleading with the crew members to reconsider and detailing why he felt that it was far safer to stay with the ship, Kane told them that their decision should be put to a vote. Confident that they would take his advice, he added that those who did decide to leave would be given whatever provisions could be spared and would be granted immunity from desertion. To his complete shock, nine of the crew, including Dr. Hayes, voted to go.

They left on August 28. In his journal, a distressed Kane, battling to keep his usually good nature intact, wrote, "So they go . . . I cannot but feel that some of them will return broken down and suffering to seek a refuge aboard. They shall find it to the halving of our last chip— but—but—but—if I ever live to get home—home! And should I meet *Dr. Hayes* or [the others]—let them look out for their skins."

His words were prophetic. In mid-December all of those who had departed returned. In their flight to safety, they had nearly died. Several had been injured. Hayes's foot had been mutilated. All were on the verge of starvation. With as much good grace as he could muster, Kane took them back aboard and shared with them the *Advance*'s supplies, which were now dangerously low.

By May 1855, the provisions were almost gone. How ironic it was, thought Kane, that the only possible, yet unlikely, way out he could think of was to follow the same plan that the "deserters" had tried to pursue. On May 20 the ship was abandoned. For the next eighty-three days, the men of the *Advance*, carrying invalid members of the crew with them, traveled over thirteen hundred miles on foot and by boat. Finally, in August, they were spotted and taken aboard a Danish whaling vessel headed for Disko Island, some 250 miles south of Upernavik. One of the men died. Kane was near death himself. But they had managed their incredible escape.

Back home, they had not been forgotten. In April, a month before the *Advance* had been abandoned, two United States naval vessels commanded by Captain Henry J. Hartstene had set sail in search of Kane. Informed by telegraph that Kane and his party were at Disko Island, Hartstene arrived there on September 13. Kane would later describe his first meeting with the captain as he and his men were being ferried from the island to Hartstene's ship. "An officer whom I shall ever remember as a cherished friend, Captain Hartstene, hailed a little man in a ragged flannel shirt, 'Is that Doctor Kane?'—and with the 'yes' that followed, the rigging was manned by our countrymen, and cheers welcomed us back to the social world of love which they represented."

Elisha Kane returned to New York on October 11, 1845. The lecture tours, speeches, and writings that would follow would make him even more famous than ever. He had not found Franklin, nor had he set foot in the Open Polar Sea. But unbeknownst to him, the route that he had followed and charted would provide the avenue for explorers to come and the eventual discovery of the North Pole.

CHAPTER 12

The

Resolute *Comes Home*

"I don't know how I did it."
—CAPTAIN JAMES BUDDINGTON, 1855

CAPTAIN JAMES BUDDINGTON simply could not believe what he was hearing. His four crew members had finally been able to return to the *George Henry* after spending three days aboard the ship that the whalemen had come upon in Davis Strait. Now they were not only telling him that they had found absolutely no one on board the other vessel but that they had discovered that the giant "ghost ship" was a British naval vessel named HMS *Resolute*.

Buddington was stunned. The *Resolute*? Wasn't that one of the ships that had been sent out in search of John Franklin? Wasn't that one of the same vessels that, according to the stories he had heard from other whaling captains, had been callously abandoned by that British commander who had been court-martialed for doing so? But that ship had been left in the ice some twelve hundred miles away. It couldn't be. How could she possibly have made her own way across the Arctic to where she now stood across from him, completely on her own?

His men must be mistaken; but he had to see for himself. Taking a small party with him, he crossed the ice to the mystery ship and boarded her. He hadn't believed his ears when his men had given him his report. Now he couldn't believe his eyes. There was the nameplate, rusted but clearly legible. There were the barrels marked *Resolute*. There were the life jackets bearing the same name. "My Lord," exclaimed Buddington to the Arctic air, "it is the *Resolute*."

As his men had done before him, Buddington then made a quick inspection of the ship. There was no question about it—the *Resolute*'s solitary voyage through ice, snow, and lord knows what else had taken its toll. The vessel's tanks had burst and its hold was filled with more than seven feet of water. Most of its rigging and sails needed to be replaced. But despite it all, the ship was still remarkably seaworthy.

From the moment he had climbed aboard the *Resolute*, Buddington could not help but be aware that, by the laws of salvage, the abandoned ship was now the prize of the owners of the *George Henry*. And what a prize she would be—far more valuable than all the whales he had not been able to catch on this stormy, ice-plagued voyage. On the other hand, the vessel was worthless where she lay. In order for it to be sold, and for Buddington and his crew to get their share of the sale, the *Resolute* would have to be sailed back to port.

Did he dare think it? Counting himself, he had only twenty-six men and that included his inexperienced sixteen-year-old son, the cabin boy. If he divided them between the two ships, it meant that he would have to sail the massive *Resolute*, a ship built to be crewed by sixty to seventy men, with, at best, only thirteen of his whalers.

For a man who, throughout his long seafaring career, had been called upon to make life or death judgments, it was, he would later state, the most momentous decision he had ever been forced to make. But he did not hesitate. He would do it. The reward was too great. Foolhardy as it might be, he would attempt to bring the *Resolute* home.

But first the ship had to be made ready to sail. The initial challenge was getting the water out of the hold. No one aboard the *George Henry* had ever seen anything like the vessel's British-made pump. No one had any idea of how to get it started. After three days of trying, Buddington himself finally managed to turn it on. For the next two weeks, crewmen manned the pump for fourteen hours a day until all of the water and the ice were finally removed.

It was only the beginning. The rigging needed to be set up, sails put in place, and the rudder repaired. After drying out the canvas that he had found aboard the British vessel, Buddington had his men attempt to rig a topmast sail, but just as they seemed to have completed the task, a strong gale blew up, taking the sail away with it. The captain would be forced to sail the vessel with just the lower masts. Finally came the backbreaking job of chopping away the ice that surrounded the ship and creating a channel that would allow the *Resolute* to make its way clear of the main pack of ice.

Somehow it was all done. But that only gave Buddington the opportunity to try to accomplish something that even many of the most experienced captains would have regarded as impossible. The weather was so bad that, as later reports would reveal, thirteen ships had given up the attempt to enter Davis Strait while the *George Henry* and the *Resolute* were anchored there. Not only would Buddington have to sail the enormous *Resolute* with a crew less than a sixth the size of that normally required, but he would have to do so through ferocious storms, with nothing close to the proper instrumentation. He had no chronometer and no chart to steer by other than a rough outline of the North American coast, drawn on a piece of scrap paper. He would be making the long, dangerous voyage with a watch, a quadrant, and what he called a "miserable compass." What he did have, he would state, were "my instincts and more than twenty years at sea."

By the third week of October, Buddington felt that he was ready to leave. Piloting the *Resolute* through the channel the men had cut, he anchored outside the ice pack waiting for the *George Henry*, captained now by his first mate, John Quayle, to appear. There he received yet another surprise. As he waited, the British bark *Alibi* suddenly appeared alongside. Informing the startled Captain Stuart of the *Alibi* of how he had recovered the *Resolute*, Buddington handed him Captain Kellett's epaulettes and asked if they could be forwarded to Kellett as soon as possible. Buddington then hastily scribbled a letter to the *George Henry*'s owners describing what had transpired and that he would be returning to New London with not one ship, but two—one of them a prize beyond the owners' imagination. Stuart promised that he would mail the letter immediately upon his arrival in Great Britain.

Three days had now passed since Buddington had begun waiting for the *George Henry*. Now, fearing that the ice would close in on him, he had to push off. He would not see his own ship again until he reached New London.

The trip back to his home port would be the most difficult of Buddington's long career. Battered by at least one storm every single day of his two-month voyage, he was continually blown off course. More than once a sudden blizzard, with its accompanying mountainous seas, threatened to destroy the undermanned ship. "I frequently had no sleep for more than sixty hours at a time," the captain would later tell friends. He was far too occupied with trying to keep the *Resolute* afloat to even think of maintaining a journal of his ordeals, but his ship's carpenter, Henry Hughes, did manage to make a few brief revealing notes in his dairy. "The falling of this ice and the thumping of the sleet make music enough for any person who is nervous . . . We have had a gale wind ever since we started for home and this is enough to make anyone out of patience," stated one entry. Another read: "So here we be knocking about on the coast of Labrador, and a hard place it is too." And on Thanksgiving Day he recorded that "there was a gale of a wind and a heavy thunderstorm . . . a dismal Thanksgiving."

But it was a much better Christmas. "I don't know how I did it," Buddington would later recall, "[but] I took the *Resolute* right into New London harbor, arriving there on the 24th of December. It took me 67 days to come . . . When I got into the harbor the news spread and there was the shore crowded with folks wondering what the ship was. I had our colours flying of course, but, out of politeness to the Britisher, I had his flag flying, too. The harbor froze over solid every night the *Resolute* lay there, with the *George Henry* on the west side. I used to say that the *Resolute* brought the ice with her."

The *George Henry* had arrived in New London some five days before the *Resolute*. She too had had a storm-tossed, difficult journey. Early on she had lost her rudder and, with Hughes, the ship's carpenter, sailing with Buddington, the skeleton crew was forced to fashion a new one as best they could. It was a process that would have to be repeated several times as one jerry-rigged rudder after another was torn away in the heavy seas. By the time the whaleship reached New London, it was almost out of control and was leaking badly. John Quayle, who had never commanded a ship before, barely made it to port.

New London, Connecticut, in 1855 was a bustling, thriving place, second only to New Bedford as the world's greatest whaling center. Ships from around the world put into its harbor. But New Londoners had never seen anything like the *Resolute*. From the moment she arrived, she became the greatest attraction ever to grace the town. "From Old England's Thames to New England's Thames" stated the headline in a Boston newspaper. Special excursion trains were run to accommodate the thousands of sightseers who came to view her.

The *Boston Daily Advertiser* described the commotion:

> *As the fine ship lies opposite the piers of that beautiful town, she attracts visitors from everywhere, and is, indeed, a very remarkable curiosity. Seals were at once placed, and very properly, on the captain's book-cases, lockers, and drawers, and wherever private property might be injured by wanton curiosity, and two keepers are on duty on the vessel, till her destination is decided. But nothing is changed from what she was when she came into harbor. And, from stem to stern, every detail of her equipment is a curiosity, to the sailor or to the landsman. The candlestick in the cabin is not like a Yankee candlestick. The hawse hole for the chain cable is fitted as has not been seen before. And so of everything between. There is the aspect of wet over everything now, after months of ventilation; —the rifles, which*

*were last fired at musk-oxen in Melville Island, are red with rust, as
if they had lain in the bottom of the sea; the volume of Shakespeare,
which you find in an officer's berth, has a damp feel, as if you had
been reading it in the open air in a March north-easter. The old
seamen look with most amazement, perhaps, on the preparations for
amusement,—the juggler's cups and balls, or Harlequin's spangled
dress;—the quiet landsman wonders at the gigantic ice-saws, at the
cast-off canvas boots, the long thick Arctic stockings. It seems almost
wrong to go into Mr. Hamilton's wardroom, and see how he arranged
his soap-cup and his tooth-brush; and one does not tell of it, if he finds
on a blank leaf the secret prayer a sister wrote down for the brother to
whom she gave a prayer-book. There is a good deal of disorder now,—
thanks to her sudden abandonment, and perhaps to her three months'
voyage home. A little union-jack lies over a heap of unmended and
unwashed underclothes; when Kellett left the ship he left his country's
flag over his arm-chair as if to keep possession. Two officers' swords
and a pair of epaulettes were on the cabin table. Indeed, what is there
not there,—which should make an Arctic winter endurable,—make a
long night into day,—or while long days away?*

"Till her destination is decided," the newspaper had stated. It was a
good question. According to the laws of salvage, the abandoned *Resolute*
now belonged to the *George Henry*'s owners. But almost as soon as she
arrived in New London, a representative of the British government
had appeared, laying claim to the vessel on behalf of the Crown. For a
while it appeared that Anglo-American relations, already strained after
a series of commercial and political disputes, would become more seriously threatened. But then one of Great Britain's favorite American citizens stepped in. Henry Grinnell had won the hearts of all Englishmen
when he had sent two expeditions out to look for John Franklin. Now
he wrote a letter to British authorities politely suggesting that, since
the *George Henry*'s owners had suffered a great financial loss when its
captain abandoned his whaling to save the *Resolute*, England should give
up its claim to the ship. Almost immediately, the British complied. To

Henry Grinnell, the compliance was but the first step in a larger plan he had for the *Resolute*. For in the miraculous recovery of the ship he saw the opportunity for the United States to truly cement its relations with Great Britain. On January 7, 1856, he wrote a letter to the United States Secretary of State:

> *I consider [this] of great importance, and that is to make every effort to cultivate and extenuate a kind feeling between this country and Great Britain and further I must say an act of comity and justice towards a brother nation . . . The ship* Resolute, *a National vessel, fitted out by the Government of Great Britain for the humane and merciful object of assisting the crews of two ships . . . for the rescue of Franklin and his party whom you well know was making explorations in the Arctic Regions, has been fallen in with by an American Whaler, abandoned, and safely brought into the port of New London. And now allow me to make a suggestion that the Government of this country take possession of that ship, convey her to the Navy Yard at Brooklyn, put her in good condition and send her properly officered and manned from our Navy to the Government she belongs to and deliver her up without any compensation. Of course compensation would have to be given to those interested in the Whaler, from what I can learn this compensation would probably be from $30,000 to $50,000.*

Grinnell's suggestion took on even greater weight when it was supported by a similar recommendation from everyone's hero Elisha Kane. After considerable debate, the United States Congress, on August 28, passed a resolution stating:

> *Whereas it has become known to Congress, that the ship* Resolute, *late of the navy of Her Majesty the Queen of the United Kingdom of Great Britain and Ireland, on service in the Arctic Seas in search of Sir John Franklin and the survivors of the expedition under his command, was rescued and recovered in those seas by the officers and crew of the*

American whale-ship, the George Henry, *after the* Resolute *had been
necessarily abandoned in the ice by her officers and crew, and after
drifting still in the ice for more than one thousand miles from the place
where so abandoned—and that the said ship* Resolute, *having been
brought to the United States by the salvors at great risk and peril, had
been generously relinquished by them to Her Majesty's government.*

    *Now, in token of the deep interest felt in the United States for
the service in which Her Majesty's said ship was engaged when thus
necessarily abandoned, and of the sense entertained by Congress of
the act of Her Majesty's government in surrendering said ship to the
salvors: Be it resolved by the Senate and House of Representatives
of the United States of America in Congress assembled, that the
President of the United States be, and he is hereby requested to cause
the said ship* Resolute, *with all her armament, equipment and
property on board when she arrived in the United States and which
has been preserved in good condition, to be purchased of her present
owners and that he send the same ship with everything pertaining to
her as aforesaid, after having fully repaired and equipped at one of
the navy-yards of the United States, back to England under control of
the secretary of the navy, with a request to Her Majesty's government,
that the United States may be allowed to restore the said ship* Resolute
*to Her Majesty's service—and for the purchase of said ship and
appurtenances, as afore-said, the sum forty thousand dollars,* or so
much thereof as may be required, is hereby appropriated to be paid out
of any money in the treasury not otherwise appropriate.*

*Some nine hundred thousand dollars today

On September 12, the *Resolute* was towed by the steam tug *Achilles*
to the Brooklyn Navy Yard, where shipwrights and craftsmen refitted
her down to the smallest detail. The entire ship was repainted from
stem to stern. All of her sails, cordage, flags, and stores were restored
or replaced. Everything that could be reconditioned was preserved,
including Captain Kellett's library, the pictures in his cabin, and his
officers' musical instruments. The *New York Daily Times* noted that

"nothing has been overlooked or neglected that was necessary to her most complete and thorough renovation." The *Times* also spoke of what was sure to be the *Resolute*'s welcome in England: "The reception which will be given to her officers and crew will, undoubtedly, be worthy of the generous conduct of the American people."

By early November, the refitting was completed and on the thirteenth, the completely refurbished *Resolute*, her U.S. colors waving proudly, left New York bound for Portsmouth, England. In command was Captain Henry J. Hartstene, the same officer who only a year earlier had brought Elisha Kane home from his second Arctic adventure.

The *Resolute* docked in Portsmouth on December 12, 1856. And her arrival caused a sensation. The ship that had carried Austin in search of Franklin; the vessel from whose decks M'Clintock had launched his already legendary sledging expeditions and whose men had found and rescued McClure; the ship from whom so many discoveries had been made; the proud vessel that the "unmentionable" Belcher had left to its own fate; and finally the ship that had become the vehicle for the vital cementing of Anglo-American relations was home. And didn't she look grand!

The magnitude of the occasion was perhaps best expressed by George McDougall, who had served as the *Resolute*'s master under Captain Kellett. "The abandonment of a ship under similar circumstances is, I believe, without precedent," he stated in a book he wrote. "Her recovery is equally novel, and her restoration unparalleled . . . Few events in annals of the civilized world are so deserving of permanent record as the restoration of H.M. *Discovery-ship 'Resolute'* to the Queen of England by our transatlantic brethren. By such a graceful proof of their affection for the old country, they have lessened party animosity, silenced the noisy declamations of stump orators on both sides of the Atlantic, and have funded a capital of good will in the hearts of all true Englishmen."

For the British public, it was a time for celebration. (The event inspired poets and songwriters to commemorate America's genorosity; see note, page 285.) And in a country famed for its pomp and circumstance, the English government went all out. The first great occasion was the visit to the HMS *Resolute* of the Queen Victoria herself. "Her majesty having expressed a wish to visit the ship, she was towed to Cowes, and there secured alongside the royal embarcation place at Trinity Wharf," McDougall wrote, continuing:

> *The* Retribution *was anchored near for the purpose of firing salutes, whilst in the Roads her Majesty's yachts,* Elfin *and* Fairy *with numerous gunboats, tended to make a holiday scene of the auspicious event. The* Resolute *was dressed in colours, the English and American ensigns floating amicably together at the peak; and on the Queen's stepping her foot on board, the royal standard was hoisted at the main.*
>
> *The royal party, consisting of Her Majesty, Prince Albert, the Prince of Wales, the Princess Royal, and the Princess Alice, accompanied by a numerous suite, were received by Captain Hartstene at the gangway, whilst grouped on either side were the officers of the ship in full uniform, as well as many distinguished American visitors, all of whom were in turn presented to the Queen by Captain Hartstene, who then addressed her Majesty in the following words: "Allow me to welcome your Majesty on board the* Resolute, *and in obedience to the will of my countrymen and of the President of The United States, to restore her to you, not only as an evidence of a friendly feeling to your sovereignty, but as a token of love, admiration and respect to your Majesty personally." The Queen, who was evidently touched by the manly simplicity of the frank and sailor-like address of the gallant captain, replied, with a gracious smile, "I thank, you, Sir."*
>
> *The Royal party then went over the ship, and examined her with manifest interest. Captain Hartstene traced her course on a map, and indicated the most important discoveries of the American Arctic Expeditions. After completing the inspection of the ship, the royal party retired amid the enthusiastic acclamations of the spectators— the Queen having invited Captain Hartstene to dine and spend the night at Osborne. . . . Her Majesty also ordered £100 to be distributed amongst the crew.*

Dec. 27, 1856.] THE ILLUSTRATED LONDON NEWS 641

Queen Victoria's personal reception of the *Resolute* and her tour of the
fully restored vessel were the high points in the lengthy and, in many
ways, unprecedented celebration that accompanied the ship's return. Here,
an *Illustrated London News* article depicts U.S. Captain Henry Hartstene
welcoming Her Majesty to the ship (top) and showing the Queen a map
(bottom) tracing the *Resolute*'s route in her Franklin rescue effort and in her
miraculous unmanned voyage.

Over the next two weeks, the celebrations continued as the *Resolute* sailed from one harbor to another, while passing ships, their cheering crews standing at attention atop the yardarms, fired noisy salutes and dipped their colors. Each evening Captain Hartstene and his officers found them- selves at a ball, a banquet, or some other type of gala. Perhaps most notable of these was the Portsmouth Banquet, whose attendees included, as one newspaper put it, "the British Officers, late of the *Resolute*."

On December 30, the final ceremony took place—the official hand- ing over of the *Resolute* to Great Britain. "Whilst the salute was being fired," McDougall wrote, "Captain Hartstene ordered the American colours to be hauled down on board the *Resolute*, at whose peak the British ensign now floated alone, whilst at her main-truck an English pendant was displayed. The salute being ended, and the change of colours effected, the American crew manned the rigging, and gave three hearty cheers, as a return for the salute, and thus did the ice-beaten *Resolute* become once more Her Majesty's ship."

Captain Hartstene, accompanied by the Chevalier Pappalardo, United States Vice-Consul at this port, and the American officers, then addressed Sir George Seymour, naval commander-in-chief at Portsmouth, saying: "Sir, the closing scene of my most pleasant and important mission has now to be performed. And permit me to hope that long after every timber in her sturdy frame shall have perished, the remembrance of the old *Resolute* will be cherished by the people of the respective nations. I now, with a pride totally at variance with our professional ideas, strike my flag, and to you, Sir, give up the ship."

One question remained: To what use was the *Resolute* now to be put? She was certainly ready to take her place in the naval fleet, more than capable of defending British honor around the world. Many thought, however, that she was now too revered for that. She should be put on permanent display, as was Lord Horatio Nelson's ship, a constant reminder of past British strivings and achievement. But one person had other ideas. Jane Franklin knew just what should lie ahead for the *Resolute*. And as usual, Lady Jane was determined to get her way.

CHAPTER 13

The

Triumph of the Fox

"O then pause on the footprints of heroic men
Making a garden of the desert wide
Where Parry conquer'd death and Franklin died."
—CHARLES DICKENS

T HE BRITISH GOVERNMENT HAD MADE IT OFFICIAL. Well before the *Resolute*'s triumphant homecoming, the Admiralty had issued this proclamation:

By Admiralty Order, 18 January 1854: It is directed that if they are not heard of previous to 31 March, 1854, the Officers & Ships companies are to be removed from the Navy List & are to be considered as having died in the service. Wages are to he paid to their Relatives to that date: as of 1 April 1854, all books and papers are to be dispensed with.

Tragic as it was, much of the public now had to agree. The facts were staggering: The British government had spent over £675,000

($40 million in today's money), the United States government had expended over $150,000, and Henry Grinnell had contributed $100,000. Lady Jane Franklin had added £35,000 of her own money to the cause. Most disheartening of all, more than ten ships had been lost in the search and at least a dozen searchers had died. Almost everybody was ready to give up. But not Lady Franklin. The tremendous cost of the search, she declared, was all the more reason to make certain that the lives, the ships, and the money had not been sacrificed in vain. Besides, it had not been proven that her husband was dead. Perhaps, for example, he was living among the Inuit, waiting to be rescued. Greater miracles had already taken place.

And now, in the latest miracle, the return of the *Resolute*, she saw a new opportunity. Hadn't this noble vessel proven that it could conquer every challenge of the Arctic? What better use could it be put to than sailing out again to at least find out for certain what had happened to her husband and his men?

From the moment the *Resolute* had dropped anchor, Jane Franklin had attended almost every official celebration. She had even baked a plum cake and had it delivered to Captain Hartstene and his crew. But she had not simply been celebrating. She had, once again, been lobbying as well. At every party, every affair, she had cornered government officials and had pleaded her case. She had even persuaded Captain Hartstene, now familiar with every foot of the *Resolute*, to command the new expedition.

She did not act alone. At her urging, both Henry Grinnell and Roderick Murchison, the president of the Royal Geographical Society, wrote letters to the Admiralty supporting her desire. Charles Dickens again devoted articles to her cause. But, for the first time, the Admiralty would not be budged. The search was over; Lady Franklin could not have the *Resolute*.

It didn't stop her. Once again she purchased her own search vessel, this time the 177-ton schooner-rigged steam yacht, the *Fox*. She then persuaded Leopold M'Clintock, who through his sledging accomplishments had become one of her personal favorites, to command the vessel.

M'Clintock was delighted. He was absolutely convinced that the search should not be abandoned until physical proof—not second-hand information—of Franklin's fate was found. And he had a strong personal motivation. He had taken part in four searches, but always as second or third in command. This was his opportunity to head a mission that he still regarded as "a great national duty." Besides, like Lady Franklin, he believed that he knew where Franklin was to be found—at King William Island, the one logical place that had not been probed.

On July 2, 1857, M'Clintock and a twenty-five-man crew set out on their mission. His second-in-command was Lieutenant William Hobson, who had been in the navy for over a decade. As a mate, Hobson had proved himself on an 1853 mission aboard the HMS *Rattlesnake*, which had been sent to supply McClure's and Collinson's 1850 search expeditions. During the mission, Hobson had also honed his sledging skills on a small but strenuous trip he undertook to search for Franklin.

Almost immediately after entering the Arctic, the *Fox* crew became caught in a predicament unlike any that previous searchers or passage-seekers had ever experienced. Entering Melville Bay, they found it almost completely filled with large packs of floating ice, and attempted to force their way through it. But the ice packs took over. Incredibly, they would spend the next eight months not in winter quarters, but being helplessly moved along by ice. Before the end of April 1858, they had drifted helplessly the full length of Baffin's Bay and all the way through Davis Strait—a distance of 1,385 miles.

Finally freed from the ice, M'Clintock and his men spent the entire summer of 1858 beginning their search, but found nothing. When the ice returned, they were forced to seek winter quarters, this time under much more favorable circumstances in the harbor at Port Kennedy, at the west end of Bellot Strait. In late February 1859, on one of the several sledging expeditions he and Hobson launched from the *Fox*, M'Clintock made his first discovery. At Cape Victoria, on the west coast of Boothia Felix, he came upon a group of Inuit, one of whom was wearing a British naval button. And the natives had a story to tell.

The Inuit told of two ships, one that had been sunk and another that had been crushed by ice, and of white men who had starved to death on an island somewhere to the southwest, a location that M'Clintock realized had to be King William Island. And, like the natives that John Rae had encountered some five years earlier, the Inuit had objects that perhaps M'Clintock would like to buy—needles, buttons, a gold chain, silver spoons, and forks. Most revealing were the knives the Inuit showed him. They had obviously been fashioned from wood and metal from a wrecked ship. Finally, the natives handed M'Clintock a silver medal, which, according to its inscription, had belonged to Alexander McDonald, the assistant surgeon aboard the *Terror*.

For M'Clintock, the Inuit's stories were a confirmation of what he had believed was the key to his search. More than ever, he was convinced that the answers he was looking for were to be found at King William Island. After returning to the *Fox*, he and Hobson set out with sledge parties to search the shores of the island. They left on April 2, and within a few days encountered another group of Inuit who told the same story of two ships, one having been sunk, the other having been driven ashore by the ice. These natives also had items that clearly had come from the *Erebus* and the *Terror*.

By April 26, M'Clintock, Hobson, and their men had reached Cape Victoria, where M'Clintock decided that they should split up. He would explore southward down the east coast of King William and then travel clockwise around the island; Hobson was to head directly to the west coast to confirm the Inuit's story of a ship having been forced ashore there.

On the seventh of May, M'Clintock came upon an Inuit village whose inhabitants also had significant items. Among them were spoons and forks bearing the crests or the initials of various *Erebus* and *Terror* personnel, including John Franklin and Francis Crozier. To M'Clintock's disappointment, despite all of the articles he had recovered, he had still not been shown a journal, a diary, or a single scrap of paper, parts of the record of the lost expedition that Franklin would certainly have compiled.

The disappointment turned into dismay when, before leaving the camp, M'Clintock was told yet another story by an elderly Inuit woman. She had seen a large group of white men slowly making their way on foot towards the Great Fish River. Many of these men had suddenly dropped in their tracks; some, she stated, had been buried; others had remained where they collapsed. It was still not evidence that he had seen for himself, but it was certainly the most devastating report he had yet received.

Leaving the settlement, M'Clintock continued south where, in another Inuit village, he saw wooden kayak paddles, spear handles, snow shovels, and tent poles. There were no trees for hundreds of miles and it was obvious to M'Clintock that the wood that had gone into the making of these items had come from the remains of a ship. A few days later he was at Montreal Island, but his explorations revealed only an empty meat tin and some pieces of copper and iron. Again, none of the hard evidence he was looking for.

M'Clintock then turned west and headed back to King William Island. There, on May 25, he made his most important find. Having decided that perhaps his next best course of action would be to follow the route he had ordered Hobson to take, in order to find out what, if anything, his lieutenant had been able to discover, he suddenly came upon a human skeleton lying face down on the frozen terrain. Close by lay a clothes brush, a pocket comb, and a notebook. A quick inspection of the book revealed that the unfortunate soul had been Harry Peglar, one of the *Terror's* officers. It was an important find—the first direct evidence of what M'Clintock was becoming increasingly certain had been a major disaster.

Meanwhile, Lieutenant William Hobson was having a terrible time of it. The several explorations he had engaged in while the *Fox* had been beset in Bellot Strait had only increased his intense dislike of sledging—the bone-numbing cold, the inevitable storms, the nights trying to sleep in inadequate tents. And this trip had already become the worst of all his sledging experiences. His men—four seamen and an Inuit guide—were suffering terribly. Since leaving the *Fox* some thirty-four days before, the temperature had averaged about 30 degrees below zero. Every one of his men had frostbite. He worried most about Thomas Blackwell, the ship's surgeon. His lower extremities had turned completely white and he had almost no feeling in them. Periodically the men would stop and attempt to warm the doctor's feet with their hands. Hobson didn't dare think of what lie ahead for Blackwell even if he was fortunate enough to return to the *Fox*.

In many ways, Hobson himself was in equally bad shape. His legs were so swollen that he could hardly walk. Most frightening, his skin had become severely blotched, his joints ached, his gums bled, and he was shaken with chills—all unmistakable signs of scurvy. And, as if that were not enough, he, like almost all his companions, had developed snow blindness from the brilliant, eighteen-hour-a-day Arctic sun. He could barely see.

Suddenly, after making his way up a rugged coastal point, he thought he saw something. His eyes were watering terribly; the landscape was appearing to him in varying colors and much in front of him seemed to be coming out of a haze. But he was sure he had seen *something*. Or was it one of the Arctic mirages? He was all too aware of John Ross's imaginary Croker Mountains.

Leopold M'Clintock's sledging expertise never served him better than during his discovery-making voyage in the *Fox*. Here, he approaches the cairn where his lieutenant William Hobson first found the note left behind by members of the Franklin expedition.

William Hobson and members of his party tear apart the cairn containing the note revealing Franklin's demise. Within weeks of the *Fox*'s return to England, publications such as the *Illustrated London News* and *Harper's Weekly* featured dramatic depictions of the expedition.

But it *was* something, something extraordinary. There, towering above the sea was a six-foot-tall stone cairn. Around it were five-foot-high mounds of clothing, blankets, mattresses, and other articles. There also were pans, kettles, and four of the type of iron stoves used on British navel vessels. Now working feverishly to clear his eyes, Hobson then discovered that the entire area was littered with scores of other objects—shovels, pickaxes, saws, and barrel hoops, all partially covered by the snow. Further on there were rusted meat tins and broken bottles, all bearing the symbol of the Royal Navy. There was no doubting it—all that he was looking at had been part of the Franklin expedition.

But a closer examination of these items would have to come later. He could not wait to tear apart the cairn. Almost as soon as he began, a sealed tin fell out at his feet. Inside was a single sheet of Admiralty record paper. Upon it was an official message printed in six languages. It read "WHOEVER finds this paper is requested to forward it to the

Secretary of the Admiralty, London, with a note of the time and place it was found." Above and below this standard message, was a handwritten note which stated:

> *28 of May 1847. H.M.S.hips* Erebus *and* Terror *Wintered in the Ice in Lat. 70°5'N Long. 98°23'W. Having wintered in 1846–7 at Beechey Island in Lat 74°43'28" N Long 91°39'15" W. After having ascended Wellington Channel to Lat 77° and returned by the West side of Cornwallis Island. Sir John Franklin commanding the Expedition. All well Party consisting of 2 Officers and 6 Men left the ships on Monday 24th May 1847.*
> — *Gm. Gore, Lieut., Chas. F. DesVoeux, Mate*

Hobson was now trembling, for he knew that he had found the first written record of the Franklin expedition. And although it had been penned almost exactly twelve years earlier, it was hopeful. "All well," it had ended. But what was the handwriting that ran all around the margins of the paper? Quickly he read it. And it was crushing. Written almost a year after the first note, it read:

> *April 25th, 1848—HM's Ships* Terror *and* Erebus *were deserted on 22nd April, 5 leagues N.N.W, of this, having been beset since 12th September 1846. The Officers and crews, consisting of 105 souls, under the command of Captain F. R. M. Crozier, landed here in Lat. 69°37'42" Long. 98°41' . . . Sir John Franklin died on 11th of June 1847; the total loss by deaths in the Expedition has been to this date 9 officers and 15 men.*
> — *James Fitzjames, Captain HMS* Erebus
> — *F. R. M. Crozier, Captain and Senior Officer*
> *And start tomorrow, 26th, for Back's Fish River.*

Hobson was devastated. John Franklin was dead. And, given the information contained in the marginal note, how could he even hope that anyone in the lost expedition could still be alive? But despite his own

H.M.S.hips *Erebus* and *Terror*

28 of May 1847 { Lat 70°5' N Long 98°23' W

Wintered in the Ice in

Having wintered in 1846-7 at Beechey Island
in Lat 74° 43' 28" N. Long 91°39' 15" W after having
ascended Wellington Channel to Lat 77° and returned
by the West side of Cornwallis Island.

Commander

Sir John Franklin commanding the Expedition.

all well

WHOEVER finds this paper is requested to forward it to the Secretary of the Admiralty, London, *with a note of the time and place at which it was found:* or, if more convenient, to deliver it for that purpose to the British Consul at the nearest Port.

QUINCONQUE trouvera ce papier est prié d'y marquer le tems et lieu ou il l'aura trouvé, et de le faire parvenir au plutot au Secrétaire de l'Amirauté Britannique à Londres.

CUALQUIERA que hallare este Papel, se le suplica de enviarlo al Secretario del Almirantazgo, en Londrés, con una nota del tiempo y del lugar en donde se halló.

EEN ieder die dit Papier mogt vinden, wordt hiermede verzogt, om het zelve, ten spoedigste, te willen zenden aan den Heer Minister van de Marine der Nederlanden in 's Gravenhage, of wel aan den Secretaris den Britsche Admiraliteit, te London, en daar by te voegen eene Nota, inhoudende de tyd en de plaats alwaar dit Papier is gevonden geworden.

FINDEREN af dette Papiir ombedes, naar Leilighed gives, at sende samme til Admiralitets Secretairen i London, eller nærmeste Embedsmand i Danmark, Norge, eller Sverrig. Tiden og Stædet hvor dette er fundet ønskes venskabeligt paategnet.

WER diesen Zettel findet, wird hier-durch ersucht denselben an den Secretair des Admiralitets in London einzusenden, mit gefälliger angabe an welchen ort und zu welcher zeit er gefundet worden ist.

Party consisting of 2 Officers and 6 Men
left the Ships on Monday 24th May 1848

It was only one page long and its most important information was scribbled all around its edges. Yet, the note containing two messages—the first dated May 28, 1847 and the second dated a year later—was the single most important piece of written evidence in the search for Franklin and his men.

ever-weakening physical condition and that of the rest of his party, he kept on searching, following the route along the island that he was now certain the survivors of the Franklin party had taken. At this point the effects of his scurvy were so bad that his teeth were beginning to fall out and he was so weak that at times he had to be pulled along in the sledge. By May 11, he decided it was folly to go on. They had to turn back.

But just as he started to do so, he made another unexpected discovery. There on the coast lay the largest lifeboat Hobson had ever seen. Together with the huge sledge upon which it rested, it had to weigh at least fourteen hundred pounds. What was inside the boat stunned him even more. Lying at the bottom of the vessel, which he now realized was the type of long, narrow vessel that both the *Erebus* and the *Terror* had carried, were two skeletons, one at the bow, the other at the stern. Between the two skeletons was an astounding array of articles—books, slippers, cigar cases, tooth brushes, various kinds of footgear, assorted tools—even a collapsible mast and sails. The only provisions were some loose tea and about forty pounds of chocolate.

To Hobson, the discovery of the skeletons, grisly as it was, was not a complete surprise. Given the note he had found, he half expected to find the remains of members of the Franklin party. What *was* astounding, however, was the nature of the articles in the boat and their accumulative weight. None of the items could be considered essential for men trying desperately to save their lives. And why in the world would they go out of their way to load the boat with so much weight when to pull it in their weakened condition would likely sap whatever energy they had left? It was yet another mystery that would never be solved, another puzzling enigma of the Franklin saga.

And it wasn't the only mystery connected with the boat. Once he started to get over his amazement at the vessel's cargo, he noticed the direction in which the boat was pointed. It was headed directly away from "Back's Fish River," where, according to Crozier and Fitzjames's note, the Franklin survivors were headed. How could that be explained?

That was not all that Hobson did not know. What he had no way of realizing was that buried directly beneath where he and his party were standing were the bones of fourteen other members of the Franklin expedition. Years later, they would be uncovered by other searchers—and would reveal a terrible secret. From the knife markings on the bones, it would be obvious that the most edible parts of the bodies had been carefully stripped away. Investigation would also reveal that the jaws of the unfortunate deceased had been carved away from their skulls, an indication that their brains, rich in protein, had been extracted. John Rae's report of cannibalism had not been mere Inuit fantasy.

His explorations completed, Hobson headed back to the *Fox*. M'Clintock, not knowing what his lieutenant had discovered, continued to follow Hobson's route. Crossing Cape Herschel, he came pon the gigantic cairn that Peter Dease and Thomas Simpsonhad erected during their 1839 discovery-filled explorations. Twelve miles from there he found a cairn that Hobson had left behind, containing a message describing the note he had found. On May 29, he spotted the lifeboat.

If anything, M'Clintock was even more shocked at the vessel's contents than Hobson had been. Later he would describe the boat and what had been packed inside it as "a mere accumulation of dead weight, but slightly useful, and very likely to break down the strength of the sledge crews." Telling himself that perhaps another explorer would some day be able to solve that part of the Franklin puzzle, M'Clintock realized that it was time to head back to the *Fox* and sail for home.

He arrived back in England during the third week of September and was hailed for having led the expedition that had finally uncovered the secrets of John Franklin's fate. Among the honors that were bestowed upon him was a request by Queen Victoria that he sail the *Fox* to her residence at the Isle of Wight, where she could personally congratulate him and view the relics he had brought back with him. (Queen Victoria inspired decades of British Arctic explorers during her sixty-three-year reign; see note, page 286). For his discoveries, William Hobson was promoted to the rank of commander. He would never realize how close he had come to proving that John Rae's report of cannibalism had sadly been all too true.

CHAPTER 14

Still Searching

"I felt that I had within my grasp the great and noble
thing which had inspired the zeal of the sturdy Frobisher,
and that I had achieved the hope of the matchless Parry."
—Isaac Hayes, 1861

THE DISCOVERIES MADE by Hobson and M'Clintock satisfied
the Admiralty that, although many questions remained, the
fate of Franklin and his men had been revealed. There would be
no more British naval searches. Nor would Lady Franklin have
the resources to mount further explorations. The Americans, on the
other hand, viewed the British withdrawal as a golden opportunity.

There were indeed questions that still remained: Were there survivors of the Franklin party still out there, perhaps among the Inuit?
What about the journals and other records of the expedition? The
passage had been found, but the other great prize, the North Pole,
still beckoned. There was still great glory to be gained and there were
Americans determined to make it their own.

Chief among them was Charles Francis Hall. The Arctic quests had featured more than their share of distinctive characters. Now the world was about to be introduced to perhaps the most unique of them all. Born in New Hampshire in 1821, Hall, a former blacksmith and owner of a small Cincinnati printing firm, was fascinated by everything about the Arctic. He had read every book and article about the region he could find. He had studied the reports and journals of all the previous expeditions, especially those of Elisha Kane, who was his hero. Unlike the frail Kane, however, the full-bearded, broad-shouldered Hall was the picture of good health. He was only five feet, eight inches tall and weighed two hundred pounds, but all of it seemed to be muscle. Above everything else, Hall had become fascinated with the Inuit.

He could not understand why, from the beginning, the British had not made a far greater effort to learn all they could from the natives. This was particularly true, he felt, of M'Clintock and Hobson. Their discoveries could not be dismissed; they were certainly the most significant yet. But why, once they had proven that King William Island was the key to unlocking the Franklin mystery, hadn't they spent more time questioning the natives? Why hadn't they combed the entire island and the surrounding area for survivors?

That is just what Hall intended to do. And, along with everything else, he had his own special motivation, one that he was not reluctant to reveal. He had received a message from above. God had come to him and told him that it was his destiny to find the Franklin survivors. He would go, and he would go as soon as possible. He knew that Isaac Hayes, the doctor who had accompanied Kane, was planning his own expedition. Hall was determined to beat him to the Arctic.

Early in the spring of 1860, Hall, having sold his business and left his pregnant wife and daughter behind, traveled to New York to seek funding for his heaven-endorsed mission. There he met with the most logical funder, Henry Grinnell, who was once again willing to put up money for an Arctic quest. But not anywhere near what Hall had hoped for. He had asked for two fully equipped ships. What he got instead was free passage aboard a steam whaleship and a quantity of supplies.

Drive by the belief that he had been personally selected by the Almighty to find the survivors of the Franklin expedition, Charles Francis Hall, through his amateur, independent expeditions, proved that it was possible for a white man to live in the Arctic for long periods of time. His untimely death added to the many mysteries attached to the Franklin saga.

Disappointed but hardly discouraged, Hall revised his plans. Once the whaleship deposited him at Baffin Island, he would spend the winter living with the Inuit, hopefully even learning their language. Then, in the spring, he would travel by boat to King William Island and make his discoveries. It was an unprecedented scheme. No explorer, not even John Rae, had ever lived alone with the Inuit for an entire winter.

Hall left for the Arctic on May 20, 1860. The whaleship upon which he was being carried was the *George Henry*—the same vessel James Buddington had used to rescue the *Resolute*. And the coincidences did not stop there. The captain of the *George Henry* was Sidney Buddington, James's nephew and the tender that had been sent to accompany the *George Henry* was the *Rescue*, the same vessel that had been part of Elisha Kane's first search for Franklin.

The *George Henry* arrived off the coast of Baffin Island in the middle of August and Buddington anchored her in what was then called Frobisher Strait, discovered by the early Arctic explorer Martin Frobisher some 285 years before. (Once Hall discovered that this body of water was actually a bay, it became known as Frobisher Bay.) At once, Hall realized that all he had read about the wonders of the North had not been exaggerated. The first iceberg he saw "appeared a mountain of alabaster resting calmly upon the bosom of the dark blue sea." Surveying the landscape, he felt that the mountains were "like giants holding up the sky . . . Never did I feel so spellbound to a spot as that whereon I stood."

His exhilaration was short-lived. Within days a horrendous storm struck the area. The *Rescue* was torn from its mooring and although its crew was saved, the vessel was completely destroyed. Somehow, Buddington was able to maneuver the *George Henry* out of the teeth of the storm and find haven in Rescue Harbor off Cumberland Sound. There the ship would remain for the rest of the year.

It was an early disaster, one that might well have diminished the spirit of even the most seasoned Arctic adventurer. But not Hall. "I was determined," he later wrote, "that, God willing, nothing would daunt me; I would persevere if there was the smallest chance to succeed. If one plan failed—if one disaster came, then another plan should be tried."

First he had to wait out the winter. And on November 2, an event occurred that would alter the rest of his days in the Arctic. As he sat in his cabin aboard the *George Henry*, an Inuit woman suddenly appeared. Introducing herself as Tookoolito, and telling him that the white man called her Hannah, she explained that she and her husband (known to the white man as Joe Ebierbing) had in the past worked with British whalers; these white men had even taken the two of them to London, where they had been presented to the Queen. Would Hall, she wanted to know, like to have the couple join him as guides and interpreters? It would be the beginning of a relationship upon which Hall would depend for the rest of his life.

In Hannah and Joe, who spoke English fluently, Hall saw his golden opportunity to learn to live like the Inuit. Guided by them, he lived for almost another full year among the natives who were camped nearby, discovering how to sustain himself on seal blubber and blood, and learning how to hunt and drive dogsled teams in temperatures

Like her husband Joe Ebierbing, the Inuit woman Tookoolito (Hannah) served Charles Hall faithfully on all three of his Arctic expeditions.

After Hannah's death, her husband, also known as "Eskimo Joe," served as Frederick Schwatka's interpreter during his 1878 search for Franklin's records.

dozens of degrees below zero. Later, Hall would describe his life in the camp as "charming for all its lack of civilized trappings—or perhaps because of its lack." (In encountering the Inuit, those who went searching for Franklin came face to face with a culture that was totally foreign to them; see note, page 287.)

In January 1861, he decided to put all that he was learning to the test. Accompanied by Hannah and Joe, he embarked upon a dogsled trip that took him all the way to Cornelius Grinnell Bay. For forty-three days he "became" an Inuit, living off whale blubber and sleeping in igloos along the way. When he returned to the *George Henry*, he found that sleeping in his cabin was far less comfortable for him than his nights in the snow houses had been.

When spring arrived, Hall made two more sledge trips. On one of them, he had the opportunity to speak with Joe Ebierbing's grandmother who, in Hall's estimation, was at least one hundred years old. The woman told Hall that as a child she had heard stories of white men who, years before, had arrived in ships and had left behind items that none of the Inuit had ever seen. From her description of these objects, Hall realized that they must have been bricks, coal, and iron. Joe's grandmother went on to relate how her ancestors had passed on stories of how the white men had first arrived in two ships, then in three vessels the following year, and finally in fifteen ships the year after. From his knowledge of Arctic history, Hall knew that what was being told to him coincided exactly with how Martin Frobisher had arrived in the region in the 1570s.

Then came his discovery. Shortly after hearing the story, Hall took a sledge journey to another Inuit village. As he and Joe made their way across the ice, he suddenly spotted an ancient red brick which, according to Joe, was exactly like the ones he had played with as a child, objects that—he too was told—had been left behind by white men many years before. Hall was overwhelmed. "This relic," he would write, "was more precious to me than the *gold* which Frobisher sought there under the direct patronage of Queen Elizabeth."

Exhilarated by his find, Hall returned to the *George Henry*, prepared to begin his trek to King William Island. But his plans were dashed by Buddington, who convinced him that the whaleboat—which had been damaged in the storm that had sunk the *Rescue*—was far too inadequate to make so long and dangerous a journey. Hall could not help but agree. He would be back, next time with a much stronger boat. Meantime, before making his way home, he would concentrate on finding more Frobisher relics.

In mid-July the ice that had imprisoned the *George Henry* finally broke, and Buddington announced that he was heading for the whaling grounds. That too was all right with Hall. Left alone with the Inuit, he was in his new element. He had learned to live like a native and in doing so had found the freedom he had always craved. Equally important, he had learned that much of the Inuit's folklore was true. His conviction had been bolstered. It would be the natives at King William Island who would lead him to whatever survivors of the Franklin party remained.

Although he probably had no way of knowing it, Hall had not been the only American searcher in the Arctic. One month after his departure from New London, Isaac Hayes had left from Boston, intent on proving that the Open Polar Sea was a reality. The goal-oriented, highly educated Dr. Hayes, now twenty-eight years old, was not only confident that this time he would find the Open Sea; he was convinced that once he sailed into it, it would lead him directly to the North Pole.

Like Hall, Hayes had hoped to secure funding for two ships, one that would serve as a depot vessel, and a second that would take him to the Pole. He intended to enter the Polar Sea by first sailing into Smith Sound. From there, with the aid of dogs, he and his crew would pull a boat across the ice until they entered open water.

Hayes attempted to raise the funds for his venture by delivering a series of lectures in which he recounted the adventures of the 1850 De Haven-Kane expedition. But he fell far short of the money he needed. Like so many others, including Hall, he turned to Henry Grinnell, who helped him purchase not two ships, but one, the 133-ton schooner *Spring Hill*, which Hayes renamed the *United States*.

The fourteen-man crew that Hayes recruited included August Sonntag, a German emigrant who had been Kane's astronomer; the Inuit Hans Hendrik, who had also been with Kane; and ship's carpenter Gibson Caruthers, who had taken part in Kane's first venture into the Arctic with De Haven. Once in Greenland, the crew would be supplemented by dog drivers, who would be recruited there.

The *United States* sailed from Boston on July 10, 1860, and by the first week of August the party had passed through Davis Strait. Hayes's plan was to stop at the Greenland ports of Prøven and Upernavik, where he would buy dogs and sign on the needed drivers. He reached Prøven on August 6, only to be told that, because of a recent outbreak of rabies, there were no animals available. He had better luck in Upernavik, where he managed to obtain three dog teams and drivers. There, in the harbor, he also encountered the Danish trading ship *Tjalfe*. After visiting the ship, which was on its way home, Hayes was also able to acquire the services of Peter Jensen, an experienced dog driver and interpreter, and two other Danish seamen, anxious for an Arctic adventure.

It should have been an auspicious beginning to the journey. But while the negotiations with the crew of the *Tjalfe* were taking place, Gibson Caruthers suddenly died in his bunk. Hayes found himself forced to convince the more superstitious members of his crew that the carpenter's passing was not a bad omen. He sadly wrote in his journal, which was published in 1867 as *The Open Polar Sea: A Narrative of a Voyage of Discovery Towards the North Pole, in the Schooner* United States:

> *A valued member of my party, Mr. Gibson Caruthers, had died during the previous night, and I called to ask the missionary to officiate at the funeral service. His consent was promptly given, and the hour of burial was fixed for the following day. The burial of a companion, at any time painful, was doubly so to us, isolated as we were from the world. The deceased had endeared himself to all on board by his excellent qualities of head and heart; and the suddenness of his death made the impression upon his late associates all the more keenly felt. He had retired the night before in perfect health, and was found dead in his berth next morning. To the expedition he was a serious loss. Besides Mr. Sonntag, he was the only member of my party who had been in the Arctic seas, and I had counted much upon his knowledge and intelligence. . . . The burial-ground at Upernavik is a sad place for human sepulture. It lies on the hill-side above the town, and is dreary and desolate past description. It is made up of a series of rocky steps, on which lie, covered over with piles of stones, (for there is no earth,) a few rude coffins,—a mournful resting-place for those who sleep here their last sleep inthe everlasting winter. The body of poor Caruthers lies upon a ledge overlooking the sea, which he loved so well, and the beating surf will sing for him an eternal requiem.*

After burying Carruthers, the expedition sailed out of Upernavik Harbor and, on August 25, reached Cape York at Melville Bay. From the time he had planned the expedition, Hayes's goal had been to sail as far north as he could before winter set in, certainly past Smith Sound and past Rensselaer Harbor, where he had spent the disastrous winter with Kane. That way the crew would have the most advantageous starting point from which to launch next summer's breakthrough to the Open Polar Sea.

It was a good plan, but it proved impossible. By the beginning of September, both ice and storms were upon them. Reluctantly, Hayes found a place to winter over in a small bay some twenty miles south of Rensselaer Harbor, which he named Port Foulke. Even for Hayes—who had experienced more than his share of Arctic conditions—the scenes he witnessed during the following difficult winter were almost beyond belief and he vividly described the dramatic environment in his journal:

> *The imagination cannot conceive of a scene so wild . . . great sheets of drifting snow rolled down over the cliffs, pouring into every ravine and gorge like gigantic waterfalls. Whirlwinds shot skywards from the hilltops, spraying dense clouds of white through the air. A glacier tumbling into a valley was obscured by a vast cloak of revolving white. The sun was just setting on a black and ominous horizon. But the wildest scene was the sea itself. A solid mass of foam lashed the cape and was hurled through the air by the wind, breaking over the icebergs and fluttering across the sea like a thick fog, rising and falling with each gust. Earth and sea are charged with bellowing sounds . . . shrieks and wailing, loud and dismal as those of the infernal blast which down in the second circle of the dammed, appalled the Italian bard.*

Eloquent as he was, Hayes concluded his entry by stating: "My pen is equally powerless."

The weather was not the only problem. In December an epidemic broke out among the sled dogs. It was so serious that by January 1, only one sledge team remained. Knowing that he would never be able to reach the Open Polar Sea without an adequate number of teams, Hayes sent Sonntag and Hendrik off to Cape York to obtain dogs from the Inuit who resided there.

The two men set out on their mission on December 21. Confident that theirs would be an easy trip, Hayes sent them off with only twelve days' provisions and no tent. A month later, they still hadn't returned. Now deeply concerned, Hayes sent out a search party, but a sudden storm forced it to return almost immediately. Then, on January 30, Hendrik finally appeared. But there was no Sonntag. From the look on Hendrik's face, Hayes knew that something had gone terribly wrong. And he was right. Because of heavy snow, Hendrik told him, he and Sonntag had been unable to find the village they were heading for and had moved on, seeking another Inuit encampment. Walking along ahead of the sledge, Sonntag had suddenly stepped upon thin ice and plunged into the freezing water. Hendrik told Hayes he had done everything he could to save Sonntag. He had pulled him out of the water, wrapped him in a sleeping blanket, and poured as much brandy as he could down the unconscious man's throat. But, as had happened with young Joseph Bellot so many years before, the Arctic waters had taken their toll. Sonntag had died the next day.

In February, Hayes was still shaken by the loss of the popular astronomer. Because of their deep shared interest in all things scientific, the two men had formed a close bond. The good-natured Sonntag had also been extremely well-liked by the rest of the crew. Hayes's spirits were revived when, blessed with the first good fortune he had received that winter, he was able to obtain the needed dogs from Inuit at a nearby encampment.

On April 3, with twelve men, two dogsleds, and a large sledge carrying the boat he intended to use to traverse the icy waters of Smith Sound, he set out for the Open Polar Sea. By April 24, he realized that the task was nearly impossible. Never could he have imagined the landscape he would encounter. One of the ice floes, by his estimation, encompassed some twenty-four square miles and towered more than

Unlike most seekers of the Northwest Passage and many of the searchers for John Franklin who refused to adopt the Inuit practice of using dogs to haul their sleds, Isaac Hayes relied on the animals on both his Arctic ventures. As this sketch—drawn by Hayes himself— reveals, there could be problems in handling the spirited animals.

twenty feet above the sea. Pushing itself to the limit, the party was only able to move forward three miles a day.

Faced with the reality of the situation, Hayes made a decision. He sent most of the men back to the ship to prepare it so that when the weather finally broke, the *United States* would be able to sail through Smith Sound as quickly as possible. With Peter Jensen and crewmen George Knorr and John McDonald, Hayes pushed on. On May 11, the team reached an enormous rock "to which," Hayes would later write, "Gibraltar is a pigmy." Fourteen days later, they had progressed only forty miles. Worse yet, their food was almost gone. At one point the dogs had gotten to their stores and Hayes managed to maintain a black sense of humor about the episode:

> *I have watched with miserly care every ounce of food; and, last*
> *night, I gave to each animal only one and a half pounds. . . . To*
> *revenge themselves, they broke into Jensen's sledge, which, owing*
> *to the fatigue of everybody, was not unlashed, but covered instead*

with three feet of snow. The brutes scattered everything around,
tried to tear open our tin meatcans with their wolfish fangs, and ate
up our extra boots, the last scrap of skin-line that was left, some fur
stockings, and made an end of Knorr's seal-skin covered meerschaum
pipe . . . Another dog tore open a seal-skin tobacco-pouch, shook out
its contents, and ate it; and another bolted our only piece of soap. This
looks bad for our future cleanliness, but thirty-two days, at these low
temperatures, have worn off the sharp edge of fastidiousness.

Less humorous, though, was Peter Jensen's health; his legs completely worn out, he could not go on. Leaving Jensen with McDonald, Hayes moved on with Knorr. He was now desperate. All of his hopes, all of his sacrifices, the deaths that had occurred on this journey be pointless if he did not find the Open Polar Sea. For the next three days the two men pushed on, but then found their way completely blocked by ice and cliffs. They could go no further. Hayes estimated that he was now only 450 miles from the North Pole. He was really more than a thousand.

But he still believed in his dream. As he looked off in the distance he was certain that the land dropped off into what was surely the Open Polar Sea. "I felt that I had within my grasp," he would write, "the great and noble thing which had inspired the zeal of the sturdy Frobisher, and that I had achieved the hope of the matchless Parry." After leaving a message in a hastily built cairn and planting an American flag, Hayes and Knorr painfully retraced their steps, recovered Jensen and McDonald, and, on June 3, arrived back at the ship. They had traveled thirteen hundred miles in two months.

On July 14, the ice at Port Foulke released the *United States*. After a difficult journey, made much longer by having to put into ports in both Greenland and Nova Scotia because of foul weather, the ship finally reached Boston in October 1861. Hayes's claim that "all the evidence showed that I stood upon the shores of the Open Polar Sea" would soon be proven completely wrong. But nobody could convince Isaac Hayes of that. He would go to his grave certain that there *was* an Open Polar Sea and that it had been within his grasp.

Charles Hall was just as certain about his own convictions. He had arrived back in New London a year after Hayes had come home, more certain than ever that there were Franklin survivors on King William Island or in its vicinity, and that his friends, the Inuit, would provide important clues as to where they were. He had found more Frobisher relics and, based on his discoveries, he would surely be able to finance a return expedition. And this time he would get a ship of his own, a vessel strong enough to challenge the ice and bring him to the island. He could not imagine returning without the aid of the skilled and faithful Joe and Hannah, and he had brought them back with him to New London. After leaving them at Captain Buddington's house, he went off to secure what he was sure would be a quick acquisition of the funding he needed.

But he was wrong. Completely out of touch with events at home while living among the Inuit, he had had no idea that the nation was now embroiled in the Civil War—a conflict that had torn the country apart. Names like Bull Run and Shiloh, not King William Island or Barrow Strait, were now foremost in Americans' minds. Once again he raised some money by lecturing and writing, but, as before, he was only able to obtain some supplies and passage aboard a whaler. It would have to do; nothing would stop him from finding the survivors.

It was not until the end of June 1864 that Hall was finally ready to depart. With Joe and Hannah aboard, the whaler *Monticello* set sail under orders to drop Hall and his companions off with a boat and their supplies at Repulse Bay. The *Monticello's* captain, however, miscalculated, and in August the party was deposited at Depot Island, many miles south of where Hall had intended to begin his search. He thought that this time he would be in the Arctic for about three years. He would actually be gone for five, almost all of it spent living among the Inuit. His sole contact with white men would take place only on those rare occasions when he was able to obtain supplies from whalers.

Hall did not expect to find traces of the Franklin party from where he had been mistakenly dropped off, but he and his Inuit companions spent the winter sledging over miles of frozen landscape, hoping they might come upon something of substance. But they found nothing. In the spring, however, Hall was ready to begin his search in earnest. On April 13, 1865, the party set out for Repulse Bay and reached it on June 10. Realizing that it was too late to begin the long trek to King William Island, he spent yet another winter among the natives.

Finally, on March 31, 1866, he was ready to make the journey to King William Island. With Hannah and Joe and a party of eight other Inuit and six of their children, he headed out. The band was immediately assaulted by a raging blizzard that lasted five days. Finally able to resume the search, they were soon rewarded when they came upon a group of Inuit who possessed a great number of relics from the Franklin disaster, including a spoon with Francis Crozier's initials, a mahogany barometer, and a pair of scissors. Most of the stories they had to tell were similar to tales that Hall and other searchers had heard—accounts of ships sinking and the bodies of white men being seen. But one of their tales was completely new. As the Inuit members of Hall's party listened in terror, the natives spoke of a fierce tribe on King William Island that killed any newcomers they encountered. Hall's companions were so frightened by the news that they refused to go on; they wanted to return immediately to Repulse Bay. Hall had no choice but to go back with them.

By May 1866, a downcast Hall was back from where he had so confidently started his main search. Two months later however, his spirits were restored when a boat sent from a New London whaler landed at his encampment carrying letters for him, including one from Henry Grinnell. In his letter, Grinnell had included a communication he had received from none other than Lady Franklin, in which she praised Hall as Grinnell's "brave and adventurous protégé." After asking the financier to share with her any news of the Franklin party that Hall might discover, no matter how tragic, Lady Franklin then offered an apology. "When [Hall's] first plan . . . was brought before me," she had written, "it was represented to me by all the Arctic people as the wildest and most foolhardy of schemes, which must necessarily fail, and with which, for the poor man's own sake, I ought to have nothing to do . . . I believe Hall is now doing exactly what should have been done from the beginning, but which no government could *order* to be *done.*"

Endorsement and encouragement from Lady Jane Franklin herself! Hall was rejuvenated. Aware that there were six whaleships that were wintering over in Repulse Bay, he visited them and extracted a promise that, in the spring, they would provide him with five men who would accompany him to King William Island. In February 1867, knowing that he would need dogs for the trek, he set out with an Inuit he had recruited to obtain the animals. He returned a month later, only to have the whaling captains tell him that the five men would not be available to him for the better part of a year.

Hall had no choice but to wait. But in the meantime he had something truly promising to occupy his attention. He had encountered a group of natives from Igloolik, who had told him that several years earlier they had met a tall white man and his short white companion near their village. Hall could hardly contain his excitement. He was convinced that the tall man must have been Crozier. A short time later, a group of Inuit from Pelly Bay told him that had come across a stone monument that had a marker pointing toward Igloolik. Now Hall was even more optimistic. In March 1868, he sledged north with Joe and Hannah and one of the whalers he had hired, intent on exploring the vicinity of the Inuit's village in hope of finding Crozier or at least evidence that he and others might still be alive. But they found nothing.

Disappointed once again, Hall returned to Repulse Bay to bide his time until all five of the whalers would be fully available to him. Then, on July 31, 1868, he became involved in the most traumatic incident of his life. On a brief sledging trip that he and five of the whalers took, two of the seamen—Patrick Coleman and Peter Bayne—became separated from Hall and came upon a group of natives from Boothia Felix. The Inuit told them that years earlier they had witnessed the ceremonial funeral of a white man. Convinced that the Inuit were describing the burial of John Franklin, the whalers questioned the natives further, eliciting every detail they could get out of them. When they reported back with the upsetting tale, Hall flew into a rage. It was he and he alone who was authorized to question the Inuit. What right had ordinary whalemen to interfere with work for which only he was qualified?

Convinced that it was Coleman who had led the questioning, Hall vehemently berated the seaman. Coleman, a large, well-built man, answered back in kind. Hall was sure that Coleman, Bayne, and the three other whalers he had hired were about to stage a mutiny. Racing to his tent, he grabbed a revolver and, pointing it at the five men, ordered them to calm down. But Coleman, according to what Hall would later write, became even more abusive and began advancing toward Hall. Without, as he would later claim, even realizing it, the threatened Hall fired the revolver, felling Coleman. Handing the weapon to a terrified Inuit onlooker, Hall helped carry Coleman to his tent where, for the next two weeks, he tried desperately to save the man he had shot. But he had been too seriously wounded. Although he would not be charged with a crime, Hall would never be able to erase the memory of the man he had killed.

Not that it prevented him from sticking to his goal. He would no longer have the services of the whalemen, and most of the Inuit in the vicinity were afraid to set foot on King William Island. He had only one option, and he took it. In March 1869, accompanied by Joe and Hannah and a group of five fearless Inuit, he set out once again for King William Island. By May they had reached the shoreline of Rae Strait, across from King William. There, in yet another Inuit village, Hall was introduced to more relics—a silver spoon bearing Franklin's crest, part of a mahogany writing desk, and some ship's planking and copper. The villagers stated that they had discovered a tent on the western shore of the island filled with weapons, ammunition, and various utensils, along with human bones. Asked if there had been any books or paper, the natives replied that they had found these items, but since they had no use for them, they had left them to be destroyed by the elements.

Hall would have liked to have spent months combing the island, but the men he had hired insisted that they could remain for only another week before heading back. Searching desperately during that short time, Hall discovered the skeleton of a man who would later be identified as Lieutenant Thomas Le Vesconte of the *Erebus*. And from a group of Inuit he encountered, he was told the most disturbing story he had yet heard. Four of their families had met a tall white man and about thirty companions who were dragging two sledges. The white men were obviously starving and had begged the Inuit to give them some seal meat, which they did. But then, the four families, having barely enough food to feed themselves, had quickly departed—leaving the white men to their fate.

Saddened both by the story and by the fact that he had to admit that there were no members of the Franklin party to found, Hall headed back to Repulse Bay. He would always believe that, of all the searchers, it was he who would have been best equipped to save any survivors from the lost Franklin expedition. "O, that I could have met Crozier and his party twenty-one years ago," he would state. "I am sure that I could have saved the whole company. I say it with no egotistical feeling but with confidence of what I know of the country."

On August 13, 1869, along with Hannah and Joe, the man who had spent five years in the Arctic on this expedition alone, the man who now knew more about the Inuit than any other white man, boarded the whaleship *Ansell Gibbs* and sailed to New Bedford. His obsession with finding Franklin survivors was over, but not his Arctic dreams. He would be back, he was sure, and he had a very different type of quest in mind.

CHAPTER 15

Drifting and Seeking

"Here we are, and here, it seems, we are doomed to remain."
—GEORGE TYSON, 1872

IKE ELISHA KANE BEFORE HIM, Charles Hall had come home to a hero's welcome. But he had also returned with a new obsession. "Neither glory nor money has caused me to devote my very life and soul to Arctic exploration," he wrote. "My desire is to promote the welfare of mankind in general under this glorious ensign—The Stars and Stripes." He intended to reach the North Pole.

He had no time to rest on the laurels that the accomplishments of his first two expeditions had brought him. Others, he knew, were also interested in reaching what now had become the ultimate prize. A German expedition had, in fact, recently tried but failed. Fortunately, the United States Congress shared Hall's desire to make the attainment of the Pole an American achievement. In 1870, it authorized a Hall expedition to the Pole and provided him with a 387-ton steam tug that he renamed the *Polaris*. Hall immediately recruited Sidney Buddington to once again act as sailing master. The Smithsonian

Institution, responsible for naming the scientist who would accompany the mission, selected Emil Bessels, a German who, at the age of twenty- four, was already an accomplished doctor and naturalist.

Because Hall had discovered that many of the young men he intended to recruit as seamen had headed to the American West to seek their fortunes, most of his crew were also Germans. He did manage to convince an articulate whaling captain who had sailed the Arctic seas for twenty years to serve as his assistant navigator. He was forty-one-year-old George Tyson, the same man who, as James Buddington's mate, had been the first to step aboard the abandoned *Resolute* fifteen years earlier. It would be Tyson's on-the-spot record of the venture that provided the most detailed and accurate accounting of Hall's fateful final expedition. Also aboard were Joe and Hannah, ready for the third time to assist Hall on one of his quests.

The party steamed out of New London Harbor on July 3, 1871, and made its first stop in Greenland, where Hall obtained several sled dogs and picked up the ever-faithful Hans Hendrik and his family. Unlike his previous expedition, in which the *George Henry* had become locked in the ice soon after reaching Arctic waters, Hall was blessed this time with good fortune. By the end of August, the *Polaris* had reached the northern mouth of Robeson Channel. Later, various members of the ship would claim different readings as to where the ship was located at this point. But whether the exact spot was 82°11' or 82°16' or 82°29', the indisputable fact was that it was farther north than any nonnative had ever been—more than one thousand miles north of the Arctic Circle, less than five hundred miles from the Pole. (The race for the Pole was fiercely competitive; see note, page 288.)

The voyage of the *Polaris* was little more than two months old, and already there had been a great achievement. But there had also been problems. Almost from the first, Hall had been having difficulty maintaining discipline. He had already had to admonish Buddington for having raided the ship's liquor supply. His biggest problem, however, was with Bessels. Bessels, small in stature, with delicate, sharp features, was highly educated; the sophisticated scientist almost literally looked down his nose at the often gruff Hall. For his part, Hall referred to Bessels as "that little German dancing master." There were attitude problems with the other German members of the crew as well, a situation that was particularly troublesome to the experienced George Tyson, who worried about the future consequences of the situation. The crew, Tyson would note, "seem bound to go contrary, and if Hall wants a thing done, that is just what they won't do."

Having reached Robeson Strait, Hall would have liked to push on even further, but now signs of the approaching winter were appearing. As the ice began to build up, the *Polaris* became trapped in the moving floes and started drifting southward. Again luck was with Hall. Within days he found a cove, which he named Thank God Harbor, a spot that was shielded from the flowing ice by a stationary iceberg that he christened Providence Berg. There they would spend the winter. It would, he knew, be a long and dark season, but having come so far north without incident, and having found a safe haven in which to wait until spring, he was more confident than ever that it would be he who would be the first to stand on top of the world. However, there was one thing he wanted to do before settling in. On October 10, he took Joe, Hendrik, and one other crew member with him on a sledging journey to scout out the best possible route to follow once the good weather returned. On October 24, he was back on the *Polaris*, absolutely certain that in the spring the Pole would be his.

Two weeks later, he was dead. As soon as he had settled back on the ship, Hall had asked for a cup of coffee. Even before finishing it, he became violently ill. At first, he thought he was suffering from an upset stomach, but for the next seven days his condition continued to worsen. In great pain, he went in and out of delirium, often crying out, accusing some of his officers of poisoning him. At one point, he called Tyson to his bedside and made him promise that if he should die, Tyson would make the journey to the Pole.

Then, what seemed to be a miracle occurred. Hall's condition improved markedly. He became clearheaded, was able to hold down food, and was even able to go up on deck. But on November 7, he suddenly collapsed and fell into a coma. He died the next day. Three days later, wrapped in an American flag and dressed in his uniform, he was buried in a shallow grave above the permafrost on the shore of Thank God Harbor. Charles Francis Hall's long Arctic odyssey was over.

Command of the expedition now fell to Captain Buddington, a man who hardly shared Hall's passion for reaching the Pole. Whether he really would have pursued the mission will never be known, for within days of Hall's burial, a violent gale set the *Polaris* adrift, driving the vessel against the Providence Berg. The crew would remain imprisoned there for the next ten months.

It would be an excruciating experience. This was no large British naval vessel whose officers, before leaving port, had planned extensive activities and entertainment to bide away the inevitable wintering over. Trapped inside the tiny *Polaris*, the men became agonizingly bored. Nat Coffin, the young ship's carpenter, went mad, imagining that some

The eternal Arctic winter darkness provides a solemn backdrop for the burial of Charles Francis Hall. The sudden and mysterious death of Hall left the North Pole expedition without an effective leader, a fact that became all too evident during the following winter's entrapment and the remarkable six-month odyssey atop the ice floes.

unknown enemy was determined to kill him. Buddington was unable to maintain discipline over the crew, and he and Bessels—who truly hated each other—were continually at odds. "Nothing has occurred that is pleasant or profitable to record," Tyson wrote in his log. "I wish I could blot out of my memory some things which I hear and see. Captain Hall did not always act with the clearest judgment but it was heaven compared to this. . . . If I can get through this winter I think I shall be able to live through anything."

By October 15, 1872, with the *Polaris* still firmly entrapped, the morale of the men had almost reached the breaking point. Suddenly, however, they were all brought to life. A wind-driven blizzard erupted, slamming huge chunks of ice against the ship. Within minutes, the engineer began shouting that water was pouring into the vessel and that it was gaining on the pumps. Later, Tyson would recall that when he informed Buddington of what was happening, "the poor trembling wretch stood there oblivious to everything but his own coward thoughts." Then, Tyson remembered, Buddington "threw up his arms and yelled out to 'throw everything out onto the ice.'"

As Tyson looked on, the crew began to toss everything overboard. Looking down, he realized that many of the precious provisions were falling between the edge of the ice pack and the vessel and were disappearing beneath the water. "I decided I had better get overboard," Tyson wrote, "calling some of the men to help me and try to carry whatever I could away from the ship so that it would not get crushed and lost." Responding to Tyson's shouts, seventeen members of the *Polaris*, including all the Germans (except for Bessels), and all the Inuit, including Hannah, Joe, Hans Hendrik, and a number of women and children, joined him on the floe.

For more than four hours, working in the darkness and the well-below-freezing temperatures, Tyson and his crew struggled to save the provisions that were thrown from the ship. Then, without warning, there was a tremendous sound as the ice between the ship and the floe on which they were perched broke completely away. As Tyson and the others looked on in astonishment, the *Polaris* broke free and, driven by the wind and the currents, sailed out of sight. At the same time, the floe began to drift.

It was utter confusion. "It was snowing at the time and it was a terrible night," Tyson wrote in his small notebook. "We did not know who was on the ice and who was on the ship . . . the last thing I had pulled away from the ship were some musk-ox skins. They were lying across a wide crack in the ice and as I pulled them toward me I saw that there were two or more of Hans's children rolled up in one of the skins. A slight motion of the ice, and in a moment more they would either have been in the water and drowned in the darkness or crushed."

He had just completed this rescue when he heard cries coming from men who, in the splintering of the ice, had become trapped on small ice packs about forty yards away from the main floe. "I took the main scow," Tyson wrote, "and went for them, but the scow was almost instantly swamped. Then I shoved off one of the whale boats and took what men I could see, and some of the men took the other boat and helped their companions, so that eventually we were all on firm ice together." By this time everyone was utterly exhausted and, despite the conditions, they all collapsed on the ice and tried to get whatever sleep they could.

At daybreak, they assessed their situation. The ice floe was much larger than Tyson had first thought, almost four miles around. The supplies they had managed to save from the *Polaris* included eleven bags of bread, fourteen hams, a can of dried apples, and fourteen cans of dried meat and lard. They also had the two small boats and two seal-skin kayaks. As best Tyson could figure, they were drifting somewhere between Ellesmere Island and Greenland. A few hours later, through the spyglass he had managed to save, Tyson spotted the *Polaris* some ten miles away. He tried to get the ship's attention by fashioning a flag, but his signal went unnoticed. Before he could make a further attempt to hail the ship, the current took the floe further south and the *Polaris* disappeared from view.

By the end of their first week on their floating ice platform, the marooned party presented an incredible sight. The Inuit had built igloos from the loose snow on top of the floe and they, Tyson, and another officer were living in them. The other men had taken up residence in a large snow house they had erected. But they were in an increasingly desperate situation. By October 28, they had run out of meat and were forced to kill and eat two of the dogs. They were bitterly cold and Tyson, who had no real authority over the group, could only look on in anguish as the Germans chopped up one of the boats for kindling. They had no seal blubber to fuel the few lamps they had managed to save, and, with the sun gone for the winter, they spent most of their time in darkness, a situation that greatly diminished their ability to hunt for food. "Here we are," Tyson jotted in his notebook, "and here, it seems, we are doomed to remain."

Soon there was another serious problem. Joe came to Tyson in the night and, handing him his pistol, stated, "I don't like the look out of the men's eyes." What he suspected was that the crewmen, desperate with hunger, were planning to kill the Inuit and eat them. It was the same suspicion that Tyson was beginning to have. Aside from his revulsion at the thought, Tyson knew that the only thing that was keeping the party alive was whatever seal the Inuit were managing to hunt down. From that moment on, he would protect the Inuit by keeping the loaded pistol at his side.

By the end of December, the stranded members of the *Polaris* were eating anything they could get down. "I have dined today on about two feet of frozen seal's entrails and a small piece of congealed blubber," Tyson wrote on New Year's Day, 1873. By February, they had drifted so far south that they began to notice cracks appearing on their floating island. Then, on March 12, in the midst of a severe storm, the "island" shattered completely apart. Huddled together, eighteen men, women, and children were now standing on an ice floe some seventy-five by one hundred yards wide.

Two weeks later, it became clear that even this floe was about to fall apart. Leaving their possessions behind, they packed themselves into the small whaleboat and rowed for twenty miles until they found a large pack. But several days after setting up camp there, that floe also began to melt and they were forced to row to yet another floating pack. Tyson, who somehow managed to keep a sense of humor through it all, noted in his journal that "this sort of real estate is getting to be very uncertain property."

Unbelievably, the worst was yet to come. Battered by April winds and rising temperatures, their latest "island" refuge began to split apart too until, as Tyson observed, there was "such a small foothold left that we cannot lie down tonight." Then, on April 20, yet another fierce storm struck, threatening to wash everyone away into the sea and certain death. In a last, desperate measure, the Inuit women and children were put into the boat while the men held gravely onto it, fighting to keep it from being swept away, a struggle Tyson described in harrowing detail:

> We stood from nine at night until seven in the morning. . . . Every little while one of the tremendous seas would lift the boat up. . . . and carry it and us forward almost to the extreme opposite edge of our piece of ice. Several times the boat got partly over the edge and was hauled back only with superhuman strength, which the knowledge of our desperate condition gave us. Had the water been clear it would have been hard enough. But it was full of loose ice rolling about in blocks of all shapes and sizes, and with almost every wave would come an avalanche of these, striking us on our legs and bodies. . . . For twelve hours there was scarcely a sound uttered except the crying of the children and my orders to "hold on," "bear down," "put on all your weight," and the responsive "Aye, aye, sir," which for once came readily enough.

Finally the storm shifted; everyone joined the women and the children in the boat and they were able to row to yet another large floe. But although they had survived this latest ordeal, all hope was now fading. Even Tyson felt that the end was near. "Fearful thoughts go through my brain," he wrote, "as I look at these eighteen souls, without a mouthful to eat."

It was now April 30 and they had drifted into the commercial shipping lanes off Labrador. It had been some six months since they had jumped off the *Polaris*. Given the vagaries of the currents and winds, they had drifted almost two thousand miles. Suddenly, they spotted first one ship and then another. But in the heavy fog no one was on deck on either vessel to hear their frantic shouts or see the flags they feverishly waved. Then they spotted a third ship that seemed anchored. It was a Canadian sealer, the *Tigress*. Hans Hendrik took to his kayak, paddled to the vessel, and brought back a rescue party.

In his journal, Tyson noted the reaction he got when he told the *Tigress*'s crew members that he and his companions had been on the ice for six months. "One of the party looked at me with open-eyed surprise and exclaimed, 'and was you on it night and day?' The peculiar expression and the absurdity of the question, was too much for my politeness. I laughed in spite of myself."

Miraculously, they had survived. But what of the *Polaris*? What had happened to the ship and its remaining crew members since Tyson had last seen them six months before? The vessel, Tyson and his companions later learned, had not been as badly damaged as the engineer had believed. It had not, in fact, been taking on more water than its pumps could handle. But it had run out of coal soon after being driven away from the party stranded on the ice and Buddington had been forced to run it aground.

Fortunately, he had beached the *Polaris* close to an Inuit village that in the past had been friendly to Arctic explorers. The natives helped Buddington and his remaining crew survive the long winter. In the spring, they built two boats, sailed south, and were soon picked up by a whaleship out of Scotland, which took them to England. Booking passage on a British steamship, they arrived in New York on October 7, 1873. Buddington had orders to go directly to a navy board of inquiry investigating the death of Charles Hall. Tyson had already given his testimony, including the fact that Hall had told him that he was being poisoned. After listening to all the witnesses, the board admonished Buddington for his failure to maintain discipline aboard the *Polaris* and for drinking while on duty. Even though Buddington had testified that he hadn't seen Tyson and his companions after the *Polaris* began to drift away, the board also criticized the captain for abandoning his shipmates.

On the larger issue of what had happened to Hall, the navy concluded that he had died of apoplexy. Many observers believed that it was a whitewash. The navy, they felt, was determined to avoid the disgrace that would have been attached to admitting that a national hero, the man who had sacrificed so much to search for John Franklin and for the North Pole, had been murdered by one of his own men.

The story does not end there. In 1968, Hall's biographer Chauncey C. Loomis, journeyed to the explorer's grave, where he took samples of Hall's hair and fingernails. Analysis at a Canadian forensic laboratory revealed "an intake of considerable amounts of arsenic by C. F. Hall in the last two weeks of his life." This fact alone, however, does not prove conclusively that Hall was murdered. As was the case with most vessels of the day, there was a good amount of arsenous compound, a common Victorian remedy for headaches and other ailments, aboard the *Polaris*. Hall himself might have accidentally taken an overdose. The real story will probably never be revealed. What we do know is that no one, including Bessels—who had had such an openly hostile relationship with Hall—was ever charged with murder.

Like many of the mysteries associated with nineteenth-century Arctic exploration, we'll never know what really happened. What we do know is that Charles Francis Hall's accomplishments were considerable. He had made significant discoveries. He had solved parts of the Franklin puzzle. He had stood at a point further north than any other non-native had ever reached. Given his fierce determination, who was to say that he would not have conquered the Pole? And, just as he had been inspired by fellow American Elisha Kane, Hall had lit a spark under other would-be explorers anxious to leave their own mark on the Arctic.

CHAPTER 16

The
Search for the Records

"Schwatka has won a splendid victory and added his own name
to a long list of illustrious names connected with this Arctic search—
names which the world will not let willingly die."
—Isaac Hayes, 1880

O NE OF THOSE WHO had been most inspired by Charles Hall was
a man who had already experienced a most interesting career.
Born in 1849 in Galena, Illinois, Frederick Schwatka graduated
from the U.S. Military Academy at West Point in 1871. As a
second lieutenant in the 3rd Cavalry of the army, he served for several
years throughout the American West, where, though portly and not
in the best physical condition, he earned a reputation as an experienced
leader. After resigning his commission, he studied law and was admitted to the Nebraska bar. Then he studied medicine and received his
medical degree from the renowned Bellevue Hospital Medical College
in New York.

But in 1877, Schwatka was not interested in practicing either law
or medicine. He wanted to "close the book" on the Franklin mystery.

Like so many others around the world, he had been captivated by the search for Sir John. He was particularly taken with one of the greatest mysteries that still remained. Scores of Inuit reports of the fate of the lost expedition had been heard. Hundreds of relics had been gathered. Graves and skeletons of members of the *Erebus* and the *Terror* had been found. But, aside from the one note that William Hobson had come upon, no written records of the sad expedition had been discovered. They had to be out there. The full story of Franklin and his men would never be known until they were uncovered—and Frederick Schwatka was determined to find them.

As England's *Nautical Magazine* had declared more than twenty years earlier: "What became of Sir John Franklin and his party . . . is a mystery; the truth will only be arrived at from the papers which, it is not unreasonable to believe, will be found . . . at the scene of this dreadful catastrophe." Schwatka could not have agreed more. His desire had grown into full-blown passion when, in 1876, whaling captain Thomas Barry returned from the Arctic with a silver spoon bearing the Franklin crest and what he swore was a reliable story that he had heard from a tribe of Inuit he had encountered. According to the natives' account, a stranger in uniform, accompanied by several white men, had visited them several years before and told them that a large quantity of papers had been left in a cairn somewhere between King William Island and Melville Peninsula.

Schwatka could not get Barry's report out of his head. If it was true, it could solve one of the most nagging mysteries that still plagued all those interested in the Franklin saga. Why had the cairn that Penny, Ross, and others had found at King William Island more than twenty-five years ago been empty? Here, perhaps, was the answer. It was certainly plausible that, for whatever reason, Franklin's men had built another cairn in the area and deposited the precious papers there.

Schwatka had not been the only one to become excited about Barry's report. James Gordon Bennett, the editor of the *New York Herald*, used his considerable influence to promote an expedition to find the documents. John Morrison, the owner of several whaling vessels,

Army officer, lawyer, physician, passionate explorer—Frederick Schwatka was arguably the most versatile individual involved in the Franklin search. His determined quest for the written records of the Franklin expedition led to what was described as "a journey unparalleled in the history of Arctic travels."

then stated that if Captain Barry would sail the vessel, he would donate the use of his schooner, the *Eothen*, to the project. Joining in, the American Geographical Society, of which Isaac Hayes was an important member, announced that it was anxious to sponsor the expedition. And it was Hayes, impressed with both Schwatka's background and his obsession with finding the papers, who successfully urged the society that the cavalry officer/lawyer/doctor be given command.

The *Eothen* sailed out of New York on June 19, 1878. Included in the crew were Henry Klutschak, who was to serve as artist and surveyor, Frank Melms, who had spent many years in the Arctic, and William Gilder, who had been named second-in-command. Hailing from a prominent Philadelphia family, Gilder had served as a major in the 40th New York Regiment, and was now a reporter for the *New York Herald*. Gilder's extensive journal of the expedition would prove to be one of the most valuable records ever compiled by an Arctic venturer, particularly his accounts of Inuit testimony and his descriptions of the various aspects of the natives' ways of life. Also aboard were Joe and Hannah who, having managed to survive the *Polaris* misadventure, were now serving under Schwatka.

On August 9, Captain Barry landed the expedition at Camp Daly near Depot Island, where Schwatka and his crew set up camp. Discovering they were there, several Inuit families soon settled near the encampment. Schwatka immediately took advantage of their presence, and throughout the fall and the winter had his men—most of whom had no experience in the North—learn everything they could from the natives about traveling and living in the Arctic.

Early in the expedition, it appeared that confirmation of Barry's report might indeed be found. In December 1878, Schwatka and his men interviewed an Inuit named Nutargeark, who told them that many years ago his father had brought a spoon with him from King William Island that corresponded in description to the one that Barry had taken to the United States. The Inuit said that it had come from one of the boat places where relics and skeletons had been found. Nutargeark firmly stated, however, that he had not given the spoon to Barry but to the wife of a friend named Sinuksook, who, in turn, had given it to a whaling captain named Potter. "We saw Sinuksook's wife a little later," Gilder wrote, "and she distinctly remembered having given the spoon to Captain Potter. It was necessary, therefore, to find this officer."

Fortune was with the expedition, for it was soon learned that Potter, now second-in-command of a whaling vessel, was wintering at Marble Island, only an eight-day sledge journey from where the Schwatka party was located. In the first week of January 1879, Gilder and Klutschak, filled with the anticipation of verifying Barry's story and perhaps even being led to the paper-filled cairn, traveled across the ice to Marble Harbor and found Captain Potter. Gilder described the encounter:

> *I asked [Captain Potter] if he remembered Captain Barry getting a Franklin spoon while with him on the 'Glacier,' and he said he had never heard anything about it until he read in the newspapers*

that Barry had sent one to Sir John Franklin's niece, Miss Craycroft,
which surprised him very much. He further said that he (Potter)
had received three spoons at that time, one of which mysteriously
disappeared shortly afterward. The published description of Barry's
spoon corresponded exactly with the one he had lost, even to its
being broken off near the bowl and mended with copper, as was the
one he had received from Sinuksook's wife. Captain Potter further
said, to one who had lived with the Esquimaux, and acquired
the pigeon English they use in communicating with the whalers
in Hudson's Bay, and contrasted it with the language they use in
conversation with each other, the assertion of Captain Barry, that
he overheard them talking about books and understood them was
supremely ridiculous. There is probably no white man in the Arctic,
or who ever visited it, that would understand them under such
circumstances unless it be one or two in Cumberland, who have
lived with them for fifteen or twenty years. In this crucible of fact
the famous spoon melted. So far as Captain Barry and his clews
were concerned, we had come on a fool's errand.

The visit to Captain Potter, if not a fool's errand, had been a major
disappointment. But Schwatka was still confident that there were papers
to be found on King William Island. On April 1, 1879, Schwatka began
his explorations. With three dog teams and seventeen people, including several Inuit women and their children, he set out for King William
Island. It would be an incredibly long and difficult trek, one which, as
Gilder would describe it, was made possible only by the Inuit hunters:

[There was] only about one month's rations of civilized food for
seventeen people, and, was in fact, nearly exhausted by the time we
reached King William Land. Our main dependence was, therefore,
the game of the country through which we were travelling; a
contingency upon which we had calculated and were willing to
rely, having full faith in the superior quality of the arms and
ammunition with which we had been so liberally equipped by

*American manufacturers. It is well for us that our faith was well
founded, for there can scarcely be a doubt that it was this that
made our expedition possible. In all other respects we were probably
in a much worse condition than any previous expedition; but the
quality of our arms put us at once upon a footing to derive all the
benefit possible from the game of the country, a benefit of which
we availed ourselves, as the unparalleled score of 522 reindeer,
besides musk oxen, polar bears and seals will show. This is what
was killed by our party from the time we left Camp Daly until
our return. The quality of our provisions was excellent, and it was
only deficient in quantity. The Inuit shared our food with us as
long as it lasted, and, indeed, that was one of the inducements to
accompany us on the journey.*

In mid-May, the party encountered its first group of Inuit, an
igloo-dwelling tribe known as Ookjooliks. There, from a man named
Ikinnelikpatolok, they heard a fascinating story. "We learned at the
interview that he had only once seen white men alive," Gilder wrote in
his journal, continuing:

> *That was when he was a little boy. He is now about sixty-five or
> seventy. He was fishing on Back's River when they came along in
> a boat and shook hands with him. There were ten men. The leader
> was called "Tos-ard-e-roak," which Joe says, from the sound, he
> thinks means Lieutenant Back. The next white man he saw was
> dead in a bunk of a big ship which was frozen in the ice near
> an island about five miles due west of Grant Point, on Adelaide
> Peninsula. They had to walk out about three miles on smooth ice to
> reach the ship. He said that his son, who was present, a man about
> thirty-five years old, was then about like a child he pointed out—
> probably seven or eight years old. About this time he saw the tracks
> of white men on the main-land. When he first saw them there were
> four, and afterward only three. This was when the spring snows
> were falling. When his people saw the ship so long without any*

one around, they used to go on board and steal pieces of wood and iron. They did not know how to get inside by the doors, and cut a hole in the side of the ship, on a level with the ice, so that when the ice broke up during the following summer the ship filled and sunk. No tracks were seen in the salt-water ice or on the ship, which also was covered with snow, but they saw scrapings and sweepings alongside, which seemed to have been brushed off by people who had been living on board. They found some red cans of fresh meat, with plenty of what looked like tallow mixed with it. A great many had been opened, and four were still unopened. They saw no bread. They found plenty of knives, forks, spoons, pans, cups, and plates on board, and afterward found a few such things on shore after the vessel had gone down. They also saw books on board, and left them there. They only took knives, forks, spoons, and pans; the other things they had no use for. He never saw or heard of the white men's cairn on Adelaide Peninsula.

Schwatka was exhilarated by the story. If Ikinnelikpatolok was telling the truth, and Schwatka was convinced he was, here was evidence not only of what had happened to at least one of Franklin's ships, but where it had met its fate. Disturbing, however, was the Inuit's account of how, despite all the articles the Ookjooliks had taken from the ship, the books had been left behind.

Moving on towards King William Island, the team came to other Inuit camps, where they heard stories of how certain of the elders had seen white men who were "very thin, and their mouths were dry and hard and black" (sure signs of scurvy). They were also told of how other Inuit had seen tents with dead bodies lying in them, and of how they had also encountered many graves. On the shore of Erebus Bay, just before crossing over to the island, they made one of their most interesting discoveries. "We secured one valuable relic here," Gilder noted in his journal, "in the sled seen by Sir Leopold McClintock, in Erebus Bay, which at that time had upon it a boat, with several skeletons inside. Since the sled came into the hands of the Inuits it has been cut down several times. It was originally seven feet longer than at present, the runners about two inches higher and twice as far apart. But even in its present state it is an exceedingly interesting memento. We have carefully preserved it in the condition in which it has been in constant use by the Esquimaux for many years." Aware of the interest that such a relic would have for the Smithsonian, which had partially sponsored his venture, Schwatka had his men pack up a remaining section of the boat to be taken back with him to the museum.

It was indeed a most valuable find, but it would be followed shortly thereafter by the most disturbing story that Schwatka, Gilder, or any of the others would hear during the entire expedition. It came from an Inuit named Ogzeuckjeuwock, who told them that several years before he had visited the site of one of the boats that the Franklin party had abandoned, where he had found skeletons and many relics. The native's story, confirmed by others in his tribe, not only provided Schwatka with

Both the long search for the Northwest Passage and the years of seeking the men of the Franklin expedition engendered hundreds of depictions of events that took place during these quests. Most were drawn by artists or individuals who took part in the happenings. Fanciful depictions also appeared, such as this one of Schwatka or one of his men gazing at a row of graves and mammoth headstones never proven to have existed.

the most probable explanation of what had happened to the sought-after books and papers, but also once again raised the ugly specter of cannibalism. "Ogzeuckjeuwock," Gilder wrote, "said he saw books [in a long boat on the island] in a tin case, about two feet long and a foot square, which was fastened, and they broke it open." Gilder continued:

The case was full. Written and printed books were shown him, and he said they were like the printed ones. Among the books he found what was probably the needle of a compass or other magnetic instrument, because he said when it touched any iron it stuck fast. The boat was right side up, and the tin case in the boat. Outside the boat he saw a number of skulls. He forgot how many, but said there were more than four. He also saw bones from legs and arms that appeared to have been sawed off. Inside the boat was a box filled with bones; the box was about the same size as the one with the books in it.

He said the appearance of the bones led the Inuits to the opinion that the white men had been eating each other. What little flesh was still on the bones was very fresh; one body had all the flesh on. The hair was light; it looked like a long body. He saw a number of wire snow-goggles, and alongside the body with flesh on it was a pair of gold spectacles. (He picked out the kind of metal from several that were shown him.) He saw more than one or two pairs of such spectacles, but forgot how many. When asked how long the bodies appeared to have been dead when he saw them, he said they had probably died during the winter previous to the summer he saw them. In the boat he saw canvas and four sticks (a tent or a sail), saw a number of watches, open-faced; a few were gold, but most were silver. They are all lost now. They were given to the children to play with, and have been broken up and lost. One body—the one with flesh on—had a gold chain fastened to gold ear-rings, and a gold hunting-case watch with engine-turned engraving attached to the chain, and hanging down about the waist. He said when he pulled the chain it pulled the head up by the ears. This body also had a gold ring on the ring finger of the right hand. It was taken off, and has since been lost by the children in the same way that the other things were lost. His reason for thinking that they had been eating each other was because the bones were cut with a knife or saw. They found one big saw and one small one in the boat; also a large red tin case of smoking tobacco and some pipes. There was no cairn there. The bones are now covered up with sand and sea-weed, as they were lying just at high-water mark. Some of the books were taken home for the children to play with, and finally torn and lost, and others lay around among the rocks until carried away by the wind and lost or buried beneath the sand.

Here then was the answer—albeit an enormously disappointing one—that Schwatka had been seeking. It was supreme irony. Records of the most advanced search for the Northwest Passage that had ever been launched had been casually destroyed by children who could not even read them. Others had been either blown or washed away. Assessing the enormity of what had been lost, Gilder stated in his journal: "It is . . . a very natural deduction that the books that were found in a sealed or locked tin case, which had to be broken open by the natives, were the most important records of the expedition."

A frustrated Schwatka was ready to go home. But first there would be two other discoveries. Coming upon a large mound of earth, Frank Melms and Henry Klutschak quickly discovered that it was a grave. Describing the burial site in his account of the journey, Schwatka wrote:

It was obvious that it had been opened and despoiled by the natives some years before. Frank and Henry had examined it closely enough to uncover a silver medal, which they brought back with them. It was about three inches in diameter. On one side was the bust of King George IV, surrounded by the inscription: "Georgius IIII., D. G. Brittanniarum Rex, 1820," and on the reverse was a laurel wreath surrounded by the inscription: "Second Mathematical Prize, Royal Naval College." Inside the wreath was cut "Awarded to John Irving, Midsummer, 1830." This then, was the resting place of Lieutenant Irving, third-ranking Lieutenant on the Terror, *the second of Sir John Franklin's ships.*

The party's second major discovery before returning to Camp Daly was made in late July. "Lieutenant Schwatka found a well-built cairn or pillar seven feet high, on a high hill about two miles back from the coast, and took it down very carefully without meeting with any record or mark whatever," Gilder wrote in his journal. "It was on a very prominent hill, from which could plainly be seen the trend of the coast on both the eastern and western shores, and would certainly have attracted the attention of any vessels following in the route of the 'Erebus' and the 'Terror', though hidden by intervening hills from those walking along the coast." Schwatka had rediscovered the cairn that had so puzzled Penny, Kane, and its other original finders. Schwatka and Gilder added their own speculation as to why there had been no message in the cairn. "The next day Frank, [Hannah], and I went with Lieutenant Schwatka to take another look in the vicinity of the cairn, and to see if, with a spy-glass, we could discover any other cairn looking from that hill, but without success," Gilder continued. "It seemed unfortunate that probably the only cairn left standing on King William Land, built by the hands of white men, should have no record left in it, as there it might have been well preserved. . . . The inference was that it had been erected in the pursuit of the scientific work of the expedition, or that it had been used in alignment with some other object to watch the drift of the ships. Before leaving we rebuilt the cairn, and deposited in it a record of the work of the Franklin search party to date."

It was now late September 1878, and it was, Schwatka felt, truly time to start back. The almost six-month return trip to Camp Daly was as demanding as the trek to King William Island had been, made even more so, in fact, by the extreme temperatures. (Frigid coldness was not the only environmental extreme with which Arctic explorers had to contend; see note, page 289). Schwatka noted the details of the harrowing trip in his journal:

It was on January 3, 1880, when Henry Klutschak noted that the thermometer had reached 71 degrees below the freezing point, coldest on the trip and the coldest I believe ever experienced by white men in the field. . . . That low temperature was not at all disagreeable, until long towards the early night when a light breeze from the south sprang up. It is not so much the intensity of the cold that determines the dangerous character of Arctic weather as it is the strength and direction of the wind. I have found it far pleasanter for travelling, hunting or sledging, with the thermometer at 60 to 70 degrees below zero, with little or no wind blowing at the time, than to face a rather stiff breeze when the little tell-tale showed a far warmer temperature.

At any temperature below zero the beard must be kept closely cut, or it will form a base for a congealed mass of annoying ice, and from 60 to 70 degrees below zero, the accumulation glues the lips and nostrils together in the most diabolical manner. The few scattering bristles that the Esquimaux grow give them quite an advantage over the full bearded Caucasian, whose flowing whiskers are decidedly more ornamental than useful.

Finally, on March 4, 1880, they reached the bivouac at Camp Daly, only to find that Captain Barry was nowhere in sight. "We had Captain Barry's word that he would await our return," Schwatka wrote. "But upon arriving at Camp Daly . . . the greater part of the party's provisions, trading material, and other stores placed in Captain Barry's charge had disappeared with him." Totally disgusted with Barry, Schwatka led his party to Marble Island, where they were able to book passage on the whaleship *George and Mary*, which brought them safely to its home port of New Bedford.

Schwatka's safe return was hailed throughout America, especially by Isaac Hayes who, at a reception honoring the explorer's achievements, stated, "Lieutenant Schwatka has performed a journey unparalleled in the history of Arctic travels. It was a bold undertaking . . . yet, by persistently following a fixed plan of operations, by never once faltering in the direct purpose of his journey, and above all by the proper exercise of a natural gift of command . . . he has won a splendid victory and added his own to a long list of illustrious names connected with this Arctic search—names which the world will not willingly let die."

Six months later, the London *Times* presented its assessment of Schwatka's accomplishment. "The importance of the results achieved by Lieutenant Schwatka's expedition has not been gainsaid by any one possessing the least acquaintance with Arctic matters. It made the largest sledge journey on record, having been from its base of supplies for eleven months and twenty days, and having traversed 2,819 geographical, or 3,251 statute miles. It was the first expedition that relied for its own subsistence and for the subsistence of its dogs on the game that it found in the locality. It was the first expedition in which the white men of the party voluntarily assumed the same diet as the natives. It was the first expedition that established beyond a doubt the loss of the Franklin records. McClintock recorded an opinion that they had perished; Schwatka recorded it as a fact."

CHAPTER 17

Remarkable Gift, Enduring Mystery

> "Man has always gone where he has been able to go.
> It's simple. He will continue pushing back his frontier,
> No matter how far it may carry him from his homeland."
> —-*Apollo 11* astronaut MICHAEL COLLINS, 1969

WHEN HE HAD OFFICIALLY turned the *Resolute* back over to Great Britain, Captain Henry Hartstene had expressed the hope that "long after every timber in her sturdy frame shall have perished, the remembrance of the old *Resolute* will be cherished." He had no idea of how dramatically his hope would be realized.

On the morning of November 2, 1880, in a time when security was minimal and the Secret Service did not exist, an express wagon hauling an enormous crate pulled up to the delivery entrance of the White House. As William King Rogers, private secretary to President Rutherford B. Hayes, signed for the crate, he tried to imagine what could possibly be inside. No packages were expected at the presidential mansion that day, certainly nothing as massive as this one. What could it possibly be?

Totally bewildered, Rogers asked the president to join him, and the two men looked on as workmen pried open the mysterious package.

Their bewilderment turned to amazement when they saw what the crate contained. It was the most magnificent desk either man had ever seen, beautifully carved, four feet deep and six feet wide. It had to weigh at least thirteen hundred pounds. Where could it have come from? Who could have possibly sent it?

They got their answer when they noticed the brass plaque attached to the front of the desk. It read:

> H.M.S. *"Resolute"—forming part of the expedition sent in search of Sir John Franklin in 1852, was abandoned in Latitude 74°41'N, Longitude 101°22' W on 15th May, 1854. She was discovered and extricated in September 1855 in Latitude 67°N by Captain Buddington of the United States Whaler "George Henry." The ship was purchased, fitted out and sent to England as a gift to her Majesty Queen Victoria by the President and people of the United States as a token of goodwill and friendship. This table was make from her timbers when she was broken up, and is presented by the Queen of Great Britain and Ireland, to the President of the United States, as a memorial of the courtesy and loving kindness which dictated the offer of the gift of the "Resolute."*

President Hayes was delighted. He had read about the *Resolute*'s heroic accomplishments during the Franklin search. He knew how the ship had been miraculously saved and then restored and given back to England. He had been disturbed to discover that, for whatever reason, the vessel had not been put back in service. But now, thanks to the generosity of Queen Victoria, the *Resolute*, in a much different form, was alive again. Immediately, the president ordered that the desk be installed in his office on the second floor of the White House.

Since Hayes, every chief executive of the United States except Presidents Johnson, Nixon, and Ford, has used the desk. Some of the nation's most important pieces of legislation have been signed upon it; many of the most memorable presidential speeches and announcements have been made from behind it.

In 1952, the *Resolute* desk was moved to the Broadcast Room on the White House's ground floor, where it was used by President Dwight D. Eisenhower for his radio and television addresses. In 1961, First Lady Jacqueline Kennedy, aware of her husband's love of the sea and its history, had the desk placed in the Oval Office. There it became the setting for the famous photograph of the young John F. Kennedy Jr., peering out from behind its open kneehole panel. From 1966 to 1977, the desk was the centerpiece of an exhibition held at the Smithsonian Institution. In January 1993, President William J. Clinton had the desk returned to the Oval Office, where it remains today.

The *Resolute* desk has twice been modified. President Franklin D. Roosevelt asked that the kneehole be fitted with a panel carved with the presidential coat of arms, but did not live to see it installed in 1945. President Ronald Regan had a two-inch base placed beneath the desk to accommodate his six-foot-two frame.

The December 11, 1880 issue of *Frank Leslie's Illustrated Newspaper* featured this illustration of the *Resolute* desk. The accompanying story heaped praise on the beauty of the desk and emphasized how Queen Victoria's generous gift was a major step in cementing British-American relations, a process that had begun with the restoration and return of the *Resolute*.

Although President Hayes had had no way of knowing it when he received the treasured gift, Queen Victoria had actually ordered that two other smaller desks be made from the *Resolute*'s timbers. One was gratefully presented to Lady Jane Franklin. The other was given to Mrs. Henry Grinnell, the widow of the man whom Charles Dickens described as having "spent a large part of his fortune in the search for [Franklin's] lost ships, when none knew where to look for them."

The brass plaque on the desk given to Mrs. Grinnell contains words similar to those on the desk residing in the Oval office, but concludes: "This table . . . is presented by the Queen of Great Britain and Ireland to Mrs. Grinnell as a memorial of the disinterested kindness and great exertions of her late husband Mr. Henry Grinnell in assisting in the search to ascertain the fate of Captain Sir John Franklin, who perished in the Arctic regions." Enhancing this desk, which now resides in the New Bedford Whaling Museum, are two ceramic figurines, one of Sir John Franklin, the other of Lady Jane, the woman who never stopped looking for him. As one publication stated, it is a desk that "symbolizes the links of sympathy not only between the nations but also between two widows, one a New York City matron, one the Queen of Great Britain."

The *Resolute* desks are not the only permanent reminders of the ship that made what has been called "the most miraculous voyage in history." The collections of the Vancouver Maritime Museum contain the *Resolute*'s bulkhead clock engraved with the name "H.M. *Barque Resolute*" and signed by its manufacturer, the English clock-maker Edward Dent, best known as the creator of London's fabled "Big Ben." The museum's collections also include a unique treasure: the playing cards used by the crew of the *Resolute*, discovered by the men of the *George Henry* when they first boarded the vessel. Made to withstand the long, damp Arctic winters, they were fashioned from the tin cans used to preserve the food brought from home. Other known *Resolute* artifacts include the ship's spyglass and sextant, housed in the New London County Historical Society, and its bell, presented in 1965 to President Lyndon B. Johnson by British prime minister Harold Wilson.

16.
Before he died at the age of thirty-seven, Elisha Kent Kane established himself as the first great American Arctic explorer, and became a national hero. Kane's achievements during his two expeditions in search of Franklin inspired generations of future polar adventurers, and one of the routes that he charted eventually led to the discovery of the North Pole.

17.
Men of Elisha Kane's 1853 expedition haul equipment across the treacherous Arctic area known as Coffee Gorge, below. Such endeavors were but part of what turned into the most potentially disastrous of all the searches for John Franklin.

18.
Captain James Buddington, right,
poses for a portrait in his sealskin gear,
1862. When Buddington left New
London in the *George Henry* on his
1855 whaling journey to the North, he
had no idea that ahead of him lay
a remarkable discovery directly linked
to the Franklin saga.

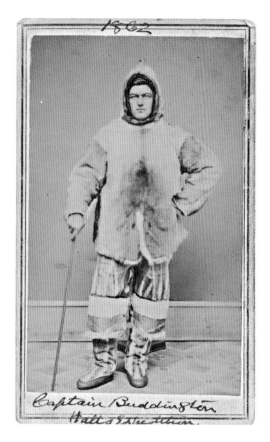

19.
She was one of New London's
most successful whaling vessels.
But the *George Henry*, below,
would gain greater fame as the
ship that discovered and recued
the HMS *Resolute* in 1855.

20.
The restoration and return of the *Resolute* to England in 1856
was hailed throughout Great Britain and notably improved Anglo-
American relations. Here, crowds gather as the queen visits her ship.

21.
The highlight of the ceremonies marking the return of the
Resolute was an inspection of the ship by Queen Victoria.
Later, Her Majesty would repay the United States with her
own special gift.

22.
One of the most dedicated of all the searchers for Franklin, and a master of Arctic sledging, Leopold M'Clintock stated that finding Sir John would be "the summit of all my waking dreams." In 1857, Lady Franklin placed him in command of the *Fox*, in which he set forth in search of more definite knowledge of Franklin's fate.

23.
The Franklin expedition boat discovered in 1859 on King William Island by Leopold M'Clintock, presented both evidence and mystery concerning the Franklin party's fate.

24.
Photographed in the Washington Navy Yard ca. 1865, the *Polaris* was the ship that carried Charles Francis Hall on one of the most unique of all Arctic adventures. After Hall died (he was probably murdered), the *Polaris* was stuck by an ice floe and driven out of control until her captain beached her. Meantime, most of the ship's crew, who had left the vessel to recover possessions that had been thrown overboard, were stranded on an ice pack that floated southward for the better part of a year.

25.
The quest for the Northwest Passage and the ensuing search for John Franklin engendered unprecedented interest in the Arctic. Dozens of books and plays dramatized the hardships faced by those who ventured north. The scene on this theater poster for a play about Arctic adventurers is reminiscent of the real-life adventure experienced by the men and women of the *Polaris* expedition of 1871–73.

26.
The obsession with the Arctic also spawned scores of songs. Their subjects included descriptions of the region, the searches for both the passage and for Franklin, and the accomplishments of individuals such as Edward Parry, Elisha Kent Kane, Leopold M'Clintock, and Lady Franklin. Songs were also written about certain ships, including the *Erebus,* the *Terror,* and the *Resolute.* This song sheet cover shows the type of message-carrying balloons used in the Franklin search.

27.
Explorers were not the only mariners to ply the treacherous
Arctic waters. Whalemen from England, the United States, Canada,
and other nations scoured the region in search of baleen-rich bowhead
whales. By the mid-nineteenth century, scenes such as this Currier &
Ives print of whalers at work had become extremely popular.

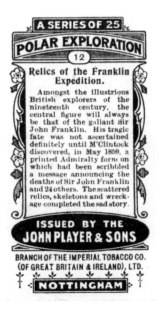

28. & 29.
Evidence of the way
in which the Arctic
adventure permeated
popular culture can be
seen in the illustrated
cards that were issued
by cigarette companies
in Great Britain and the
United States. Many of
the cards featured like-
nesses of the various
explorers. By the 1860s,
cards depicting dramatic
moments in the Franklin
search became sought-
after, particularly those
showing relics of the lost
expedition that had been
discovered—such as the
card shown here in both
front and back view.

30.
John F. Kennedy Jr. playfully peers out from from the kneehole panel in the Resolute Desk, while his father, President Kennedy, smiles. This iconic image was taken in October 1963 by White House photographer Stanley Tretick. In 1961, First Lady Jacqueline Kennedy moved the desk to the Oval Office from the Broadcast Room, where President Eisenhower had used it to deliver radio and television addresses.

31.
The Resolute Desk, shown above in the Oval Office of the Biden White House, has been used by every American chief executive—except Lyndon Johnson, Richard Nixon, and Gerald Ford—since President Hayes received it in 1880.

The fashioning of the desks signaled the final chapter in the story of the *Resolute*. There would be no mystery attached to what happened to the ship destined to play such an integral role in the Franklin saga. The same could not be said of the 128 men that she had tried so desperately to find. M'Clintock's and Hobson's discoveries had done much to begin the unraveling of the mystery. The Inuit testimony gathered by Hall and Schwatka filled in important pieces of the puzzle. But major questions remained. Where exactly had Franklin steered the *Erebus* and the *Terror* before he and his men had met their fate? Most important, what had really happened to them? How could such an unprecedented human tragedy have taken place? How exactly had they died?

Given Sir John's determination to complete his mission, it is most likely that he would have tried to cover as much distance as possible before winter set in. And, in fact, we know that both he and John Barrow fully expected that he would find the passage and sail through it in a single season. That might explain why initially he did not interrupt his voyage to stop and build cairns containing news of his progress.

It can be assumed that, as his orders dictated, he steamed through Lancaster Sound and then moved on through Barrow Strait. Ahead of him would have been Cape Walker, the last spot of land on his map. Looking to the southwest, he would have seen the unexplored territory that he had been told to investigate. But, in all probability, he found that ice barred his way in that direction. His orders mandated that if he was unable to proceed southwest, he was to turn north through Wellington Channel, which, knowing the man and his strict devotion to following orders, he would have done.

As Franklin headed north through the unknown territory surrounding Wellington Channel he would eventually have encountered the then-uncharted Grinnell Peninsula, which would have turned him to the northwest. By this time, ice would have been building up in the area, and eventually his way would have been completely blocked. He would have been forced to retreat to Barrow Strait but would have found his way to the west also blocked. Most Arctic experts agree that what probably happened next is that Franklin then found a passageway

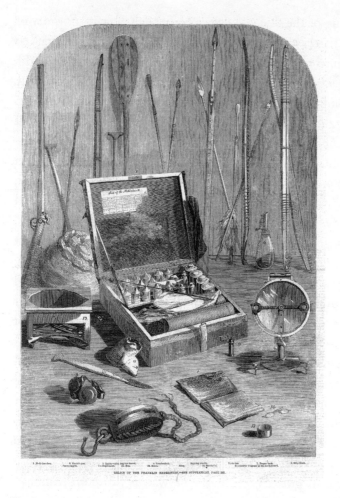

The discovery of thousands of relics from the Franklin expedition—begun in earnest with John Rae's acquisition of objects from the Inuit—captivated the public. The items in this illustration of objects found near the cairn discovered by William Hobson includes a medicine chest, a stove, a prayer book, sun goggles, a gun, and a flag.

that he was confident would take him close to King William Land (he would not have known that John Rae and others had discovered it was an island). This must have truly excited him, for what we know for certain is that, based on his own previous Arctic explorations and those of others—particularly Simpson and Back—he truly believed that from there, it was clear sailing to open western waters. Later, colleagues back home would remember how before setting sail, Sir John had placed his finger on that area of the map, declaring, "If I can get down there my work is done; thence it's plain sailing to the westward."

By now, however, the ice would most assuredly have been building up. He would have had to find a haven for the winter. That he found it in the harbor at Beechey Island is another fact that we know for certain. The three graves and the scattered relics bear indisputable testimony. And there, at Beechey Island, is where the real mysteries begin.

Why was there no message in the cairn found on the island? Almost every passage-seeker who had been forced to winter down had built cairns and had placed messages within them detailing where he had been, what had transpired, and what he planned to do once he was released from the ice. It was standard naval procedure. And no one adhered to accepted procedure more than John Franklin. Was he so confident that once spring came he would gallantly sail away to the open sea and the glory beyond that leaving a message behind seemed superfluous? Some have suggested that perhaps the weather broke so suddenly in the spring that Franklin, anxious to get underway while he could, simply had no time to prepare a document. But he had been on the island for months. Why would he not have prepared a message long before then? It has also been speculated that Sir John might have indeed deposited a note in the cairn but that it had been stolen by natives. This too is highly unlikely since there were no Inuit on or near barren Beechey Island. The frustrating answer to all these questions is that we will probably never know.

What we can be pretty sure about is that, in the spring of 1846, Franklin, adhering to his orders, probably set out for Cape Walker. As Arctic authorities have pointed out, he would not have known that he was heading straight for one of the great phenomena of the north— the gigantic impenetrable stream of ice that, in the spring, pores down from the Beaufort Sea. Once he ran up against this moving barrier with its one-hundred-foot thick packs of ice, he would have had to turn back. To the south of him lay the unexplored and hitherto unnavigated Peel Sound, which, Franklin believed, led to King William Land.

He was right. When he completed his Peel Sound passage he would have actually been able to see the northern tip of King William Land. It was only one hundred miles away (see map, page 76).

But, as we know from the note that Hobson found—the only message that would ever be discovered—the ice then set in, and on September 12, 1846, the *Erebus* and the *Terror* were once again imprisoned. Nine months later, Franklin was dead. How did he die? Where was he laid to rest? Certainly his burial would have been treated with great ceremony. Was it at sea or in a grave that has never been found?

In many ways, even greater mystery surrounds Francis Crozier, the officer who assumed command of the expedition once Franklin was gone, the man whom Schwatka believed was the white stranger the Inuit swore they had seen wandering near their villages. In the years following the search for Franklin, there would be even more rumors about Crozier than there had been about Franklin. Some had him living among the Chipewyans. Others had him wandering aimlessly through- out the north where he had spent most of his life. Whatever finally happened to him, it was Crozier who inherited the burden of trying to save the expedition after its leader and twenty-four of its men had died.

It was a staggering total. Of all those who had gone out in search of the passage since 1818, only seventeen had perished. And with his men dying every day, Crozier knew it was going to get much worse. His options were limited. Should he stay where he was, hoping that by May or at least June, the ice would break up and he could head for home? Or should he abandon the ships and head for the Great Fish River, hoping that it would take him either to where the whaling fleet would be that summer or to the Hudson's Bay Company Trading post on Great Slave Lake? One thing was for certain: Any hope of completing the search for the passage was gone. His one goal had to be saving as many members of the expedition as he could.

He chose to leave the ships and head for the river. To this day, there is disagreement as to whether it was a horrendous mistake. As George Back had discovered, the Great Fish River was incredibly difficult to navigate, and Crozier's men were in a weakened condition, to say the least. In Crozier's defense, he probably counted on the river being ice-free, relieving his men of the burden of having to drag heavy boats over the ice. There would also be fish in the river and perhaps game along its banks, another important consideration for men who were rapidly running out of food. And Crozier knew that before they had left England, Franklin had been informed that if, by any chance, the expedition had not been heard from by the spring of 1848, the Hudson's Bay Company would launch a search for it. Crozier may well have thought that he might encounter help even before reaching the company outpost at Great Slave Lake.

A mystery also attaches itself to the almost eight-hundred-pound boat that Hobson and M'Clintock discovered, loaded to the gunwales with seemingly superfluous supplies. M'Clintock simply couldn't understand what Crozier and his fellow officers had been thinking in hauling all that equipment off the ships if they were to be abandoned. But here again, Crozier might have had what to him were plausible reasons. Over the years, for example, much has been made of the fact that among the equipment found on shore were four heavy iron boat stoves, which had been dragged from the ships. Why in the world had that been done? It seemed ludicrous, especially to M'Clintock and Hobson.

In his 2000 book *Ice Blink*, however, Scott Cookman offered an intriguing explanation. Did Crozier, knowing that the boat stoves cooked much faster than the single immovable stoves on the *Erebus* and the *Terror*, have them placed ashore so that biscuits could quickly be made to help sustain the men in their long march in hope of rescue? M'Clintock and Hobson were also amazed to find such "unnecessary," items as curtain rods among the equipment. But, as Cookman has also speculated, Crozier, aware that lightning posed a serious threat in that flat open region, may well have carried the curtain rods along to be used as improvised lightning rods.

All this, of course, is based on educated speculation. And new theories continue to appear. Of these, the most compelling by far is that put forth by oceanographer and author David C. Woodman. After spending ten years researching and analyzing Inuit testimony collected by the various searchers for Franklin, Woodman published his conclusions. Most intriguing among them is his belief that not all of Franklin's men died in 1848 or 1849, and that it was not until 1851 that the last of the survivors left the area where the *Erebus* and the *Terror* were abandoned. From his investigations, Woodman also concluded that Inuit, in all likelihood, actually visited the ships while Franklin's men were still aboard and that some of them were eyewitness to the sinking of one of the ships. (The enigma of what really happened to Franklin and his men continues to fascinate people; see note, page 291).

All of the speculations are, of course, a major part of the Franklin mystique. They will end only if conclusive firsthand accounts are discovered. Not that this is out of the realm of possibility. As Woodman and others have reminded us, in 1973 a clearly legible note, written in 1851 by a Franklin searcher, Commander Charles Phillips, was found at Cornwallis Island. And in 1871 a similarly legible letter, written by Dutchman William Barents, one of the first of the northern explorers, was found in the Arctic. It had been written 1595.

It is not inconceivable that one day a twenty-first or twenty-second century adventurer will turn over a stone slab or find a long-hidden cairn and all will be revealed. Until then, the exact place and time of the death of their crews will remain a mystery.

Ironically, the one thing that does not remain a mystery is how the men of the Franklin expedition probably died. Scurvy was undoubtedly a major factor. As Pierre Berton, author of the *The Arctic Grail*—the landmark 1988 book on all of nineteenth century British Arctic exploration—pointed out, the lack of fresh vegetables and meat, combined with the huge amounts of salt that the Franklin party consumed, led, without question, to the outbreak of the debilitating and often fatal disease of scurvy. "One thing that went wrong," Berton wrote, "was they ate too much salt meat. Even the birds they shot, they salted down. This killed the vitamins and left them susceptible to scurvy . . . If you take only salt meat and no fresh vegetables or fresh food, by the third year you'll come down with scurvy. This was true for every expedition that went to the north. . . . These explorers were not hunters. As Englishmen, they were used to shooting grouse on the moors. They didn't know anything about shooting big game and didn't have the weapons for it. Not only that, but they made absolutely no contact . . . with Eskimo hunters who could have brought them [fresh] meat."

Scurvy was indeed a major cause of the Franklin tragedy. But it was not the only one. In 1852, in evidence he gave to the British government concerning the graves that he and others had discovered at Beechey Island, Captain Erasmus Ommanney of the *Assistance* stated, "We know that three of their men . . . died the first year, from which we may infer that they were not enjoying perfect health. It is supposed that their preserved meats were of inferior quality." And even before Franklin and his ships left port, James Fitzjames, second-in-command aboard the *Erebus*, stated his alarm over the fact that the Admiralty had purchased so many of the expedition's provisions from an unknown supplier because he had quoted them the lowest price.

Fitzjames was referring to Stephan Goldner, the man who had been given the contract to provide the eight thousand tin containers of meats, vegetables, and soups for the Franklin expedition. Fitzjames was aware that, about a year before Goldner had been given that contract, a supply of preserved meat that he had sold to another vessel had gone bad. Later, when the full extent of the Franklin tragedy became known, the *Times* would declare: "If Franklin and his party had been supplied with such food as that condemned, and relied on it as their mainstay in time of need, the very means of saving their lives may have bred a pestilence or famine among them, and have been their destruction."

It was a statement sadly more prophetic than the *Times* itself realized. At the time when Goldner had been awarded his contract, the tin container was a relatively new invention, only little more than a year old. Cooking the contents of the cans properly was a demanding process. Food inside small two-to-four pound tins needed to be cooked from seven to eleven hours at a consistent temperature of over 250 degrees. Larger cans required much longer cooking. Sealing the cans was a whole other issue. The solder used in these earliest days of canning was made of a combination of 10 percent tin and 90 percent lead. Early canners had no idea of how deadly lead could be if it leached into the food.

Later it would be revealed that because Goldner had fallen so far behind in delivering the eight thousand cans to the *Erebus* and the *Terror*, he had taken disastrous short cuts. Instead of cooking the contents of the smaller cans for seven to eleven hours, he had cooked them for only thirty to seventy-five minutes. And, in his haste, he had cooked them at a temperature some fifty degrees below that which was required. Equally disastrous was the fact that, to save time, Goldner had decided to put much of the food in larger tins. Although they obviously required a longer cooking time, Goldner prepared them in the same, inadequate time as the smaller cans. To make matters much worse, he was totally careless in how the cans were sealed. As investigations would later prove, his hasty, sloppy sealing process resulted in much of the lead-filled solder leaking into the food.

In the 1980s, University of Alberta anthropologist Owen Beattie and author and filmmaker John Geiger led an expedition to the three graves at Beechey Island in order to investigate just how the first of the 129 men of the Franklin expedition had died. After exhuming the bodies of the three men and performing a painstaking, scientific analysis of their remains, particularly their hair, Beattie and Geigier concluded that the three sailors had died from lead poisoning. Their specific conclusion, published in their 1989 book *Frozen in Time: The Fate of the Franklin Expedition*, was that the cans that Goldner had supplied had been so improperly sealed that the lead solder had run down inside of the tins, poisoning the food that the men had eaten.

Beattie and Geiger's investigations also resulted in another important finding. While at Beechey Island, they had come upon the stone tent circle that the men of the Penny, Ross, and De Haven expeditions had discovered. Scattered outside the circle, Beattie and Geiger found more than thirty human bone fragments, including parts of a skull that, as tests would reveal, had come from a single Caucasian male who had been between twenty and twenty-five years old when he died. From the knife marks on the bones, the way in which the skull had been taken apart, and the results of forensic tests that were conducted on all the remains, there was only one conclusion that could be drawn. Modern science had confirmed the veracity of the various Inuit accounts.

Further proof that the desperate men of Franklin's lost expedition had resorted to cannibalism came in 1992 when, on King William Island, anthropologist Anne Keenleyside and archaeologist Margaret Bertulli discovered more than four hundred human bones which, they determined, were part of the remains of from eight to eleven persons. From the nature of the large collection of relics they also found at the site, it was obvious that they had discovered yet further evidence of the Franklin party's stay at the island.

Using a powerful electron microscope, the two scientists were able to trace the pattern of the cut marks on the bones and determine conclusively that the flesh from the remains had been deliberately cut away by the types of knives carried by Franklin's men. "This evidence," reported Keenleyside, "is strongly suggestive of cannibalism among these Franklin crewmembers. I don't see any other possible explanation that would account for these cut marks." More than one hundred years after Rae and Schwatka had issued their controversial reports, Keenleyside and Bertulli's tests corroborated the Inuit accounts.

We will, in all likelihood, never know exactly how the men of the Franklin expedition died or if indeed scurvy and lead poisoning were the only major factors. What becomes obvious is that—added to all the mysteries that consumed a nation and much of the world—there are several supreme ironies, including the fact that, in the end, it became clear that there was not one, but several Northwest Passages, various winding routes, all of them treacherous, that are open or closed according to the ice, wind, weather, and tides during any particular season. Perhaps the greatest irony of all is the fact that after all the expeditions, all the frustrations and sufferings, and after all the deaths, the final conclusion was that an Arctic water route from the Atlantic to the Pacific never had been—and probably never would be—commercially viable.

Robert McClure is still given credit for having been the first to prove the passage's existence, although there are those students of the

Arctic experience who believe that, in their desperate march south to the Great Fish River, those of Franklin's men who were still alive might have spotted the final link before McClure.

The first actual navigation of the Passage was not achieved until 1906. Despite John Barrow's obsession, it was not accomplished by an Englishman, but by the Norwegian explorer Roald Amundsen. Nor was it done, as Barrow had believed it would be, in a single season. It took Amundsen three torturous years sailing in the tiny converted herring boat *Gjöa* to complete the voyage. "We bungled through zigzag as if we were drunk," the explorer would write. "It was just like sailing through an uncleared field." Sixty-one years had elapsed between Franklin's final attempt and Amundsen's three-year accomplishment. It would be another thirty-four years before, in 1940, the first single-season passage was achieved by the *St. Roch*, a Royal Canadian Mounted Police steam schooner, commanded by Henry Larsen.

The greatest test as to whether the passage would ever be commercially viable occurred in 1969, when the supertanker SS *Manhattan* set out to test the feasibility of the waterway for the transport of oil by attempting to bring the first cargo of Alaskan crude oil to refineries on the East Coast. The *Manhattan* was a supertanker in every sense of the word—670 feet long, with a 125-foot steel-armored bow that weighed over 5,000 tons. Its hull was covered with nine-foot-thick and thirty-foot-deep protective steel. Unlike the *Erebus* and the *Terror*, the *Manhattan* knew its exact route, thanks to computers, satellite photographs, and hydrographic maps. Yet despite all these modern advantages, the ship became imprisoned in the ice in McClure Strait. Badly damaged, it was finally freed by icebreakers and had to spend months in dry dock while extensive repairs were made.

In a prime example of the way in which Arctic waters are almost never the same from one year to the next, several ships actually completed a navigation of the passage in 2000, a year in which the polar ice was thinner than at almost any time in memory. This development led to the speculation that one of the few benefits of global warming might be the opening of the passage for increasing periods of time.

As the supertanker SS *Manhattan* discovered in 1969, one of the great ironies of the more than four-hundred-year search for the Northwest Passage was that, in the end, it was proven to be a commercially unviable route because it was frozen over so much of the year.

Most scientists have come to believe that that is highly unlikely. And for those who have devoted themselves to Arctic matters, the notion of a commercially viable Northwest Passage raises a most intriguing issue. In a television interview, Pierre Berton was asked to comment on what, to him, would be the result if increasing ice melt-off made the passage more navigable. "I'm afraid," Berton responded, "a commercially viable Northwest Passage would detract from the romance of the region. Not too many years ago I sailed through the Panama Canal. Before my cruise I read up on the building of the canal and the horrific problems, the wildness of the region and so forth. You can imagine my disappointment when I finally made the passage and could easily have mistaken it for a cruise up the Hudson River. I expect that a tamed Northwest Passage would produce the same result. Already GPS, snowmobiles, and the like have jaded us, and, I think make it difficult to appreciate [the Arctic explorers'] accomplishments."

Berton's comments go to the heart of the enduring fascination with the entire Franklin saga. For it is almost impossible to consider all that took place between Barrow's launching of the first expeditions in 1818 and Franklin's final attempt without realizing that, for so many of those who sought the passage, the great attraction was not the prize itself but the challenge and romance of seeking it. It was the doing, not the gaining, that drove this unique breed of men.

Given the results, it would not be difficult to dismiss the entire endeavor as a failure. From the very beginning, it was marked with tragic mistakes, colossal blunders, lessons never learned, even outright lunacy—all enveloped in an unwavering arrogance. Most expedition organizers never understood that expeditions could simply be too large. Nor, despite all they had been told, would they accept the fact that conditions in one area of the Arctic could be totally different from year to year. Most commanders exhausted their men by insisting that they, not dogs, pull the sledges. Almost all continued to dress inadequately for the Arctic climate. And not until the expeditions of Hall and Schwatka did they begin to truly listen to the Inuit, who had so much to tell them, not only about surviving in the North, but about what they had seen and heard regarding the lost expedition.

But these same men, willing to sail into the unknown, willing to endure years of hardship wintering in the ice, waiting for the thaws that might allow brief periods of exploration, willing to face the harshest climate imaginable, gave the world a lesson in courage, daring, and dedication to duty. When the search for both the Northwest Passage and Franklin was over, geographical and scientific exploration had been advanced as never before and almost all the Arctic archipelago—once totally unknown—had been revealed.

Perhaps the greatest legacy of all was the way in which these men inspired future generations of seekers and adventurers, willing to make the same types of sacrifices for the romance of challenging the unknown. No one said it better than Roald Amundsen, the man who was the first to sail the passage and the first to reach the South Pole. As a young man he had immersed himself in the tales of Parry, the Rosses, Kane, Hall, and others. Their stories, he stated, "thrilled me as nothing I had ever read before. What appealed to me most were the sufferings that John Franklin and his men had to endure. A strange ambition burned within me, to endure the same privations . . . I decided to be an explorer."

"There is nothing worth living for but to have
one's name inscribed on the Arctic chart."
—ALFRED LORD TENNYSON, ca. 1855

Dr. Alexander Armstrong

Armstrong, who stood beside Robert McClure in October 1850 as
they became the first to view the final link in the Northwest Passage,
went on to a distinguished career both as an author and as a medical
administrator. Unlike McClure's self-serving published account of
the extraordinary experiences of the *Investigator*—in which he omitted almost all negative aspects of the voyage—Armstrong's *Personal
Narrative of the Discovery of the North-west Passage* was totally unem-
bellished. Armstrong's other book, *Observations on Naval Hygiene and
Scurvy, More Particularly as the Latter Appears During a Polar Voyage*,
was a major medical contribution. During the quarter century following the publication of that book in 1858, Armstrong, among other
appointments, served as superintendent at the naval hospital in Malta
and as the director general of the medical department of the Royal
Navy. Knighted in 1871, he died four years later.

Horatio Austin

After returning from his 1850–51 expedition, Austin never regained the level of esteem he had held before taking his five-vessel fleet out in search of Franklin. Although a special committee, convened to look into the dispute that had arisen between Austin and the whaling captain William Penny, decided that Penny was probably the chief instigator of their argument, the committee, made up of five naval veterans, privately felt that Austin had ended his search far earlier than was necessary.

Austin was never again asked to lead an Arctic search, and spent the last fifteen years of his career first as superintendent of the Southampton packet service, then as superintendent of the Deptford Dockyard, and finally as head of the Malta Dockyard. Despite his removal from the public eye, he was promoted to vice admiral in 1864 and was knighted in March 1865, some eight months before his death.

George Back

When George Back somehow managed to beach the crippled *Terror* on the coast of Ireland after the vessel had been trapped for the better part of nine months atop an ice floe, he was barely alive. Although he was only forty at the time, he would never fully regain his health, and the traumatic voyage marked the end of his naval career. Now recognized, along with Samuel Cresswell, as the most accomplished of the Arctic shipboard artists, Back was rewarded for his achievements—particularly his heroics during the first Franklin overland expedition—with a knighthood in 1839.

He spent much of his later years actively involved in the Royal Geographical Society and was, for seven years, its vice president. He would be remembered by his fellow explorers as one of the most arrogant and self-important of men. His reputation as a "ladies' man" would also remain with him, perhaps best summarized by one observer who stated, "If he was in love with himself, he had not right to suppose every lady he met [felt] the same."

Frederick William Beechey

At one point early in his career, Beechey, the geologist who accompanied John Franklin on the *Trent* in his 1818 North Pole expedition, seemed destined to become one of the most prominent of the naval explorers. Yet he never approached that status. From 1835 to 1847, he was engaged in conducting surveys for the Admiralty along the coast of South America and the coast of Ireland. He did become a member of the Arctic Council and for three years served as an aide-de-camp to Queen Victoria. In 1855, a year after being promoted to rear admiral, he was elected president of the Royal Geographical Society, but died shortly thereafter. Beechey Island, the site of the first significant discoveries in the Franklin search, was named for his father, the acclaimed artist Sir William Beechey, the official portrait painter to Queen Victoria.

Edward Belcher

Following his court-martial and the added ridicule he received when the *Resolute* was found, and then refurbished and given back to England by the Americans, Belcher devoted the rest of his life to writing and to scientific research. His books included the three-volume novel *Horatio Howard Brenton*, which many are certain provided the inspiration for C. S. Forester's immensely successful Captain Horatio Hornblower series. The fact that Forester's wife was a Belcher, and that the first name of his title character was the same as that of Belcher's main character, and that the fictitious Hornblower rose through the ranks of the British navy in much the same manner as Belcher, almost assuredly makes the connection more than a coincidence.

Although it is difficult to explain, Belcher's disgraceful performance in the Arctic, the ridicule he received from both public and press, and the silent reprimand he received from the Admiralty did not prevent his being showered with honors. Promoted to vice admiral in 1861, he was raised in rank to admiral eleven years later. He was also made a Knight Commander of the Order of the Bath. Ironically, Belcher, who died in 1877, went to his grave having received more honors than many of those who had served with far greater distinction.

David Buchan

After returning from his unsuccessful 1818 search for the North Pole, David Buchan spent most of the rest of his life in Newfoundland. For several consecutive winters he served as governor of the province, filling in for the senior official who left for warmer climes during the cold winter months. In 1825, Buchan became Newfoundland's high sheriff, and during the next seven years was involved in attempting to settle the complex disputes that continually arose in a region just beginning to move toward representative government. In the late 1830s, for reasons still unknown, Buchan left Newfoundland and signed on with the East India Company. In December 1838, he was aboard that company's vessel *Upton Castle* as it set out from Calcutta to the Arctic. Neither the ship nor Buchan was ever heard from again.

James Buddington

The man who found the *Resolute* had a long and fruitful life after rescuing the ship. Less than a year after his remarkable voyage back to New London, he took the *George Henry* back to Davis Strait, this time returning with his hold filled with bone and oil. Two years later he completed another successful whaling voyage.

Following the whale hunt, he decided he had had enough of the sea and headed west to Illinois to take up the life of a farmer. But the sea was in his blood and, little more than a year later, he was back on the Connecticut coast. In 1871, the United States government, impressed by his knowledge of the Arctic, hired him to serve as ice pilot on the supply ship *Congress* when it was sent to Greenland to bring supplies to Charles Francis Hall's *Polaris* expedition, for which his nephew Sidney was sailing master.

In 1876, the government hired Buddington again, this time to captain the former whaling vessel *Era* on a five-month expedition to Hudson Bay in search of mica. By this time, his son James, Jr., who had been the *George Henry*'s cabin boy when the *Resolute* had been found, had become one of the nation's leading sealing captains. In 1887, at the age of seventy, Buddington signed on as a first mate on one of his son's expeditions. For Buddington, it wasn't a pleasant experience. "I couldn't stand that," he wrote to his daughter. "Those little seals are almost human."

Two years after returning from this trip he sailed again with his son but this time in a hunt for whales. It was his last voyage. Retiring to Staten Island, Buddington had much to reflect upon. At the age of ninety he wrote, "I do not belong to any church. I believe [that] nature's God is good. He has cared for me when I was almost sure there was no hope. I have nothing to say against folks who like to worship God under a roof. That's there. But I like to sit out here and look at the sea and sky. That's an open Bible any man can read to suit himself."

James Buddington died on December 23, 1908, exactly 53 years to the day on which he brought the *Resolute* into New London Harbor.

Richard Collinson

Richard Collinson never forgave Robert McClure for his deceptions during what was supposed to be a joint search for Franklin in 1850. He fully believed that if McClure had stayed with him, they not only would have *jointly* found the Northwest Passage but would have found Franklin as well. Angry as well with the Admiralty for not awarding him a share of McClure's prize, he never requested another command. He did remain active, however, and provided important counsel to Lady Franklin as she organized the *Fox* expedition.

Promoted to rear admiral in 1869 and then knighted, Collinson spent much of his later years involved in the activities of Trinity House, the organization that maintained navigational aids such as lights and buoys along England's rivers and its coastline. In 1875 he became head of Trinity House and remained deeply involved in the work of that establishment until his death in 1883.

Samuel Cresswell

As artist aboard the Ross and McClure expeditions, Cresswell produced many of the most beautifully rendered and revealing depictions of the Arctic adventure. His *Series of Eight Sketches in Color . . . of the Voyage of the H.M.S.* Investigator, published in 1854, and his illustrations for

McClure's *Discovery of the North-West Passage by the H.M.S.* Investigator, published in 1856, were hailed throughout Great Britain and captured the personal attention of Queen Victoria. Cresswell later served in the Baltic during the Crimean War and in the China Seas where he was promoted to the rank of captain. He died in 1867, a few months after retiring.

Peter Dease

Peter Dease never received the level of acclaim for the achievements of his 1837–39 Arctic expedition given posthumously to his partner Thomas Simpson. But if it had not been for the mild-mannered Dease's organizational abilities, his skill with the natives, and his ability to keep the bombastic Simpson under control, the expedition, in all probability, would not have been nearly as successful. Two years after returning from his exploration, Dease retired to a farm near Montreal where, for the next twenty years, he lived surrounded by his large family.

Edwin De Haven

After returning from leading the first Grinnell Expedition, Edwin De Haven had had enough of the Arctic. For a short time he served in the U.S. Coast Survey, but then found true satisfaction by spending the rest of his career serving under famed oceanographer Matthew Maury at the U.S. Naval Observatory. Failing eyesight caused him to retire in 1862 and he died three years later.

Jane Franklin

Even after she was shown proof that her husband was dead, Lady Jane Franklin, the woman who never gave up, continued to press the Admiralty to search for the *Erebus* and the *Terror* and for the remains of the Franklin expedition. Although all of her requests were politely denied, she remained an Arctic force, with her advice continually being sought by young explorers such as Sherard Osborn. In 1860 she was awarded the prestigious Gold Medal of the Royal Geographical Society.

Accompanied by her niece Sophia, she continued to travel extensively, visiting Alaska, Hawaii, Canada, the United States, South America, China, Japan, and India. When she died in 1875, the pallbearers included Leopold M'Clintock and Richard Collinson. Her most appropriate tribute was the inscription placed under the statue of John Franklin in Westminster Abbey. Written by the Dean of Westminster, it reads, "This monument was erected by Jane, his widow, who, after long waiting, and sending in search of him, herself departed to seek and to find him in the realms of light, July 18, 1875, aged 83 years."

She did not depart without eventually adding yet another mystery to the Franklin saga. Years after she died, her heirs left her personal papers to the Scott Polar Research Institute with the proviso that the institute was to "take out whatever is of polar interest and burn the rest." What was it about Lady Jane Franklin that they did not want us to know?

Henry J. Hartstene

The life of the man who brought the *Resolute* home to England would have taken a much different turn had Lady Franklin been granted her wish to have him take the ship back to the Arctic on yet another search for her husband. Instead of potentially being the man to make the startling discoveries on King William Island, Hartstene returned to his naval duties and was involved in taking soundings for the laying of the transatlantic telegraph cable. When the Civil War erupted in 1861, Hartstene, a devoted South Carolinian, resigned his commission and became an officer in the Confederate Navy. A year later, for reasons never determined, Henry Hartstene went insane.

Isaac Hayes

The man who thought he had discovered the Open Polar Sea came home to find his nation on the brink of civil war, and during the conflict served as an army surgeon at Satterlee Hospital in Philadelphia. After the war, he conducted another brief expedition to Greenland. Upon returning home, he moved to New York City. From 1876 until his death in 1881, he was a member of the New York State Assembly.

William Hobson

Upon returning to England in the Fox after finding the only written evidence of Sir John Franklin ever discovered, William Hobson was treated to a hero's welcome. In 1860, he was given command of the HMS *Pantaloon* and in 1862 took command of the HMS *Vigilant*. Advancing to the rank of captain, he retired in 1872. He died eight years later, still hailed as having made the most important discovery in one of history's greatest searches

Edward Inglefield

Following his several Arctic explorations and adventures, including bringing the Belcher expedition home, Inglefield served in the Crimean War where he took part in the Siege of Sevastopol. A multitalented man, he spent much of his later life producing highly acclaimed marine paintings. An inventor as well, he introduced the hydraulic steering gear and the Inglefield anchor. Regarded as one of the most devoted of all British explorers, he was knighted in 1877 and named a Knight Commander of the Order of the Bath ten years later. He died in 1894.

Elisha Kent Kane

Kane, who was sickly all his life, never recovered from the rigors of his second Arctic expedition. Aware that, more than ever, his days were numbered, he worked feverishly to compile his account of the voyage, a two-volume work titled *Arctic Explorations . . . 1853, '54, '55*. When completed in 1856, it contained nine hundred pages and was illustrated with ink sketches of the expedition that Kane had drawn. In its first year, the book sold an astounding sixty-five thousand copies.

The enormous energy that Kane poured into the project proved to be his final undoing. A year after he finished it, he died in Havana. He was thirty-seven years old. The rites attendant to his passing were unlike anything that America had ever witnessed. The governor of Cuba personally escorted Kane's funeral cortege to New Orleans. From there, the man who had come to be known as the "American Columbus" was taken by boat up the Mississippi to Cincinnati. All along the way, the banks of the river were lined with mourners. The train trip from Cincinnati to Philadelphia took four days because of long delays caused by the thousands of additional mourners who spilled over onto the tracks. When Kane's body finally reached Philadelphia, it lay in state for two weeks in order to accommodate the throngs who came to pay their last respects. The funeral itself was the largest in American history until that of President Abraham Lincoln. The frail man whose adventures in the Arctic had initiated American polar exploration had left his mark.

Henry Kellett

Captain Kellett's epaulettes, which James Buddington had found aboard the *Resolute*, were successfully returned to him. But Kellett—the man who from 1825 to 1854 had devoted his life to Arctic exploration and the search for Franklin, the man who had captained the *Resolute* and instigated the search that led to the rescue of McClure and his men, the man who had bitterly opposed Edward Belcher's decision to abandon his four seaworthy ships—never received the amount of acclaim heaped upon others with lesser accomplishments. Appointed commodore in 1854, he spent the rest of his life as commander of the British naval station in China, where he died in 1875.

William Kennedy

Only a year after Kennedy returned in 1852 from taking the *Prince Albert* in search of Franklin, Lady Franklin sent him out again. His mission was to sail through Bering Strait and scour the western and Russian Arctic. The expedition, however, came to a halt when Kennedy's crew mutinied and he had them put into prison. Unable to find a new crew because of the outbreak of the Crimean War, Kennedy was forced to call off the expedition.

He spent the rest of his life in his native Canada where, in the late 1850s, he served as a director of the North-West Transportation Navigation and Railway Company. In 1860 he settled permanently at Red River where he and his brother owned and operated a store.

Settling into the life of his province, he served as both a member of the Manitoba board of education and a magistrate. He died in 1890.

George Francis Lyon

Lyon, who, before serving as second-in-command to Edward Parry on his 1821 attempt to find the passage, had undertaken an unsuccessful attempt to find the African River Niger, experienced one of the most unfortunate "afterlives" of all the naval explorers. Upon his return from the Parry expedition he was given sole command of the HMS *Griper* for another voyage to the Arctic, but unfortunately met with some of the worst weather yet encountered in the North. His mission was aborted after only five months, and was never given another naval command.

By 1825, Lyon had found himself almost destitute, a situation that was made even worse when the ship carrying him home from a temporary job in a Mexican mining company sank, carrying down with it what little remained of Lyon's possessions. Upon finally making his way to England, he received far more tragic news: His wife had died and he was left to raise their only child.

In 1827, desperate for work, Lyon took a low-paying job inspecting the gold mines of a large conglomerate in Brazil. But five years later his misfortunes continued when his eyesight began to seriously fail and he was forced to seek passage home to find medical attention. The ill-starred Lyon did not complete the voyage. He died en route, having never come close to realizing the early potential that John Barrow and others had seen in him.

Leopold M'Clintock

Leopold M'Clintock brought the *Fox* home to a hero's welcome in 1859. Celebrated wherever he went, he received honorary degrees from England's three most prestigious universities, a medal and fellowship from the Royal Geographical Society, and was knighted by the Queen.

His days in the North, however, were not quite over. In 1860, he made his final voyage to the Arctic when he was sent to explore the possibility of laying an underwater telegraph line from Scotland to Labrador, by way of Greenland. Ironically, it was a voyage in which the man who had survived so many hardships in his quest for the passage and his search for Franklin nearly lost his life. His vessel, the *Bulldog*, was nearly wrecked and M'Clintock barely made it home.

One year later he was back at sea, and between 1861 and 1868 he commanded three different naval ships that sailed the waters of the Mediterranean, the West Indies, and the North Sea. In 1872, he was named superintendent of the Portsmouth Dockyard. His final naval appointment came in 1879, when he was named commander-in-chief of the North America and West Indies Station. Through it all, M'Clintock maintained a strong interest in Arctic matters. He oversaw the fitting out of George Nares's North Pole–seeking expedition and was an important member of the Admiralty's Arctic Committee. He died in 1907, having been promoted to the rank of admiral.

Robert McClure

The man who, by luck, deception, and unyielding resolve, had proved the existence of the Northwest Passage, never backed down from his declaration that he had not needed to be rescued and that, left to his own devices, he would have extricated the *Investigator* from the ice and sailed her through the passage. In the account of his voyage that he published, McClure never admitted any mistakes and never mentioned the danger that he had constantly put his men in.

But he was the man who had found the passage and he was honored as such. He was knighted and eventually promoted to the rank of vice-admiral. He never returned to the Arctic, but spent the remainder of his naval career in the Pacific where, in 1857, he led a battalion of marines at the capture of Canton. He died in 1873.

George Nares

Nares—who had taken part in the 1870 *Challenger* expedition that had "invented" modern oceanography, and who had broken several records while searching for John Franklin on the *Resolute* and the North Pole on the *Alert*—remained a naval man to the end. Elected a fellow of the Royal Society in 1875, he was knighted on his return from his polar search and was later awarded the gold medal of the Royal Geographic Society and of France's Société de Géographie.

In 1878, he again commanded the *Alert* while conducting surveys of the Magellan Strait and the waters off Australia. He ended his career as the Admiralty's marine adviser to the board of trade.

Sherard Osborn

The man who had been placed under cabin arrest by Edward Belcher experienced a full and active career after a court-martial absolved him of any wrongdoing. Along with the articles he wrote, he edited both Robert McClure's and Leopold M'Clintock's journals and arranged for their publication.

His days at sea did not end with his search for Franklin. During the Crimean War, he was given command of the HMS *Vesuvius* and served with such distinction that he was promoted to captain and awarded medals from England, Turkey, and France. In 1857, he was involved in yet another conflict when he commanded the HMS *Furious* during the Second Opium War against China.

In the years following the war, Osborn continued to travel the world, first commanding the HMS *Donegal* in Mexican waters and then leading a fleet on a voyage to China. In 1863, after serving as an agent for the Great Indian Peninsular Railway in Bombay, he began a seven-year stint as managing director of the Telegraph Construction and Maintenance Company and oversaw the laying of an underwater cable that ran from England to India to Australia.

It was Osborn who, early in the 1870s, first suggested that the Admiralty launch a renewed search for the North Pole, an expedition in which he hoped to participate. Failing health, however, prevented him from actively taking part in the search, and he had to content himself with working with Leopold M'Clintock to prepare George Nares for the venture. He died in 1875, shortly before the Nares expedition was launched.

Edward Parry

No British naval explorer has received greater or more enduring acclaim than Edward Parry. When he died in 1855, the London *Times* proclaimed that "no successor on the path of Arctic adventure has yet snatched the chaplet from the brow of this great navigator. Parry is still the champion of the North."

After his days in the Arctic were over, Parry, arguably the most devout of all the naval explorers, spent much of his time writing religious tracts which he dedicated to his wife, "the chief comforter of my earthly pilgrimage—the sharer of every joy, and the alleviator of every sorrow—but a faithful counselor and friend, through many a rough and thorny path in our journey." He kept busy right to the end. The Admiralty first appointed him to reorganize its Packet Service and then placed him in charge of its Steam Department. In 1846, he became captain superintendent of the large naval hospital at Haslar, where his senior physician was John Richardson. There, his unqualified support of Richardson's medical innovations helped facilitate significant advancements in nursing practices and the care of the insane.

William Penny

The only whaling captain to have been given command of a British naval vessel, Penny, because of what was regarded by the Admiralty as a premature return from his 1850–51 search for Franklin and his open dispute with Horatio Austin, was never again asked to join in the rescue effort. He returned to whaling and, in 1853, became the first whaling captain to purposely winter in the Arctic, where he introduced the practice of floe whaling. One of the earliest promoters of the construction of steam whaling ships, he made his last whaling voyage in 1863. He died in 1892.

Bedford Pim

The man who found Robert McClure had an extremely full life after serving aboard the *Resolute*. He remained in the navy and served in wars in Russia and in China, during which he was wounded six times. Promoted to the rank of commander in 1858, he was sent to the Isthmus of Suez, where he studied the possibility of building an inter-ocean canal. After retiring from the Navy in 1870, he studied law and was called to the bar in 1873. The author of several books and magazine articles, he died in 1886.

W. J. S. Pullen

Although Lieutenant W. J. S. Pullen had spent most of his time in the Arctic cast in the relatively unglamorous role of commander of a supply ship, he had, in the course of his duties in 1849, led a party of small boats on a courageous journey along the northern Alaska coast in search of Franklin, but had found nothing. In 1855, Pullen commanded the HMS *Falcon* in the Balkans in the campaign during the Crimean War. For the rest of his naval career he was involved in coastal patrols and conducting surveys for the laying of underwater telegraph lines. Promoted to the rank of vice admiral in 1879, he died in 1886.

John Rae

After Rae received his £10,000 reward for having found evidence of the Franklin expedition, he spent a portion of the prize outfitting a ship for further Arctic exploration. But the ship sank in the Great Lakes. Back in the Hudson's Bay Company's employ, he spent the better part of the 1860s leading long, arduous explorations. In 1861, he conducted a survey for a telegraph line that was to run between Great Britain and America, through Scotland, the Faroe Islands, Iceland, and Greenland. In 1865 he led another survey party as it plotted a route for a telegraph line between St. Paul and Vancouver Island.

Despite the cannibalism controversy he had spawned and the disfavor he often found himself in because of his adoption of Inuit dress and ways of life, Rae received many honors for his accomplishments. Two universities, McGill and Edinburgh, granted him honorary degrees. He was elected a fellow of the Royal Society of London and was awarded the Founder's Gold Medal of the Royal Geographical Society. His book, *Narrative of An Expedition to the Shores of the Arctic Sea in 1846 and 1847*, and his many other writings describing his Arctic travel were well received. An expert marksman, he even found time to represent the London Scottish Regiment in shooting competitions at Wimbledon and other sites. Rae died in 1893.

John Richardson

Of all the scores of individuals who played central roles in the Franklin saga, John Richardson may well have ended up leading the most distinguished life of all. The man who accompanied John Franklin on both his first and second expeditions and who, along with James Clark Ross, was the first to go out in search of Franklin, had three separate careers—Arctic explorer, surgeon, and naturalist.

Richardson's influence in Arctic matters continued long after he returned home from his search for Sir John. His participation in the Arctic Council, in particular, made him a major force in northern affairs. But his accomplishments as a naval surgeon were even more profound. A close friend of Florence Nightingale, he called upon her for advice while helping to raise British standards of nursing. Before he retired from active duty in 1855, he also played a major role in transforming the treatment of the mentally ill from pure confinement to humane, rehabilitative care. And when ether and chloroform were introduced, Richardson established himself as a pioneer in the use of general anesthesia in naval surgery.

Significant as all these accomplishments were, it was in the field of ichthyology that John Richardson made his greatest contribution. His friend Charles Darwin continually came to him seeking information about Arctic flora and fauna. So too did James Audubon. His two monumental books, *Fauna Boreali-Americana* and *Flora Boreali-Americana*, based on specimens he had colleted during his two Franklin overland expeditions, became instant classics and opened up the brand new field of geographical natural history.

By the time he died in 1865, Richardson had been knighted and had received the awards and acclamation of scientific societies around the world. Many animal and plant species have been named for him, as well as an Arctic mountain, river, lake, and bay.

James Clark Ross

Unlike many of his fellow naval explorers, who found second or even third lives after their Arctic traveling days were over, Ross spent his remaining years in the country at Buckinghamshire, totally immersed in the company of his wife Ann and their four children.

Although his uncle's marriage ended in abandonment and scandal, the man who had found the Magnetic North Pole was blessed with one of the happiest of unions. "I am bound to say," the editor of *Literary Gazette* would write, "that a more perfect state of married felicity could not be imagined . . . enjoying what they wished of neighboring society and entertaining friends at home, surely their life was a pleasant one, and, above all, their tastes and habits and opinions were ever in accord . . . if ever an observer affirm there were two human sympathies concentrated in one, it might have been affirmed of Sir James Ross and Lady Ross." When Lady Ann Ross died in 1857, her husband went into a steady decline and died in 1862.

John Ross

John Ross's life following his final venture into the Arctic at the age of seventy-two was as controversial and tumultuous as his earlier years had been. Never a favorite of many of his fellow explorers, his relations with them became even more strained when, in a pamphlet he published in 1855, he vociferously criticized almost everyone involved in the Franklin rescue effort.

Meanwhile, his personal life was hardly sanguine. His wife, many years younger than he, had run off with his lawyer after Ross had been accused of molesting two young servant girls. Ross vehemently denied the accusations, claiming that he was totally innocent and that the girl who was pregnant had been put into that condition by her brother. Nonetheless, he never saw his wife again. All this had happened when he was almost seventy years old.

John Ross would remain a controversial figure until his death in 1856. His great "Croker Mountains" mistake would long be remembered. The truly significant achievements of his second expedition would, for the most part, be credited to his nephew. But his had been a career that had begun with the very first expeditions that John Barrow had launched and had not ended until the first real evidence of the Franklin expedition's fate had been discovered.

William Scoresby

Despite being treated as a pariah by John Barrow, Scoresby—explorer, scientist, and the greatest of all English whalemen—never lost the respect of Arctic veterans such as Edward Parry, who, in a letter to Scoresby, informed him that he would always be regarded as one of "us Arctic men." When Barrow died, the Arctic Council, "being aware of your great experience in all matters connected with the Polar Sea and of the value that consequently attaches to your opinions," openly sought his advice.

Scoresby remained active until the day he died. At the age of forty, he received a calling to become a minister and entered Cambridge University, where he earned a Doctor of Divinity degree. He began his religious duties as chaplain of the Mariners' Church in Liverpool, and then became the longtime vicar of a church in the industrial town of Bradford. Among his innovations was the establishment of a floating chapel, which became highly popular with mariners.

Scoresby never lost his interest in science and, in his later years, his work in magnetism led to the creation of some of the most effective compasses yet developed. He also took a personal interest in the new phenomenon of hypnosis, and earned a reputation as one of its most effective practitioners. Always restless, he made two trips to America and one to Australia. When he was almost seventy, he astounded his fellow passengers, by climbing high into the rigging to check the effectiveness of one of the compasses he was developing. He died in Toronto in 1857.

Frederick Schwatka

Schwatka's 1878–79 expedition established beyond a doubt the loss of the written records of the Franklin expedition. In 1883, the U.S. Army sent Schwatka, now a lieutenant, on a journey of exploration down the

Yukon River. With a small group of men, he traveled the length of the river, from its head to its mouth, a distance of more than thirteen hundred miles. It was the longest raft journey that had ever been made. Within months of completing the record trip, Schwatka resigned from the army. Beginning in 1896, he led five separate private expeditions, two to Alaska and three to northeastern Mexico. His lectures and writings describing the customs of the people he met on these trips and the flora and fauna he recorded were highly popular.

In the early 1890s, Schwatka began to suffer from a painful stomach ailment, probably brought on by his years of heavy drinking. Resorting to the use of laudanum, he died on November 2, 1892, from an overdose of the drug.

Parker Snow

After returning from his brief search for Franklin aboard the *Prince Albert*, the colorful and flamboyant Snow spent most of the rest of his life absorbed in literary pursuits. One of them involved Charles Francis Hall who, upon finding himself without funds after completing his first expedition, decided to write a book to help finance his next Arctic search. Hall asked Snow to help him write the volume. When it was finished, Snow claimed that he had written most of it, which was probably not true, since the majority of the book was based directly on quotations from Hall's journals. Before Hall left on his second expedition, he was sued by Snow, who claimed that Hall owed him money for his work. To Snow's dismay, the court summarily dismissed the suit.

Snow's many other works were far less controversial and continue to be regarded as important geographical writings. Included in his canon are: *Voyage of the* Prince Albert *in Search of Sir John Franklin: A Narra-tive of Every-Day Life in the Arctic Seas* and *A Two Years' Cruise off Tierra del Fuego, the Falkland Islands, Patagonia, and in the River Plate.* Snow also authored a popular tract in which he advocated the migration of the English working class to British Columbia. Several of his articles appeared in such prestigious publications as the *Atlantic Monthly*.

By the last decade of the 1900s, although the British Admiralty had long ceased searching for the Franklin expedition, determined individuals and organizations continued to seek answers to what had become one of the greatest maritime mysteries of all time. The chances of finding any survivors of the now internationally famous expedition had, of course, long since passed, but in many circles, finding the *Erebus* and the *Terror* remained an obsession. This was particularly true in Canada, where the two ships had been such an important part of both Arctic exploration and Canadian culture. In 1992, although the vessels were still very much missing, the Canadian government designated them a National Historic Site of Canada to protect them from harm in the event they were ever found.

In 2008, Parks Canada, the government agency that oversees Canada's natural and cultural heritage, relaunched a major renewed effort to find the two ships. And from the moment that the agency began, there was an enormous difference in the way it approached the mission. Starting with the earliest seekers of the Northwest Passage, few of those who had risked their lives to seek this Holy Grail had ever thought it important to ask the Inuit who lived in the frozen Arctic about the nature of the weather there, the topography, or anything else that might help in the search. The same was true of those who sought Franklin, his men, and their ships. They made little or no attempt to understand the Inuit, harbored an almost total lack of respect for them, and seldom sought their opinion.

Parks Canada took a quite different approach. The agency made it a major practice not only to listen to the Inuit but to seek them out to learn anything they might know about the ill-fated expedition.

And Parks Canada was also aware that among the Inuit's descendants was a highly respected elder, oral historian, and schoolteacher named Louie Kamookak. Before Kamookak died in 2018, he had devoted almost forty years to seeking answers to the mystery of the lost ships and missing men. As author and Franklin saga expert Russell Potter has written, "In the history of the modern revival of interest in the fate of the Franklin expedition, there's really only one man whose presence links it all together: Louie Kamookak."

Kamookak was born in a seal-hunting camp on the Boothia Peninsula in 1959 and raised in nomadic camps for the first ten years of his life. He grew up hearing stories passed down from Inuit elders about two tall ships and distressed white men. John Geiger, chief executive officer of the Royal Canadian Geographical Society, has called him "the last great Franklin searcher."

"I first started hearing [Franklin] stories as far as I start remembering," Kamookak stated, "maybe age six or seven. When I started going to school . . . that's when the teachers started talking about the Franklin expedition. How it happened on King William Island. How all of them died. They didn't get back. The ships were never found."

The stories his teachers told him matched the ones that his great-grandmother had passed on to him, and it was not long before

seeking out these accounts became an obsession. "If it was a Franklin story," he recalled, "I was always there to listen." And Kamookak new from earlier accounts that the *Erebus* would be discovered on or near the place where he had spent most of his life—the hamlet of Gjoa Haven on the southeast coast of King William Island.

Louie Kamookak photographed for the December 2014 issue of *Up Here.*

In the 1980s and 1990s, Kamookak spent a good amount of time teaching young people about the importance of oral history. "He was concerned," says John Geiger, "that the stories be passed along to young Inuit and that they wouldn't be lost. He wanted to preserve the wisdom that comes from people who have lived for centuries on the land and understand it innately." Also during this time, Kamookak provided expedition members with information about the territory and shared the stories he had heard about Franklin, his men, and the two huge ships.

It was in September 2014 that the long sought-after breakthrough was made on a tiny island in Wilmot and Crampton Bay, some ninety-five miles southwest of Gjoa Haven. A group of metal objects, one of them large and heavy—part of the boat-lifting gear of a British naval vessel—was suddenly discovered by a Government of Nunavut archaeology team who had been working side by side with Parks Canada. Nearby, a Parks Canada boat was conducting its search; immediately Ryan Harris, the underwater archaeologist leading the project, began laying out a new search grid in the area where the discovery had been made.

On September 2, 2014, Harris put a side-scan sonar unit to work and sat back with the rest of the crew to watch the images being relayed to the screens on their Parks Canada boat, *Investigator*. They had hardly settled back when one of the images caused them to jump to their feet: a live picture of a large British discovery vessel. "That's it!" Harris screamed. "That's it!"

It was truly a glorious moment. After one of the greatest maritime searches in history, one that had gone on for almost 170 years, it was almost certain that one of Sir John Franklin's two ships had been found. After it was determined that the ship was resting only about thirty-six feet below the surface, a remotely operated vehicle was sent down to take a closer look. Among the first things the team noticed was that part of the vessel's stern was missing, and various small parts of the ship were scattered about the seafloor. They also found two brass six-pounder guns lying off the stern.

But, preserved by the frigid water, the timber of the ship was in good condition. On the *Erebus*'s upper deck, divers found something much more important—the ship's bell. Certainly, they thought, the bell would have the vessel's name on it. However, it did not. But it *was* inscribed with the British government's official broad-arrow marking and the figure 1845—the year that the *Erebus* and the *Terror* set sail for the Arctic.

The dimensions of the wreck were then compared with the plans of the two ships which, since they were built, had been housed in the National Maritime Museum in Greenwich, England. And it was confirmed: HMS *Erebus*, John Franklin's flagship, had been found.

Meanwhile, the search for the *Terror* continued. And on September 3, 2016, exactly two years and one day after the *Erebus* was found, the *Terror* was discovered by the crew of the R/V *Martin Bergmann*, a ship of the nonprofit Arctic Research Foundation. And it may not have happened had it not been for a story told by a newly hired crewmember about what he'd seen on a hunting and fishing trip a number of years earlier.

Bronze bell in situ on upper deck of HMS *Erebus*, September 2014, with the distinctive Royal Navy broad arrow and date "1845" visible.

The storyteller's name was Sammy Kogvik, a Canadian Ranger and a native of Nunavut. As the *Martin Bergmann* was heading west with the intention of searching for the *Terror* in Cambridge Bay, Kogvik made a fateful decision. He decided he should tell the expedition's leader, Adrian Schimnowski, about something he had seen on a trip he'd taken with his friend known as "Uncle James" more than six years ago in Terror Bay.

"When I was getting off the snowmobile, I looked to my left and saw something [pretty strange]," Kogvik told Schimnowski. "I looked to my left and saw a [mast] sticking out of the ice. I told [Uncle James] it might be one of those old ships that they've been looking for." Kogvik then related how he took out his camera, gave the mast a huge hug, and had Uncle James take a picture of him and the mast.

But then shortly afterward, Kogvik lost his camera along with the film inside. "I told Uncle James don't tell anybody because we don't have any proof. . . . We do not want to keep secrets, but it might seem like lies to people, because we don't have any proof."

Schimnowski and his search expedition were headed in a much different direction than toward where Kogvik said he had seen the mast, but the expedition leader was brought up short by the man's account. "I guess because I was listening, he started opening up and telling me the story about the mast," he recalled. "The way he was telling the story, the look in his eyes, [and] the sound of his voice, [I was convinced] he saw something and that it was real." Adding to Schimnowski's conviction was the fact that members of the *Bergmann's* crew told him that they had heard stories from the Inuit about native people seeing the silhouette of a tall-masted ship at sunset.

Without nearly as much hesitation as one might have imagined, Schimnowski, ordered the *Bergmann* to join the Parks Canada–led search and head to Terror Bay, on the west flank of King William Island, where Kogvik and his companion had seen the mast. Like the discovery of the *Erebus*, the finding of the *Terror* was almost anticlimactic. Once in the bay, it took the searchers just two-and-a-half hours to find the ship that had been missing for so long. It lay on the sea floor under seventy-eight feet of water, about two times farther down than where the *Erebus* had met its fate. Not only were the *Terror*'s three masts still partly standing and most of its hatches closed, but there were unbroken panes of glass in the windows of Captain Crozier's cabin. While the *Erebus*'s sets of davits (equipment for lowering and raising its boats) had been broken off, those of the *Terror* had remained intact.

Although the authority to enter the sunken *Terror* rested with higher officials, Schimnowski sent a remotely operated vehicle (ROV) down to the vessel where it entered the ship through an open hatch. The ROV was able to explore cabins and even the food storage room. Everything that could be seen was neatly stowed, all of which led to an initial speculation: before it was abandoned, a few remaining crewmembers had closed down the *Terror* and then may have sailed the *Erebus* some forty-five miles to the south where she had been discovered.

The *Terror* appeared to be in remarkably good condition, given that it had lain sunken in one of the most inhospitable locations in the world—a place so challenging that the entire immense area remains covered with thick ice for all but a few months a year. (This makes traditional summer marine operations impossible, but Parks Canada notes that underwater archaeological work can be done very productively through the ice.) Parks Canada dived the wreck in September 2016 and officially confirmed its identification as *Terror*. They then mounted a major ROV-based study of the wreck from an ice camp in April 2017. Two years later they returned to the site in August 2019 and continued their study of the wreck, including an interior exploration with a micro-ROV. Working overtime to take advantage of surprisingly clear conditions, donned in thick neoprene dry suits and lobster claw–shaped gloves, and led by Ryan Harris, the searchers did not personally enter the *Terror*. They used the ROV to obtain footage—to not only get the first good "look" at the interior of the vessel, but also to help them plan how to recover the hundreds of important artifacts that lay within it.

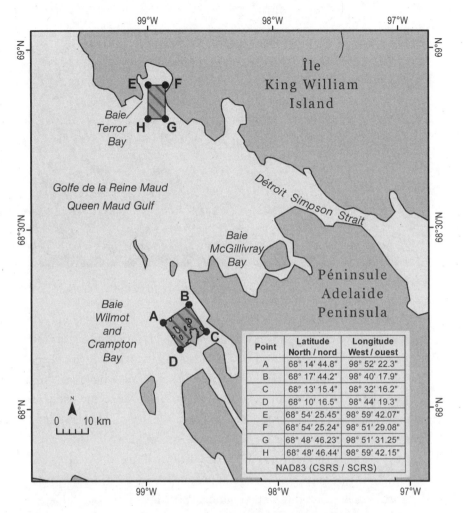

This map shows the location of the wrecks of the HMS *Erebus* and HMS *Terror*, a National Historic Site of Canada located in the Kitikmeot Region of Nunavut. Both vessels were trapped in the ice in September 1846, deserted by their crews in April 1848, and sank sometime thereafter.

As reported in an August 29, 2019, *Smithsonian* magazine article, the video footage they obtained on that search clearly revealed such objects as unbroken blue-and-white china stacked neatly on the shelves in the room where the *Terror*'s crew took their meals, rusted firearms hanging securely on the walls, glass bottles sitting upright in storage rooms, and wash basins and chamber pots sitting undisturbed in officers' rooms.

Ceramic plates stowed on shelves along the starboard side of the forecastle on the lower deck of HMS *Terror*, August 2019.

Harris later told reporters that, thanks to the unusual clarity of the water and the penetration of light from the surface, divers were, for the first time, able to see clearly to the sea floor on which the ship lay perched. This led to an important observation once the footage was studied. The *Terror*'s propeller was down. "It looks," Harris stated, "like the ship was in operating trim and then somehow maybe unexpectedly it sank. With all the shipboard articles lining the shelves on both sides of the ship, it gives the appearance that the wrecking was not particularly violent. It settled almost vertically on the sea floor."

The most intriguing sight of all was in Captain Crozier's cabin: his sediment-covered desk with its drawers tightly closed. Could they at last provide papers that conclusively reveal why and when the *Erebus* and the *Terror* split from each other, how they got to their final resting places, and what happened to the men? (As of this writing, due to the buildup of sediment, the cabin has still not been accessed.)

In another important development in this amazing saga, the *Erebus* and the *Terror* are not the only long-lost ships in the Franklin story to have been discovered, and not the first. In July 2010, members of a Parks Canada expedition found the *Investigator*. This is the ship that had discovered the Northwest Passage while also searching for Franklin, before itself becoming trapped in the ice for almost three years.

Unlike the *Erebus* and the *Terror*, the events surrounding *Investigator*'s icy imprisonment and the details of the rescue of its officers and sixty-six-man crew by a search party from the *Resolute* are not a mystery. The *Investigator*'s captain, Robert McClure, wrote an official account of the harrowing voyage and the vessel's surgeon, Alexander Armstrong, published an unofficial account (see page 231). However, her exact location remained unknown for over 150 years because of the extreme difficulties in reaching the area, which is almost always iced over.

In July 2010, a team of Parks Canada scientists, archaeologists, and surveyors began searching for the *Investigator* in Mercy Bay at the northern tip of Aulavik National Park. Based on old charts and journals, the expedition, which was the first to search specifically for the ship, had a good idea of where they believed the sunken vessel was when it was abandoned. But they had no idea how far it might have drifted after so many years. So certain were they that finding the *Investigator* would, if even possible, be extremely difficult, that they had planned to search for sixteen hours a day for two full weeks.

The expedition was also armed with stories long told by the Inuit. According to these accounts, the abandoned *Investigator* was an important source of copper, iron, and wood for the people living in the area. (A fact later corroborated when many metal nails were found to be missing from the remains of a smaller boat from the expedition found onshore when the *Investigator* was discovered.) The Parks Canada searchers were also aware that when Canadian anthropologist Vilhjalmur Stefansson came upon Mercy Bay during his 1915 Arctic voyage, he had seen no remains of the *Investigator*. In Stefansson's 1921 book, *The Friendly Arctic*, he recounts that an Inuit had told him in 1910 that "one year she had still been on the beach and the next year she was gone without a trace."

A 2010 side-scan sonar image of the wreck of HMS *Investigator*. The bow is at the left of this image.

On July 22, 2010, the Parks Canada team, using a torpedo-shaped sonar scanner towed from an inflatable boat, began their search based on the original Royal Navy records of the position of the ship when it was abandoned. And in what must be an Arctic search record, in less than fifteen minutes from the time they started, they found the *Investigator* some 490 feet off the shore of Banks Island, its hull partially buried in silt with its deck approximately twenty-six feet below the surface.

The search for the Northwest Passage was an epic quest and a historic discovery. But despite the monetary reward and the attention that Robert McClure and his men received, they never got the amount of acclaim they would have gotten if England and much of the rest of the world had not been so focused on—even obsessed with—the searches for Franklin. Ryan Harris hopes that this discovery will eventually change that. "Our goal," he has stated, "is to remove the *Investigator* from the margins of history."

The discoveries of the *Erebus*, *Terror*, and *Investigator* have provided the long sought-after answers to where each of these vessels sank beneath the sea. And in the better part of two centuries since the Franklin saga began, answers to other questions have emerged.

Scientists, archaeologists, and anthropologists for example, have proven that the tin cans in which much of the expedition's food supply was contained—while in many cases improperly sealed—were *not* the cause of death of many the men on Franklin's ships. Also, an increasing amount of evidence has revealed conclusively that despite the vehement denials of Victorian England in general and famous individuals like Charles Dickens in particular, cannibalism *was*, toward the end, a sad part of the story of desperate men struggling to survive.

Still, as Arctic and Franklin expedition experts have pointed out, many other intriguing questions remain including: Were the *Erebus* and the *Terror* sailed to where they were discovered, or were they carried they by wind, tide, and the same ice that had entrapped them? What caused the ships to sink? Why has Franklin's grave never been found? Certainly, he would have been buried with more than the usual trappings. What really caused the men of the *Erebus* and the *Terror* to die? These are just some of the remaining questions, that cry out to be answered. There will most assuredly be others.

Most significantly, the greatest and most perplexing of them all remains—the same question that has confounded those who have looked for Franklin, his ships, and his men from the very beginning: Why, with the exception of the one note in 1859, has no other written evidence of the ill-fated expedition—letters, accounts, reports, documents—still not been found? Hopefully, by the time the challenging excavations of the *Erebus* and the *Terror* are more fully carried out, such documentation may well have been discovered. Until then, searchers will continue their quest for answers and the Franklin story will continue to be an inspiring saga of determination and persistence; it will remain not only one of history's greatest and most heroic adventures, but one of its greatest mysteries as well.

APPENDIX I

Timeline

1818   John Ross commands his first voyage in search of the Northwest Passage, aboard the *Isabella*, with Edward Parry (*Alexander*) as second-in-command. They turn back at Lancaster Sound.

1819   David Buchan, commanding the *Dorothea*, seeks the North Pole, with John Franklin (*Trent*) as his second-in-command.

1819–20   Edward Parry leads his first passage-search expedition, commanding the *Hecla*, with Matthew Liddon (*Griper*) as his second-in-command. They pass 110° W longitude in September 1819, and discover Melville Island.

1819–21   John Franklin leads his first overland expedition to Point Turnagain; eleven members of the expedition die.

1821–23   Parry, aboard the *Fury*, conducts his second search for the passage, with George Lyon (*Hecla*) as his second-in-command.

1824–25   Parry makes his third and final search for the passage. The *Fury* is grounded during a storm on July 30, 1825, and subsequently abandoned on Fury Beach at Somerset Island.

1825–27   John Franklin leads his second overland expedition, to the mouth of the Coppermine River. He and John Richardson map more than a thousand miles of coastline.

1827   On June 1, Edward Parry leaves Spitzbergen, Norway, on the *Hecla*, in search of the North Pole. His second-in-command is James Clark Ross. He reaches 82°45'N, a record that will not be broken for fifty years.

1825–28   Frederick Beechey sails to the Arctic in the *Blossom* in an attempt to provide both the Parry and Franklin expeditions with supplies.

1829–33   Gin merchant Felix Booth sponsors John Ross's second expedition (*Victory*) to search for the passage. His nephew, James Clark Ross, is second-in-command. With assistance from the Inuit, Ross and his crew survive four Arctic winters. Clark Ross discovers the magnetic North Pole on June 1, 1831.

1833–4   George Back leads an expedition to search for John Ross; after Ross is found alive, he begins to map the Great Fish River.

1836   Back leads an expedition to the Canadian Arctic, but his ship, the *Terror*, becomes trapped for ten months in an ice field.

1837–39   Hudson's Bay Company explorers Thomas Simpson and Peter Dease conduct an overland expedition to explore remaining unknown areas of the Northwest Passage.

1845   Under command of Sir John Franklin, the *Erebus* and the *Terror*, with 128 men aboard, leave England in search of the Northwest Passage—they vanish into the Arctic.

1848   The Admiralty offers a £20,000 reward for the rescue of the lost Franklin expedition.

1848–49   James Clark Ross leads the first expedition in search of the lost expedition. Under Ross are Leopold M'Clintock and Robert McClure, commanding the *Enterprise* and the *Investigator*. The expedition is unsuccessful; six men die.

1848–51 John Richardson, with John Rae as his second-in-command, lead an unfruitful overland search expedition.

1848–51 W. J. S. Pullen, on the *Herald*, and Henry Kellett, on the *Plover*, sail to Bering Strait in search of Franklin and to act as supply depots for the Richardson/Rae expedition.

1850–53 Robert McClure in the *Investigator* and Richard Collinson in the *Enterprise* leave in search of Franklin, sailing via the Bering Strait. On October 26, 1850, McClure discovers the last link in the Northwest Passage. The *Investigator* becomes trapped in the ice in Mercy Bay.

1850–51 William Penny sails in search of Franklin, commanding the *Lady Franklin* and the *Sophia*; the graves of three members of the Franklin expedition are discovered on Beechey Island.

1850–51 Horatio Austin leads a four-ship expedition in search of Franklin: the *Resolute*, the *Assistance*, the *Pioneer*, and the *Intrepid*.

1850–51 John Ross sails in search of Franklin on a privately funded expedition.

1850 Charles Codrington Forsyth leads Lady Franklin's privately funded search for her husband aboard the *Prince Albert*.

1850–51 The first US expedition funded by the American shipping magnate Henry Grinnell, is led by Edwin De Haven commanding the *Advance* and the *Rescue*, with Elisha Kent Kane as medical officer.

1851–52 Lady Franklin privately funds a second *Prince Albert* expedition, with William Kennedy and Joseph René Bellot in command. They do not find Franklin, but explore more than one thousand miles of the Arctic.

1852–54 Edward Belcher commands a five-ship Admiralty expedition: the *Assistance*, the *Pioneer*, the *Resolute*, the *Intrepid*, and the *North Star*.

1853 Elisha Kane sets out on an American expedition to search for Franklin.

1853 Men of the *Resolute*, led by Bedford Pim, rescue Robert McClure and the crew of the *Investigator*, which is abandoned.

1853–55 Elisha Kent Kane leads the second Grinnell expedition in search of Franklin, aboard the *Advance*. The ship's doctor is Isaac Hayes.

1854 John Rae, while on a surveying mission for the Hudson's Bay Company, discovers relics of the Franklin party and hears stories from the Inuit concerning the expedition's fate, including accounts of cannibalism.

1854 The *Resolute and the Intrepid* are iced in; Belcher orders that they be abandoned and that their crews sail back to England on the North Star.

1855 Connecticut whaler James Buddington, sailing in the Davis Strait aboard the *George Henry*, finds the *Resolute*—a ghost ship adrift 1,200 miles from where she was abandoned. He sails it back to New London, Connecticut, with only eight men, through a hurricane.

1856 The *Resolute* is purchased by the United States government, reoutfitted, and returned, with much fanfare, to Queen Victoria.

1857 The *Fox*, commanded by Leopold M'Clintock and funded by Lady Franklin, leaves in search of the lost expedition.

1859 Lieutenant William Hobson of the Fox discovers a note describing the early fate of the Franklin expedition. Hobson and M'Clintock find other vital evidence of men of the *Erebus* and *Terror*.

1860 American Charles Francis Hall sets out on his first expedition to search for Franklin party survivors. He sails on the *George Henry*, captained by Sidney Buddington, the nephew of James Buddington.

1860 Isaac Hayes leads an expedition in search of the Open Polar Sea.

1864–69 Charles Hall leads his second expedition in search of Franklin survivors. He lives and travels with the Inuit, and discovers important artifacts from the lost expedition.

1871–73 Charles Hall leads an expedition in search of the North Pole, aboard the *Polaris*. Four months into the journey, he dies of suspected foul play. In 1872, eighteen of the crew are stranded on an ice floe and drift for six months before being rescued by a Canadian sealing ship.

1875 George Nares, commanding the *Alert* and the *Discovery*, sets out in search of the North Pole. He breaks several records for reaching farthest north.

1878–80 The American officer Frederick Schwatka leads a search for the records of the Franklin expedition. The team makes the longest sledging journey to date, and discovers relics and skeletons from the Franklin Expedition. It confirms that the Franklin records had been destroyed.

1879 Queen Victoria orders the *Resolute* to be decommissioned. The ship's best timbers are made into a desk, and two secretaires.

1880 The *Resolute* desk is presented to President Rutherford B. Hayes.

1984 Anthropologist Owen Beattie and author and filmmaker John Geiger lead an expedition to the three graves at Beechey Island. Forensic tests prove conclude that the sailors had died from lead poisoning. Testing on bone fragments confirm the reports of cannibalism.

1992 Anthropologist Anne Keenleyside and archaeologist Margaret Bertulli discover more than four hundred human bones on King William Island; they, too, corroborate the report of cannibalism in the Franklin expedition.

1992 Canadian government designates the *Erebus* and the *Terror* as a national historic site of Canada to protect them if they are found.

1990–2014 Searches for the written evidence of the Franklin expedition and for the remains of the *Erebus* and the *Terror* continue.

2008 Parks Canada enters the search for the *Erebus* and the *Terror*.

2011 HMS *Investigator* found by Parks Canada in collaboration with Inuit communities.

2014 HMS *Erebus* found by Parks Canada in collaboration with Inuit communities.

2016 HMS *Terror* found by the crew of the R/V Martin Bergmann, a ship of the nonprofit Artic Research Foundation in collaboration with Inuit communities.

2018 The United Kingdom gifts Canada the remaining items gathered from the wrecks of the *Erebus* and *Terror*; the national historic site will be co-managed by Parks Canada and the Kitikmeot Inuit Association (KIA).

APPENDIX II

Plans of the HMS Resolute

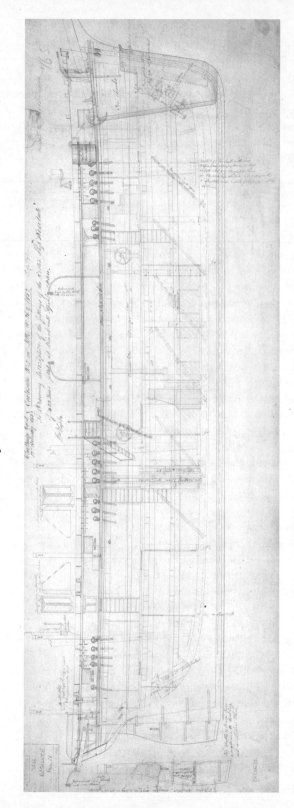

This rare British naval drawing shows the side view of the HMS *Resolute*, and is titled *A Drawing descriptive of the fittings of the Arctic ship Resolute of 422 tons fitted at Blackwell, April 1850.*

As the plan reveals, the *Resolute* was specially fitted to survive the challenges of making its way through ice floes and surviving the inevitable winters locked in the ice. This can be seen most clearly in the attention paid to reinforcing the ship's bow with "ice chocks" and with thick galvanized-iron plates all "filled in between with 2-inch fir and caulked." The plan also shows the strong "Canadian elm stringer" that ran the length of the middle of both the port and starboard sides of the vessel, and the iron plate 5⁄16" thick that also reinforced both sides of the ship.

Among other features shown in this side view are: the storage space for the "spare rudder, may be used as long or short rudder," the "boat's skid," the "temporary or portable hood over captain's ladder," the "temporary or portable hood over officer's ladder," and the "portable roundhouse." Note how the drawing also indicates the location of the anchor and the all-important ship's bell.

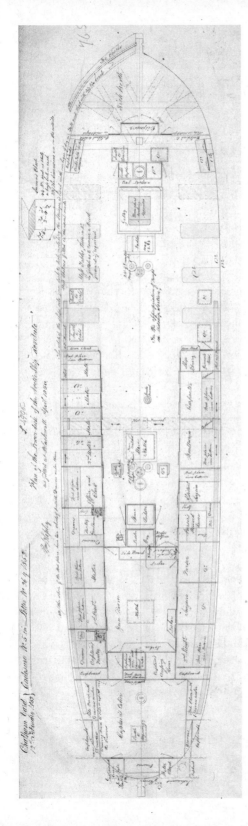

This companion drawing to the side view on the opposite page shows the official plan of the lower deck of the *Resolute*. Indicative of the designer's and builders' awareness of the hardships the crew of the vessel was bound to face on its long voyages in the frozen North, one of the largest spaces on the ship was reserved for the sick berth. The exalted position of the captain in the British naval system is revealed by the size of the "Captain's Cabin" with its adjoining "Captain's Pantry" and "Captain's Dressing Room." The importance of rank is also revealed by the space allotted for the private cabins of the 1st lieutenant, the ship's master, the vessel's clerk, the 2nd master, the mates, the 2nd lieutenant, the surgeon, the purser, the assistant surgeon, the boatswain, and the vessel's carpenter.

Interesting is the fact that the plan includes both a special notation stating that "the whole of the bed place have two chests of portable Drawers under them" and a detailed drawing of that staple of all naval officers and sailors, the seaman's chest. That the *Resolute* was designed and built for Arctic exploration is indicated by the drawing of the layers of wood called "Ice Chocks" fitted at the bow of the ship.

Note also the indication of the "Hot air Tunnel" along both sides of the vessel. It was this system of keeping the crewmen warm while encounterng Arctic temperatures that astounded the men of the *George Henry* when they discovered the abandoned "ghost" ship.

APPENDIX III

Excerpt of Instruction addressed to

Captain Sir John Franklin, K.C.H., Her Majesty's Ship "Erebus,"

dated 5th May 1845,

By the Commissioners for executing the office of Lord High Admiral of the United Kingdom of Great Britain and Ireland.

1. Her Majesty's Government having deemed it expedient that further attempt should be made for the accomplishment of a north-west passage by sea from the Atlantic to the Pacific Ocean, of which passage small portion only remains to be completed, we have thought proper to appoint you to the command of the expedition to be fitted out for that service, consisting of Her Majesty's ships *"Erebus"* under your command, taking with you Her Majesty's ship *"Terror,"* her Captain (Crozier), having been placed by us under your orders, taking also with you the *"Barretto Junior"* transport, which has been directed to be put at your disposal for the purpose of carrying out portions of your provisions, clothing and other stores.

2. On putting to sea, you are to proceed, in the first place, by such a route as from the wind and weather, you may deem to be the most suitable for dispatch, to Davis' Strait, taking the transport with you to such a distance up the Strait as you may be able to proceed without impediment from ice, being careful not to risk the vessel by allowing her to beset in the ice. . . .

4. As, however, we have thought fit to cause each ship to be fitted with a small steam-engine and a propeller, to be used only in pushing the ships through channels between masses of ice, when the wind is adverse, or in a calm, we trust the difficulty usually found in such cases will be much obviated, but as the supply of fuel to be taken in the ships is necessarily small you will use it only in cases of difficulty.

5. Lancaster Sound, and its continuation through Barrow's Strait, having been four times navigated without any impediment by Sir Edward Parry, and since frequently by whaling ships, will probably be found without any obstacles from ice or islands. . . it is hoped that the remaining portion of the passage, about 900 miles, to the Behring's Strait may also be found equally free from obstruction; and in proceeding to the westward, therefore, you will not stop to examine any openings either to the northward or southward in that Strait, but continue to push to the westward without loss of time. . . .

6. We direct you to this particular part of the Polar Sea as affording the best prospect of accomplishing the passage to the Pacific, in consequence of the unusual magnitude and apparently fixed state of the barrier of ice observed by the *"Hecla"* and the *"Griper"* in the year 1820, off Cape Dundas, the south-western

extremity of Melville Island; and we, therefore, consider that loss of time would be incurred in renewing the attempt in that direction; but should your progress in the direction before ordered be arrested by ice of a permanent appearance, and that when passing the mouth of the Strait, between Devon and Cornwallis Islands, you had observed that it was open and clear of ice; we desire that you will duly consider, with reference to the time already consumed, as well as to the symptoms of a late or early close of the season, whether that channel might not offer a more practicable outlet from the Archipelago, and a more ready access to the open sea, where there would be neither islands nor banks to arrest and fix the floating masses of ice; and if you should have determined to winter in that neighbourhood, it will be a matter of your mature deliberation whether in the ensuing season you would proceed by the above-mentioned Strait, or whether you would persevere to the south-westward, according to the former directions. . . .

8. Should you be so fortunate as to accomplish a passage through Behring's Strait, you are then to proceed to the Sandwich Islands, to refit the ships and refresh the crews, and if, during your stay at such place, a safe opportunity should occur of sending one of your officers or dispatches to England by Panama. . . .

9. If at any period of your voyage the season shall be so far advanced as to make it unsafe to navigate the ships, and the health of your crews, the state of the ships, and all concurrent circumstances should combine to induce you to form the resolution of wintering in those regions, you are to use your best endeavours to discover a sheltered and safe harbour, where the ships may be placed in security for the winter . . . and if you should find it expedient to resort to this measure, and you should meet with any inhabitants, either Esquimaux or Indians, near the place where you winter, you are to endeavour by every means in your power to cultivate a friendship with them, by making them presents of such articles as you may be supplied with, and which may be useful or agreeable to them; you will, however, take care not to suffer yourself to be surprized by them but use every precaution, and be constantly on your guard against any hostility: you will, by offering rewards, to be paid in such a manner as you may think best, prevail on them to carry to any of the settlements of the Hudson's Bay Company, an account of your situation and proceedings, with an urgent request that it may be forwarded to England with the utmost possible dispatch.

10. In an undertaking of this description much must be always left to the discretion of the commanding officer, and, as the objects of this Expedition have been fully explained to you, and you may have already had much experience on service of this nature, we are convinced we cannot do better than leave it to your judgement, in the event of your not making the passage this season, either to winter on the coast, with the view of following up next season any hopes or expectations which your observations this year may lead you to entertain, or to return to England to report to us the result of such observations, always recollecting our anxiety for the health, comfort and safety of yourself, your officers and

men; and you will duly weigh how far the advantage of starting next season from an advanced position may be counterbalanced by what may be suffered during the winter, and by the want of such refreshment an refitting as would be afforded by your return to England. . . .

19. For the purpose, not only of ascertaining the set of the currents in the Arctic Seas, but also of affording more frequent chances of hearing your progress, we desire that you frequently, after you have passed the latitude of 65 degrees north, and once every day when you shall be in an ascertained current, throw overboard a bottle or copper cylinder closely sealed, and containing a paper stating the date and position at which it is launched. . . .

21. In the event of any irreparable accident happening to either of the two ships, you are to cause the officers and crew of the disabled ship to be removed into the other, and with her singly to proceed in prosecution of the voyage, or return to England, according as circumstances shall appear to require . . . Should, unfortunately, your own ship be the one disabled, you are in that case to take command of the *"Terror,"* and in the event of any fatal accident happening to yourself. Captain Crozier is hereby authorized to take command of the *"Erebus"* placing the officer of the expedition who may then be next in seniority to him in command of the *"Terror."* Also, in the event of your own inability, by sickness or otherwise, of any period of service, to continue to carry these instructions into execution, you are to transfer them to the officer next in command to you employed on the expedition. . . .

22. You are, while executing the service pointed out in these instructions, to take every opportunity that may offer of acquainting our secretary, for our information, with your progress, and on your arrival in England, you are immediately to repair to this office, in order to lay before us a full account of your proceedings in the whole course of your voyage, taking care before you leave the ship to demand from the officers, petty officers, and all other persons on board, the logs and journals they may have kept, together with any drawings or charts they may have made, which are all sealed up, and you will issue similar directions to Captain Crozier and his officers. The said logs, journals or other documents to be thereafter disposed of as we may think proper to determine.

Given under our hands, this 5th day of May 1845.
(signed)   *Haddington.*
          G. Cockburn
          W. H. Gage
          Sir John Franklin, K.C.H. Captain of H.M.S. *"Erebus"* at Woolwich
By command of their Lordships.
(signed)   *W. A. B. Hamilton*

source: (Official Report on the Franklin Expedition): *Arctic Expedition,* Ordered by the House of Commons, to be Printed 13 April 1848

NOTES

The Northwest Passage. The Spanish called it the Strait of Anian and the British termed it the Northwest Passage, but whatever it was called, the quest for a commercial route to the East occupied the hearts and minds of men for centuries. Long before John Barrow came upon the scene, pioneer explorers had experienced the adventures, the mysteries, the frustrations, the discoveries, and the tragedies that would characterize the search.

The first of these explorers was the Italian Giovanni Caboto who, in 1497, sailing for England's Henry VII under the name John Cabot, reached the northeastern coast of North America. In the first of endless misconceptions related to the search, Cabot, having heard reports of people living to the north of where he had landed, thought surely that these people must be residents of Cathay. Cabot's voyage, coupled with Vasco da Gama's discovery the next year of a sea route around Africa to India, and Ferdinand Magellan's passage around Cape Horn into the Pacific Ocean, intensified the search for a shorter route to the riches of the Orient.

In 1534, Frenchman Jacques Cartier landed on the shores of Labrador. He did not find the passage, but succeeded in penetrating as far inland as the Gulf of St. Lawrence. In 1576, the inveterate Elizabethan adventurer Martin Frobisher reached what he named Frobisher Bay on Baffin Island. Although he found no trace of a Passage, he brought back ore thought to contain gold. This discovery led to two successive larger Frobisher expeditions in 1577 and 1578, launched to mine the gold. Unfortunately, after the explorer's third voyage, the ore was found to be worthless.

Frobisher had been backed by Sir Humphrey Gilbert—a half brother of Sir Walter Raleigh—and, in 1583, Gilbert undertook his own voyage, landing in Newfoundland and claiming the territory for Great Britain. Between 1585 and 1588, another English passage-seeker, John Davis, made three journeys to the Canadian Arctic where his searches took him along the coasts of Greenland, Baffin Island, and Labrador.

British attempts to find the passage continued in the early 1600s. Most notable were the voyages of Henry Hudson, Luke Foxe, and Thomas James. In 1609, Hudson sailed up the river that bears his name and discovered Hudson Bay. Later in his voyage, when his crew mutinied and he and eight others were cast adrift in a boat and never heard from again, Hudson became arguably the first of hundreds who would lose their lives in the legendary search. In 1631, rival explorers Luke Foxe and Thomas James made their attempts. Foxe explored the western shore of Hudson Bay and Baffin Island while James reached Hudson Bay's southern shores. Although neither man would suffer as tragic a fate as Hudson, Foxe was forced back to England by scurvy and James had to endure an almost disastrous winter trapped on Charlton Island.

While almost all these voyages produced new discoveries, not one even approached achieving the sought-after prize. Enthusiasm for the search waned even further when reports of some of the adventurers' experiences were published. "It would be sometimes so extreme that it was not endurable," James wrote of the life-threatening temperatures he had encountered, "no clothes were proof against it; no motion could resist it. It would, moreover, so freeze our eyelids that we could not see; and I verily believe that it would have stifled a man in a very few hours." Thanks to such reports, no other serious attempts to find the passage were made for almost one hundred years.

In 1774, however, the English parliament, anxious to outdo rival nations by finding a more profitable route to the East, rekindled enthusiasm for the search by offering a £20,000 reward to anyone who found it. But tragedies continued. In 1776, James Cook, at the time acknowledged as the world's most accomplished navigator, tried his hand. He reached the Bering Strait by sailing up the West Coast but had to turn back when the waters ahead of him were completely blocked by ice. Later in the same long voyage, Cook would lie dead on a Hawaiian beach, fatally clubbed and stabbed by natives.

All of these quests were but a prelude to the seemingly endless succession of nineteenth-century searches initially promoted and launched by John Barrow, quests which, before the century was three-quarters over, would make the trials and consequences of the earlier searches seem mild in comparison.

CHAPTER 2

William Baffin. Early British explorer William Baffin (1584–1622) was pilot on two passage-seeking expeditions sent out by a company boldly calling itself the Company of Merchants of London, Discoverers of the North West Passage. On his first voyage in 1615, in which the expedition vainly attempted to find a channel in Hudson Bay, Baffin deduced the first longitude ever calculated at sea. A year later, passing up Davis Strait, his second search resulted in the exploration of what was called Baffin Bay and the northeast shore of what Edward Parry later named Baffin Island "out of respect to the memory of that able and enterprising navigator." Despite its discoverer's claim, the existence of Baffin Bay was long discredited, perhaps because, after two unsuccessful attempts, Baffin was vocal in expressing his belief that there was no Northwest Passage, a proclamation that discouraged many would-be explorers from Arctic exploration.

Even though John Ross's life would be filled with future Arctic adventures, some of them never equaled, the ridicule that he received because of his mirage-inspired abandonment of John Barrow's first attempt to find the passage would follow him for the rest of his days. But his confirmation of William Baffin's discovery of a body of water that would prove vital in the Arctic quest was a major achievement.

CHAPTER 3

Samuel Hearne. John Franklin was not the first to make an overland journey through the Canadian Arctic. Fifty years earlier, British explorer and fur trader Samuel Hearne made three arduous treks through the unexplored territory and, in the process, discovered many of the places that formed the backdrop of the Franklin expedition.

Born in London in 1745, Hearne entered the British navy when he was only eleven years old and took part in several battles of the Seven Years War. In 1766 he was hired by the Hudson's Bay Company and served aboard two of the Company's ships. The desire to explore was in his blood and when informed of native reports of a great river and large copper mines that lay in the Canadian wilderness, he volunteered to lead an expedition to discover them. In the annals of all the British expeditions that would follow, his experiences in the Arctic were unique. No other explorer would ever be asked to entrust his life so completely to the natives as Samuel Hearne.

In 1769, Hearne, accompanied by two Company employees and a group of Chipewyan Indians, set out to find the river and the mines. From the beginning, Hearne underestimated the magnitude of the task he had undertaken. Like all other white men, he had no idea of the expanse of the Canadian wilderness or the severity of its climate. After traveling two hundred miles and continually facing death by starvation or exposure, the Chipewyan pleaded with Hearne to return with them to the fort from which they had started. When he refused, all of the Indians, save one, abandoned him and Hearne's first expedition came to an ignoble end.

A year later he was at it again. This time he was better equipped and had a larger band of Chipewyans with him. Once again, coping with the weather and finding enough food were major challenges, but by sheer determination Hearne penetrated deeper into the American subarctic than any other white man and drew the first maps of the interior of northern Canada ever made. Despite the severe conditions, he daily grew more confident of success. But it was not to be. Having left a temporary campsite for a day's hunting, Hearne returned to find that a newly arrived band of Indians had run off with his quadrant and other gear. Hearne and two Chipewyans tracked them down and recovered the items, but it was a temporary reprieve. Shortly afterwards, when Hearne had mounted his quadrant on a rock to take a reading, a huge gust of wind blew the vital instrument over, smashing it beyond repair. With no means of verifying positions or determining distances, Hearne was once again forced to stop short of his goal. Again he would not admit defeat. Encouraged by the progress he had made on his second journey, the Hudson's Bay Company agreed to finance yet another attempt, this time supplying Hearne with as many supplies as he—and an even larger contingent of Chipewyans—could carry.

Hearne's third expedition set out in December 1770. Despite being better supplied, his long trek would still require his party to continually hunt and fish for food. Several times the weather turned so bad that even Hearne considered turning back. But he made himself go on and became the first white man ever to cross the enormous open tundra that became known as the Barren Grounds. Along the way he discovered and named a number of lakes and other landmarks. Then he found Great Slave Lake—so-named after the native Slavey tribe, who lived in the area—and beyond it the goal itself. Standing on the banks of what would be called the Coppermine River, he noted in his journal: "We have finally arrived at the long wished-for spot."

Hearne's triumph had come only after he had suffered through one of the worst experiences of his life. Just weeks before he had discovered the Coppermine, his party had come across an Inuit settlement. The Chipewyans, bitter enemies of the Inuit, had attacked the settlement in the dead of night and brutally massacred twenty men, women, and children in their sleep. The site would become known as Bloody Falls, the same spot where fifty years later, Franklin's Indians would abandon him.

Hearne had been helpless to stop the massacre and years later would note in his journal that he still wept over the memories of what he had witnessed. But now he stood at the Coppermine. Canoeing northward along it, he navigated its 525 miles, charting it along the way, and reached its mouth at the Arctic Ocean. He was still not done. Traveling back along the river, he found the copper deposits. But they were a disappointment. As far as he could determine, they were nowhere near as rich as they had been rumored to be.

Nonetheless, Hearne had accomplished what he had set out to do. He had discovered and mapped the Coppermine River and had traced it to the Arctic Ocean. He would remain in the North for the next fifteen years where, among other accomplishments, he would establish Cumberland House, the Hudson Bay's first interior trading post, a place which, half a century later, would provide a lifesaving haven for John Franklin and his men.

CHAPTER 4

Scurvy. Caused by a lack of vitamin C, scurvy first emerged as a problem for maritime explorers when they began to make extended voyages into the Pacific and Indian Oceans. In 1499, while sailing to India, Vasco da Gama lost two-thirds of his crew to the disease. Twenty years later, more than 80 percent of Ferdinand Magellan's men died from scurvy while crossing the Pacific. A British report, issued in 1600, estimated that in the previous twenty years, some ten thousand mariners had been killed by what adventurer Sir Richard Hawkins called the "plague of the sea" and the "Spoyle of Mariners."

By the early 1800s, scurvy had become so pernicious and widespread that, at times, as much as one-third of the Royal Navy was incapacitated by it. The problem was that no one knew what caused it. Its symptoms—including malaise, lethargy, shortness of breath, and, in the later stages, fever, convulsions, and emotional disturbances—were so varied that it was commonly mistaken for syphilis, dysentery asthma, or even madness.

Actually, the first breakthrough in determining both the cause and the means of preventing scurvy took place as early as 1747, when the British naval doctor James Lind conducted an experiment on six pairs of sailors who were seriously afflicted with the disease. Lind fed each of five of the pairs a different "cure"—cider, vinegar, distilled sulfuric acid, garlic-mustard paste, and seawater. None had any effect. But the sixth pair of seamen, who had been fed two oranges and a lemon every day, recovered completely within a week. Despite this discovery by one of its own physicians, however, it took the Royal Navy some fifty years before it began regularly supplying its vessels with lemon juice as a preventative against the disease. (The fact that the British commonly referred to lemons as "limes," coupled with the use of lime juice as well as lemon juice, led to the emergence of the nickname "limey" for British sailors).

More than the British Admiralty ever realized, the nineteenth-century Arctic expeditions were particularly susceptible to scurvy. Unlike their whaling counterparts, whose global pursuit of the migratory whales most often enabled them to put into ports to take on fresh vegetables and meat, the passage-seekers, ensconced in northern waters for years at a time, had no such opportunity. And even those commanders who were wise enough to store lemon or lime juice aboard their vessels had no way of knowing that vitamin C loses its potency over time, thus making it less effective during the long polar explorations. Seriously compounding the problem was the fact that many of the commanders, particularly when forced to winter in the ice, mistakenly instituted antiscurvy practices that, instead of preventing or alleviating the disease, actually caused or hastened its progression. Edward Parry was typical of scores of well-intentioned commanders when he regularly doled out rations of beer and instituted a strict regimen of exercise aboard his ship. It would not be until a century later that it would be discovered that both practices caused a hastening of the disease. Ignorance of ways to prevent scurvy was, in fact, so widespread that John Ross was actually criticized for copying the Inuit by feeding his men a regular diet of vitamin C–rich fresh salmon whenever he could during the four winters between 1829 and 1833 that his ships were icebound—this, despite the fact that when he finally was able to return to England, his entire contingent was relatively scurvy-free.

It was not until 1912, when vitamins were discovered—and later, when it became possible to diagnose deficiency diseases—that anyone understood which fresh vegetables, meats, and fruits prevented scurvy, and why they did so. By that time, the enigma of the Northwest Passage and the mystery of the disappearance of its most famous seeker had been thoroughly explored, most of the Arctic was no longer unknown, and more brave souls engaged in unlocking these riddles had died of scurvy than from any other cause.

George Back. By the mid-nineteenth century, the Northwest Passage had still not been found and gigantic blunders had been made, yet the earlier expeditions led by Edward Parry, John Franklin, and John Ross had unlocked significant pieces of the Arctic puzzle. Other seekers of glory had also made notable voyages before the most anticipated and optimistic search of all was launched by John Franklin in 1845.

Significant among them were two journeys made by George Back, voyages that were a microcosm of the often consecutive achievements and disasters experienced by those who challenged the Arctic. A vain and often cantankerous man, Back had severely tested the patience of John Franklin, whom he had served under during the latter's first two ventures into the Arctic—and Franklin was patient and easygoing to a fault. Most of the other early nineteenth-century explorers had found Back equally difficult. But no one could question his courage. He had proved his bravery beyond a doubt when twice his heroics had prevented Franklin's overland journey from becoming a total disaster.

In 1833, Back was given his first command, one directly connected with John Ross's four-winter misadventure. By 1832, Ross had been gone for three years. Not a word from him or about him had been heard. The same question was increasingly being asked throughout England: What had happened to John Ross? The Admiralty was sure that he and his men were dead. But not Ross's brother George, the father of James Clark Ross. A furor erupted when George Ross began to publicly decry the government's reluctance to send a rescue party in search of his brother and his son. Was their disappearance being ignored because John Ross, out of favor with John Barrow, had launched his own private expedition? Informed of the controversy, George Back interrupted his vacation in Italy, rushed home, and volunteered to head a rescue mission. Reluctantly giving in to mounting pressure from the public and the press, the Admiralty granted Back his wish. His modest party of twenty included fellow officer Dr. Richard King, three soldiers, and men recruited from the Hudson's Bay Company.

In 1820, when Back had been with Franklin in Canada, he had sat enthralled as an elderly Indian warrior told stories of a mysterious river that the natives called the Great Fish. Now, Back's plan was to find this river, follow it to its mouth, cross over to Prince Regent Inlet (where he was sure that Ross had gone), and conduct his search for the missing party. The Hudson's Bay Company men, as well as King, were certain that Ross and his men had long since died. Nor did they believe that the mysterious river existed. But it did. And Back found it. Early in 1834, just as he was about to begin following it, he received a dispatch with the startling news that Ross and his men had been found alive. Back now found himself with the opportunity of exploring the unknown territory through which the river passed. Perhaps he would even find the passage.

As he moved down the Great Fish River (now the Back River), Back encountered what he later described as "a violent and tortuous course of five hundred and thirty geographical miles, running through an iron robbed country without a single tree on the whole line of its banks." The river, he discovered, emptied into a number of lakes that gave him a clear view of distant vistas. He also discovered a body of water that he named Chantrey Inlet. Now he could see the lands that John Ross had named Boothia Felix and King William Land. If he could have explored them, perhaps he would have confirmed John Clark Ross's contention that Boothia Felix was a peninsula and would have found that King William Land was an island, information that would have changed the entire nature and outcome of the search for the passage. But by this time he was running out of supplies and had to make his way back to England.

He arrived back in England in 1835, and a year later he returned to the Arctic, this time in the 340-ton *Terror*. His intention was to spend the winter in Repulse Bay and then explore the far shore of Melville Peninsula. What followed was one of the most horrifying experiences that any of the Arctic adventurers had yet endured.

Back and his crew sailed from England in June 1836. Only six weeks later they became surrounded by an enormous ice field. They would remain trapped in the field for the next ten months. For four of these months the *Terror* would sit precariously perched atop what Back would describe as "an icy cradle," continuously lifted in and out of the water onto the floes. In the spring, when the ice began to break up, Back and his men, who had accomplished nothing on their journey except barely managing to survive, were, for the first time, hopeful of at least returning safely home. Suddenly, however, when they were still deep in the Arctic, the *Terror* was struck by a submerged iceberg that splintered the ship. Realizing that he had no chance of reaching England safely, Back headed for the Irish coast. Miraculously, he was able to ground his vessel on an Irish beach just before it fell apart. He would never return to the Artic.

CHAPTER 6

Setting the Stage for Franklin. Between 1837 and 1839, two Hudson's Bay Company men, Thomas Simpson and Peter Dease, had completed an expedition that many believed had resulted in a survey of much of the remaining unknown areas of the Northwest Passage. John Franklin's orders, in fact, called for him to travel along the large part of the Arctic coastline that Simpson and Dease had mapped.

Although the Hudson's Bay Company had been formed primarily as a fur-trading enterprise, from the beginning it had engaged in the exploration of the North, as witnessed by Samuel Hearne's significant achievements. Also, on several occasions the company had provided important aid to the Admiralty's passage-seekers. And although its original charter dealt mostly with matters relating to the fur trade, it also mandated that the company should do whatever it could to discover a northwest passage.

The two men that the Hudson's Bay Company selected to conduct the 1837 expedition were not strangers to the northern wilderness. As secretary (and cousin) to the company's governor, George Simpson, Thomas Simpson had accompanied his relative on tours throughout the Hudson Bay territory. Extremely fit and energetic, Thomas Simpson was one of the most ambitious men in the company's employ. A much calmer man than Simpson, Peter Dease had a past history with John Franklin. It was he who had supplied Sir John with important information about the topography and the weather during Franklin's first overland Arctic expedition. And it was he who had contributed to the success of Sir John's second expedition by providing counsel regarding the supplies that Franklin needed to take with him.

Starting out in February 1837, the first objective of the Simpson-Dease expedition was to travel on foot and by small boat from the Athabasca region to Point Barrow. By July 31, 1837, the small party was about halfway there, but Dease and some of the others had become totally exhausted. Refusing Dease's plea that they turn back, Simpson, with five men, plunged on, tracing and mapping the Arctic coast as he went. On August 4 the Point was reached, an accomplishment that Simpson, in a classic overstatement, would celebrate by proclaiming, "I and I alone have the well-earned honour of uniting the Arctic to the great western ocean."

Making his way back from Point Barrow, Simpson reconnected with Dease and during the next two years they traced the Arctic coast from north of the Coppermine River all the way to the Gulf of Boothia. When they were finished, a considerable amount of the remaining blank spaces on the Arctic map had been filled in. Neither Simpson nor Dease would ever receive the acclaim of a Parry or a Franklin or a James Clark Ross, but, in truth, they had unlocked Arctic mysteries as important to finding the passage as those uncovered by any of their predecessors.

In the fall of 1839, buoyed by what he had accomplished (he never gave any credit to Dease), Simpson was certain that he was on the verge of finding the passage. One more expedition should do it. Stating that "I feel an irresistible presentiment that I am destined to bear the Honourable Company's flag fairly through and out of the Polar Sea," he petitioned the Hudson's Bay Company for permission to undertake another exploration as soon as possible. This time he wanted no Peter Dease to accompany him. "Fame I will have," he wrote, "but it must be alone."

It was fame that the Company was only too happy to try to give him. Nothing would please its directors, and particularly its governor, George Simpson, more than snatching the great prize away from the British navy. In response to his request, the Company sent a letter to Simpson, congratulating him on his accomplishments, approving the next expedition, and granting him sole command.

Simpson would never receive the letter. While it was on its way, he met a sudden and violent death. To this day, it is not clear exactly what happened. What is known is that on June 14, 1840, while riding through Dakota Sioux country with a group of four heavily armed, mixed-race porters, he died from a bullet wound to the head. Was it suicide, as an official report would later conclude? Or had the cantankerous Simpson angered his traveling companions one time too many? The "fame alone" he sought would never be his. But nothing could take away the fact that he had, it seemed, set the final stage for others to sail into glory.

CHAPTER 7

George Simpson & the HBC. The Hudson's Bay Company (HBC), one of the oldest commercial organizations in the world (and today Canada's largest department-store retailer), was formed shortly after two English-sponsored French fur traders and explorers, Médard Chouart, Sieur des Groseilliers, and his brother-in-law Pierre Esprit Raddison, made a profitable trading expedition to Hudson Bay. HBC's charter, granted by England's King Charles II in 1670, gave the company a trading monopoly covering an enormous region that included much of present-day western Canada and parts of what is today the northern United States. Building the company meant opening up trading posts throughout the vast region, and that meant exploring territory into which no other white men had ever set foot. In establishing these posts, early HBC adventurers such as Henry Kelsey (the discoverer of the Canadian plains) and Samuel Hearne (the discoverer of the Coppermine River), established a tradition of courage and daring that would be the hallmark of scores of company men who followed.

The beginning of the Hudson's Bay Company's rise to commercial success can be traced to 1820, when George Simpson assumed the first of several positions that quickly led to his being appointed governor of HBC operations in North America, a post he would hold for more than forty years. An able administrator, Simpson was also a skilled negotiator and, shortly after becoming governor, he scored one of his greatest achievements. For years, the Hudson's Bay Company's one major North American competitor was the North West Company. It was a rivalry so bitter that on several occasions it had erupted into open warfare. Simpson immediately saw the necessity of bringing North West into HBC's fold. Through skilled and iron-fisted maneuvering he was able to do just that. When this had been accomplished, he held a dinner to bring the former enemies together.

It was an extraordinary event—men who had tried to kill each other, who had, on occasion, held each other captive, sitting down to dine as members of the same organization. One observer described it this way: "Men found themselves vis-à-vis, across the narrow table, who had lately slashed each other with swords, and bore the mark of combat. I noticed one Highlander . . . whose nostrils seemed to expand as he glared at his mortal foe, and who snorted, squirmed and spat . . . he and his enemy opposite being as restless as if each was sitting on a hillock of ants." Somehow, Simpson not only kept the dinner from turning into a bloodbath, but was able to attain the improbable goal of getting the men from both organizations to work together for the good of the now greatly enlarged Hudson's Bay Company.

He was equally successful in the establishment of the trading posts. Nicknamed the "Little Emperor" because he was short in stature and long on giving orders, he was a stern taskmaster who pushed his traveling crewmen to extremes, demanding that they journey quickly from one trading post to another. Equally demanding on himself, he visited every wilderness post in his realm and twice traveled completely across the continent. His travels were made mainly by canoe and were accomplished in a style befitting his imperial manner. As he toured his vast empire in his own nar-row-beam, twenty-six-foot, banner-waving "Express Canoe," he was accompanied by a crew of eight expert Iroquois voyageurs and his personal bagpiper and bugler.

George Simpson would play an important role both in the hunt for the passage and the search for Franklin. Always painfully blunt, he had been openly critical of Sir John's leadership of the 1821 overland expedition, and even more of Franklin's selection as commander of the most ambitious search yet launched. "Lieut. Franklin, the officer who commands the party," he had written, "has not the physical powers required for the labor of moderate Voyaging in this country; he must have three meals per diem, Tea is indispensable, and with the utmost exertion he cannot walk Eight miles on one day."

Simpson was, in fact, critical of the way in which, in his opinion, most of the British navy's passage-seeking expeditions had been bungled and was convinced that his two Company men, his nephew Thomas Simpson and Peter Dease, had accom-plished more toward unlocking the secrets of the passage than any of John Barrow's explorers. When pressed, however, he was willing to lend support to the Admiralty, and his willingness to permit the Company's John Rae to join in the Franklin search would eventually prove a major contribution to finally solving the mystery of Sir John.

CHAPTER 8

A Ballad of Sir John Franklin. By the 1850s, the search for John Franklin had so captured worldwide attention that dozens of songs were written, lamenting his loss and praying for his safe return. Most were sung to the tune of traditional folk melodies. One of the most popularly published of the songs, written by George H. Boker was titled "The Ballad of Sir John Franklin," written in 1851, excerpted here:

Whither sail you, Sir John Franklin?
Cried a whaler in Baffin's bay.
If to know between the land pole
I may find a broad sea-way.

I change you back Sir John Franklin
As you would live and thrive:
For between the land and the frozen pole
No man may sail alive.

But lightly laughed the stout Sir John
And spoke unto his men—
Half England is wrong, if he is right;
Bear off to westward then.

O, wither sail you brave Englishman?
Cried the little Esquimaux
Between your land and the polar star
My goodly vessels go.

Come down if you would journey there
The little Indian said;
And change your cloth for fur clothing
Your vessel for a sled.
But lightly laughed the stout Sir John
And the crew laughed with him
    too—
A sailor to change from ship to sled,
I ween, were something new!

All through the long, long polar day,
The vessels westward sped;
And wherever the sail of Sir John was
    blown
The ice gave way and fled.

Gave way with many a hollow groan,
And with many a surly roar;
But it murmured and threatened on
    every side,
And closed where he sailed before.

Ho! see ye not, my merry men,
The broad and open sea?
Bethink ye what the whaler said,
Think of the little Indian's sled!
The crew laughed out in glee.

Sir John, Sir John, 'tis bitter cold,
The scud drives on the breeze,
The ice comes looming from
    the north,
The very sunbeams freeze.

Bright summer goes, dark winter
    comes— We cannot rule the year;
But long ere summer's sun goes down,
On yonder sea we'll steer.

The dripping icebergs dipped and rose,
And floundered down the gale;
The ships were staid, the yards were
    manned,
And furled the useless sail.

The summer's gone, the winter's come,
We sail not on yonder sea:
Why sail we not, Sir John Franklin?
A silent man was he.

The cruel ice came floating on,
And closed beneath the lee

Till the thickening waters dashed no
    more;
'Twas ice around, behind, before—
My god! there is no sea?
What think you of the whaler now?
What of the Esquimaux?
A sled were better than a ship,
To cruise through ice and snow.

Sir John, the night is black and long,
The hissing wind is bleak,
The hard, green ice is strong as
    death—
I prithee, Captain, speak!

What hope can scale this icy wall,
High over the main flag-staff?
Above the ridges the wolf and bear
Look down with a patient, settled
    stare
Look down on us and laugh.
Oh! when shall I see my orphan child?
My Mary waits for me.
Oh! when shall I see my old mother,
And pray at her trembling knee.

Be still, be still, my brave sailors!
Think not such thoughts again.
But a tear froze on his cheek;
He thought of Lady Jane.

Oh! Think you, good Sir John Franklin,
We'll ever see land?
'Twas cruel to send us here to starve,
Without a helping hand.

Oh! whether we starve to death alone,
Or sail to our own country,
We have done what man has never
    done—
The open ocean danced in the sun—
We passed the Northern Sea!

CHAPTER 9

Kennedy and Bellot. Nothing could have more dramatically demonstrated Lady Jane Franklin's unyielding resolve than her funding of a second *Prince Albert* rescue effort launched almost immediately after the vessel returned from its unsuccessful 1850 search. The two men she selected to head the new expedition were after neither fame nor money. They had come to her, motivated by nothing desire to help her find her husband.

Canadian native William Kennedy, who would head the rescue effort, had been born at Cumberland House in Saskatchewan and, as a child, had actually met Franklin during the latter's first overland expedition. In 1833 he had joined the Hudson's Bay Company and had spent more than ten years traveling the Canadian wilderness in its employ. Highly religious, Kennedy had resigned from the company in 1846 over its policy of selling liquor to the Indians.

Joseph René Bellot was a lieutenant in the French navy who had begged leave to join the search for Franklin. As her friends would point out, there was no question that, in the devoted, young Bellot, Jane Franklin had found the son she never had.

Lady Franklin could not have chosen two more different men to carry forth her hopes. Kennedy, the hardened son of a Hudson's Bay fur trader and a Cree woman, had never been to sea. Bellot, an animated, tender soul, had never been anywhere near the Arctic. Their crewmen would always remember the sight of Kennedy sledging ahead in his Inuit clothing accompanied by the somewhat foppish Bellot in his pink tunic, high seaboots, and white leggings. Yet despite their obvious differences, the two would get along well together and theirs would turn out to be one of the most harmonious of all Arctic partnerships.

In June 1851, the *Prince Albert*, for the second time in two years, headed out in search of the lost expedition. Among its seventeen-man crew was a fifty-seven year old veteran of northern exploration: John Hepburn, who, in 1820, had come close to starving with Sir John. He too had volunteered for the mission.

According to the orders that Lady Franklin had given him, Kennedy was to search for her husband both in Prince Regent Inlet and in the area southwest of Cape Walker, which was in Barrow Strait. A month out, near Upernavik, Greenland, the *Prince Albert* had its encounter with De Haven's ships trying to make their way home. Boarding the *Prince Albert*, Elisha Kane was taken aback at the sight of Bellot. "I have seen many things here to surprise me," the American exclaimed, "but what I least expected to find here was a French officer." Kane and Bellot quickly discovered that they had much in common, and, in the days that the ships were anchored near each other, exchanged several visits. Later, Kane would remember his conversations with the sensitive Bellot as one of the few pleasant experiences of his first venture into the Arctic.

By September, Kennedy had succeeded in moving through Lancaster Sound and into Prince Regent Inlet. A few days later, he and four of his men went ashore at Port Leopold intending to conduct a spirited search for Franklin. Suddenly, offshore, there was a violent shift in the ice, carrying Bellot and the rest of the crew aboard the *Prince Albert* away to the south. Finally regaining control of the ship, Bellot just managed to put into Batty Bay before he became completely icebound.

For a man who had never been in the Arctic, it was a terrifying experience. But Kennedy and his four companions had to be rescued. Over the next five weeks, Bellot and several crewmen made three laborious attempts to reach their marooned comrades. Finally they found them and led them back to the ship. Ahead of them all lay an icebound winter in Batty Bay.

But neither Kennedy nor Bellot was to be deterred. Late in February 1852, they and twelve of their crew members set out on a dog-sledge journey to search the Boothia Felix area. After passing Fury Beach and reaching Brentford Bay, eight of the crewmen returned to the *Prince Albert* while Kennedy, Bellot, and the four remaining crew moved on along the coast of Somerset Island. On April 7, they made their most important discovery—a new channel that Kennedy later named Bellot Strait.

Together on their trek, Kennedy and Bellot mapped all of Somerset Island and much of Boothia Felix (which would later be renamed Boothia Peninsula). By the time they returned to their ship, they had completed a journey of more than 1,100 miles. They left for home early in November. Although they, like those before them, had not found Franklin, they had added much to the knowledge of the Arctic and had completed their hazardous undertaking without losing a single man.

CHAPTER 10

1. Sledging. Throughout the long years of searching for John Franklin and for those who had themselves become lost in the search, more discoveries were made—and more knowledge of Arctic geography gained—through sledging than could ever have been accomplished by ships and boats alone. One of the liveliest and most accurate descriptions of this vital form of travel, exploration, and rescue appeared in the July 11, 1856, *Boston Daily Advertiser*.

"The sledge is in general contour not unlike a Yankee wood-sled, about eleven feet long. The runners are curved at each end. The sled is fitted with a light canvas trough, so adjusted that, in case of necessity, all the stores etc. can be ferried over any narrow lane of water in the ice. There are packed on this sled a tent for eight or ten men, five or six pikes, one or more of which is fitted with an ice chisel, two large buffalo skins, a water-tight floor-cloth which contrives a double debt to pay floor by night, the sledge's sail by day.

"There are, besides, a cooking apparatus, of which the fire is made in spirit or tallow lamps, one or two guns, a pick and shovel, instruments for observation, pannikins, spoons, and a little magazine of such necessaries, with the extra clothing of the party. The provisions, the supply of which measures the length of the expedition, consist of about a pound of bread and a pound of pemmican per man per day, six ounces of pork, a little preserved potato, rum, lime-juice, tea, chocolate, sugar, tobacco, or other such creature comforts. The sled is fitted with two drag-ropes, at which the men haul. The officer goes ahead to find the best way among the hummocks of ice or masses of snow.

"Sometimes on a smooth floe, before the wind, the floor cloth is set for a sail, and she runs off merrily, perhaps with several of the crew on board, and the rest running to keep up. But over broken ice, it is a constant task . . . You hear 'one, two, three, haul' all day long, as she is worked out of one ice 'cradle hole' over a hummock into another. Different parties select different hours for traveling. Captain Kellett finally considered that the best time, when, as usual, they had constant daylight, was to start at four in the afternoon, travel till ten P.M., breakfast then, tent and rest four hours; travel four more, tent, dine, and sleep nine hours. This secured sleep when the sun was highest and most trying to the eyes. . . .

"Each man, of course, is dressed as warmly as flannel, woolen cloth, leather, and sealskin will dress him. For such long journeying, the study of boots becomes a science and our authorities are full of discussions as to canvas or woolen, or carpet or leather boots, of strings and buckles. When the time to tent comes, the spikes are fitted for tent poles, and the tent set up, its door to leeward, on the ice or snow. The floor-cloth is laid for the carpet. At an hour fixed, all talking must stop. There is just enough for the party to lie side by side on the floor-cloth. Each man gets into a long felt bag, made of heavy felting, literally nearly half an inch thick. He brings this up wholly over his head and buttons himself in. He has a little hole in it to breathe through. Over the felt is sometimes a brown holland bag, meant to keep out moisture.

"The officer lies farthest in the tent as being next to the wind and . . . hardship [is considered] the point of honor. The cook for the day lies next to the doorway, as being first to be called. Side by side the others lie between . . . No watch is kept, for there is little danger of intrusion.

"Some thirty or forty parties, thus equipped, set out from the *Resolute* while she was under Captain Kellett's charges. As the journey of Lieutenant Pim to the *Investigator* . . . was that on which turned the greatest victory of her voyage, we will let that stand as a specimen of what has been accomplished through sledging."

2. Edward Inglefield. Edward Inglefield, the man who helped bring the ill-starred Belcher expedition home, was a navy man to the core. The son of a rear admiral and the grandson of a captain, he joined the navy at the age of fourteen and by the age of twenty-five had performed so gallantly, particularly during operations off the Syrian coast, that he was promoted to the rank of commander.

While most of his colleagues were obsessed with finding the Northwest Passage, Inglefield had a different ambition. He wanted to be the first to reach the Geographic North Pole. A great admirer of John and Lady Franklin, he was also determined to take part in the search for Sir John. Perhaps if fortune smiled his way, he thought, he could accomplish both goals.

He got his chance in 1852 when Lady Franklin, who had already twice sent the private yacht *Prince Albert* to look for her husband, bought yet another small private vessel, the *Isabel*, and equipped it to join the search. Inglefield, who firmly believed that his hero Franklin was still alive, took leave from the navy and volunteered to captain the rescue ship.

Almost as soon as he reached Arctic waters, Inglefield made an important contribution. When John Ross had returned home from his search for Franklin, he had brought with him a tale that had been related to him by his interpreter, Adam Beck, that Franklin and his men had been killed by Inuit and that their bones lay buried underneath a cairn north of Umanak, Greenland. Jane Franklin who, among other Arctic observers, never believed the story, had responded by sarcastically thanking Ross for "having murdered my husband." As soon as he reached Greenland, Inglefield found the cairn, tore it apart, and saw that it contained only animal bones. The disturbing rumor had been put to rest.

Sailing on, Inglefield entered Smith Sound at the head of Baffin Bay, filled with what he later described as "wild thoughts of getting to the Pole—of finding our way to Behring Strait—and most of all reaching Franklin and giving him help." He did not reach the Pole and, in fact, was blocked more than 850 miles short of it. But the route he had followed through Smith Sound—one that Elisha Kane would also pursue in 1853—would nonetheless, as later explorers discovered, provide the avenue to reaching the North Pole.

Having been blocked to the north, Inglefield then sailed southward through both Jones and Lancaster Sounds. Along the way he discovered and named several islands and capes, including Littleton Island and Cape Sabine. Although he had found no trace of Franklin, he returned home to high acclaim for his discoveries and his valiant effort.

In 1853, he was back in the Arctic, this time as commander of the steam-powered supply ship *Phoenix*. After bringing provisions to Edward Belcher's depot ship, the *North Star*, Inglefield became involved in a heroic rescue when his sister supply vessel, the *Breadalbane*, became crushed in the ice and all of her crew had to be taken aboard the *Phoenix*. Shortly afterwards, Inglefield sailed back to England, taking with him the *Investigator*'s Lieutenant Samuel Cresswell, whose father had helped instigate the Belcher expedition. It was Cresswell who would be the first to break the news that the Northwest Passage had, at last, been found.

Within months, Inglefield had retuned to northern waters, charged with again supplying the Belcher party. He arrived at Beechey Island just in time to re-lieve the *North Star* from the enormous and dangerous burden of having to transport all of the men from Belcher's abandoned ships along with the crew of the *Investigator*, who had been rescued by the men of the *Resolute*. He never reached the Pole; nor did he ever find any trace of Sir John. But Edward Inglefield made himself an important player in the Franklin drama.

Cannibalism. Since first being described in the Bible in regard to the 723 BCE Siege of Samara (2 Kings 6:26–30), cannibalism has been surrounded by myth, mystery, fear, and speculation, and has been regarded in most cultures as the ultimate taboo. Although there is evidence of early ritualistic cannibalism among certain ancient groups such as the Aztecs and Easter Islanders, most anthropologists believe that accounts of such practices were greatly exaggerated. More common and more clearly documented have been the instances of cannibalism undertaken as a last resort by individuals literally on the verge of starvation.

The first documented case of mariners engaged in cannibalism was that of the survivors of the French ship *Medusa*, who in 1816 resorted to the practice after being adrift on a raft for four days. Arguably the most famous case of all took place in 1820, after the Nantucket whaleship *Essex* was sunk by a whale. The twenty members of the crew took to the vessel's three open boats and set out for South America, the nearest landfall, some two thousand miles away. After several months, one of the boats was struck by a storm and disappeared, never to be seen again. Later, with food and drinking water totally gone, the men in the other boats began to resort to cannibalism. By the time that the last of the eight survivors of the horrific voyage had been rescued in April 1821, seven crewmen had been eaten.

Another famous case took place in 1846–47 (almost the same time that Franklin's men were icebound at King William Island). Trapped by record snowfall in the Sierra Nevada mountains, the remaining members of the eighty-nine-person Donner Party were forced to sustain themselves by eating the corpses of those who had starved to death. When finally rescued, only forty-nine people remained alive.

Modern examples of cannibalism include documented accounts among Japanese soldiers trapped on Pacific islands during World War II; the case of the Uruguayan rugby team, who were stranded for more than two months when their plane crashed in the Andes in 1972; and numerous reports from North Korean defectors and refugees about the practice during the height of the disastrous famine in that country in the 1990s.

The cannibalism that occurred in 1821 during John Franklin's first overland expedition was but the first known instance of the eating of human flesh during Arctic ventures. In 1881–84, members of the American polar expedition led by Lieutenant Adolphus Greely found themselves marooned for three years in a primitive hut high above the Arctic circle. When rescuers finally found Greely and seven other survivors of the twenty-six-man party, they discovered indisputable evidence that they had kept themselves alive by eating the remains of those who had died.

CHAPTER 12

The Affair of the **Resolute.** The discovery of the *Resolute*, Buddington's heroics sailing her to New London, and the ship's triumphant return to England occasioned numerous songs and poems. "The Affair of the *Resolute*" was written by English poet Martin Tupper and was reprinted many times on both sides of the Atlantic.

I

A gracious and generous action
Outweighing all sins on each side
Outshaming the treasons of faction,
Ambition, and folly, and pride.
No jealousies now shall be rankling
No silly suspicions intrude
But 'round the rememb'rance of Franklin
Our brotherly loves be renewed.

II

The *Resolute* lying forsaken
The sport of the winds and the ice
By luck to America taken
Is nobly restored without price.
Not only refusing all ransom
But, fitted anew for the Queen
In a manner more generous and
    handsome,
And kinder, than ever was seen.

III

We, too, were not lacking in honor
For, waiving all claim to the ship
When Buddington's flag was upon her
We flung away quibble and quip.
"He saved her, and so let him take her,"
But handsome America said,
"I guess, Cousin, that we can make her
A prettier present instead."

IV

"With thousands of dollars we'll buy her
With thousands of dollars repair
(Diplomacy cannot take fire
That here at least all isn't fair)
In honor of Britain's ice-heroes
Of Franklin and Ross and McClure
To gentle Victoria the Sea-Rose
Her *Resolute* thus we restore!"

V

Huzzah for this generous meeting
Huzzah, too, for Grinnell and Kane
And all the kind hearts that are
    beating
So nobly, from Kansas to Maine.
Our instincts are all for each other
(Though both have a tincture of heat)
And truly as brother with brother
Our bosoms in unison meet.

VI

When craft diplomacy's blindness
So often does harm in the dark
One plain, international kindness
Comes, just as the dove, to the Ark.
O, wisdom, above the astuteness
Of placemen, by cunning defiled
O, better than manhood's acuteness
This kindliness, as of a child.

CHAPTER 13

Queen Victoria. "We are not interested in the possibilities of defeat. They do not exist." These words, spoken by England's Queen Victoria, symbolized the spirit of what came to be known as the Victorian Age, an era in which everything seemed possible, national pride was at its zenith, and the discovery of the Northwest Passage was regarded as a British right and an inevitability of English achievement.

Born in Kensington Palace on May 24, 1819 (the same month and year that Edward Parry set out on his first search for the passage and John Franklin embarked on his first overland expedition), Alexandria Victoria inherited the throne from her childless uncle King William IV when she was eighteen years old. Despite her youth, she was determined to resist the influence of her domineering mother and, from the beginning, demonstrated a surprising maturity and an unexpected firmness of will.

The most powerful influence on her during the early years of her reign was that of her prime minister, William Lamb, 2nd Viscount Melbourne. But it would be another man who would eventually become the central figure in her life. In 1840, Victoria married her first cousin Prince Albert of the House of Saxe-Coburg-Gotha. Immediately, Albert, upon whom the queen bestowed the title Prince Consort, established himself as much more than husband and companion. His influence shaped Victoria's political, as well as personal, thinking. By 1850, when the search for Franklin was in full blossom, Victoria was demanding that government officials consult with her on British affairs to a far greater degree than had been the case with her predecessors.

It was in another area, however, that Albert's influence had arguably its greatest impact. A man of unbending sexual morality, he persuaded Victoria to introduce strict sexual decorum in the court and together they made straitlaced behavior the order of the day. It was a development that made the revival of public morality synonymous with the Victorian Age—an era also marked by extraordinary industrial progress, symbolized in particular by the Great Exhibition of 1851, conceived and organized by Prince Albert to showcase England's industrial and economic might.

In 1861, Victoria's life abruptly changed when Albert died of typhoid fever. Totally devastated, she entered a period of mourning and self-imposed seclusion that lasted for almost fifteen years. In 1887, her life took another dramatic turn when the Golden Jubilee, the celebration of her fiftieth year as queen, took her out of her shell and she once again entered public life. (Some students of the monarchy believe that the rekindling of her sprit actually took place some years earlier through her relationship with her manservant John Brown. There is evidence that suggests that romance was involved and that even a secret marriage might have taken place.)

Queen Victoria died on January 22, 1901. She had ruled for sixty-three years, the longest reign in British history. By the time of her passing, she had contributed significantly to creating the climate that made exploration and discovery a national obsession. And she had played a unique role as far as the HMS *Resolute* was concerned as well.

CHAPTER 14

Inuit Life. One of the most comprehensive descriptions of the Arctic natives' way of life was written by *New York Herald* correspondent William Gilder, who accompanied Frederick Schwatka in 1878 on what became the final search for survivors of the lost Franklin expedition. The following are excerpts from Gilder's lengthy journal:

"The government among the Inuit tribes, where they have any at all, is patriarchal, consisting of advice from the older and more experienced, which is recognized and complied with by the younger. Parental authority is never strictly enforced, but the children readily defer to the wishes of their parents—not only when young, but after reaching man's estate. The old people are consulted upon on all matters of interest. The authority of parents in their family, and of the chief, or *ish-u-mat-tah*, in his tribe, is enforced without fear of punishment or hope of reward.

"The Esquimaux are polygamists, no distinction whatever being placed upon the number of wives a man shall have. I have never, however, known any instance of one having more than two at a time. This is very common, however, among the Iwilliks and Kinnepatoos, where there is a surplus of women. At least half of their married men have two wives. Every woman is married as soon as she arrives at a marriageable age, and whenever a man dies his wife is taken by someone else, so that with them old maids and widows are unknown.

"There are no wedding ceremonies among the Esquimaux, and hardly anything like sentiment is known. The relation of man and wife is purely a matter of convenience. The woman requires food, and the man needs some one to make his clothing and to take charge of his dwelling while he is hunting. Marriages are usually contracted while the interested parties are children. The father of the boy selects a little girl who is to be his daughter-in-law, and pays her father something. Perhaps it is a snow-knife, or a sled, or a dog. . . . The children are then affianced, and when arrived at a proper age they live together. The wife then has her face tattooed with lamp-black and is regarded as a matron in society. . . . The forehead is decorated with a letter V in double lines, the angle very acute, passing down between the eyes almost to the bridge of the nose, and sloping gracefully to the right and left before reaching the roots of the hair. Each cheek is adorned with an egg-shaped pattern. . . . The most ornamented part, however, is the chin, which receives a gridiron pattern. . . .

"The natives of Hudson's Strait dress very much like the others, the difference being in the women's hoods, which, instead of being long and narrow, are long and wide, and provided with a drawing string. Instead of the long stockings, they wear a pair of leggings that reach about half-way up the thigh, and trousers that are much shorter than those of the western tribes. The Kinnepatoos are by all odds the most tasteful in their dress, and their clothing is made of skins more carefully prepared and better sewed than that of the others. . . .

"It would astonish a civilized spectator to see how many people can be stowed away to sleep in one small igloo and under one blanket; but the proverbial illustration of a box of sardines would almost represent a skirmish line in comparison. Each one is rolled up into a little ball, or else arms, legs and bodies are so inextricably interwoven, that it would be impossible for any but the owners to unravel them. And these bodies are like so many little ovens, so that, no matter how cold it be, when once within the igloo, the snow-block door put up and chinked, and all stowed away in bed, Jack Frost can be successfully defied."

CHAPTER 15

George Nares. Charles Francis Hall was not the only explorer to seek the North Pole during the 1870s. In 1875, George Nares—who, while serving aboard the *Resolute*, had distinguished himself by sledging 665 miles in sixty-nine days in one search for John Franklin, and 586 miles in fifty-six days on another—also made a notable attempt. Five years before that, however, Nares made what would be his greatest contribution when he captained the *Challenger*, a ship employed in a scientific expedition which, during its groundbreaking voyage, laid the foundations of almost every branch of oceanography as we know it today.

A joint venture of the Admiralty and the Royal Geographical Society, the mission of the *Challenger* expedition, organized at a time when scientific investigation of the oceans was in its infancy, was highly ambitious. At 362 sampling stations in the Atlantic, Pacific, and Indian Oceans, the *Challenger*'s scientists were to determine the ocean depth, the composition of both the shallowest and deepest water, and the speed and direction of surface currents. They were also to determine if there was any animal life in the ocean depths and were to collect whatever sea life they could.

The three-masted, square-rigged *Challenger* had been originally designed as a British warship—outfitted with seventeen guns and a steam engine capable of delivering twelve hundred horsepower. For its unprecedented scientific journey it had been radically modified. All of its guns had been removed, and laboratories for natural history and chemistry, along with workrooms, extra cabins, and a special dredging platform, had been installed. Along with Captain Nares, the vessel's crew included six civilian scientists headed by Dr. C. Wyville Thomson, twenty British naval officers, and 216 crewmen. Nares also brought along his nine-year-old son.

During its four-year journey, the *Challenger* circumnavigated the globe and traveled almost seventy thousand miles. Its scientists sounded the ocean bottom to a depth of 26,850 feet, determined the patterns of ocean temperatures and currents, and charted the contours of the great ocean basins. They also discovered and cataloged over four thousand previously unknown animal species. The scientific results of the voyage were published in a fifty-volume, 29,500-page report that took twenty-three years to compile. When it was finally published, it was hailed as "the greatest advance in the knowledge of our planet since the celebrated discoveries of the fifteenth and sixteenth centuries."

By the time it ended in 1876, the long and demanding voyage had taken its toll. Seven people had died, twenty-six had been left in hospitals along the way, and several had deserted the ship at various ports of call. Nares himself did not complete the journey. In 1874 he was abruptly recalled by the Navy to take command of two ships, the *Alert* and the *Discovery*, which the Admiralty was about to send out in search of the North Pole.

The two vessels arrived in Franklin Bay in late August 1875, where the *Discovery* was left in winter quarters while the Alert, under Nares's command, sailed on, enabling Nares to become the first explorer to take a ship all the way north through the channel between Greenland and Ellesmere Island (now named Nares Strait). On September 1, Nares reached latitude 82°27', a new record for northward travel. Here he was able to, once and for all, disprove the theory of the Open Polar Sea. There was nothing there but a vast wasteland of ice. In spring 1876, Nares sent out sledging parties seeking a route to the Pole, and on May 12, one of the expeditions, led by Albert Hastings Markham, set another record when he planted the British flag at latitude 83°20'.

Nares was now agonizingly close to the Pole, but, by this time, scurvy among his men had developed to the point that many of their lives were in jeopardy. He had no choice but to return home. He would be criticized for not having taken proper precautions against the disease, but no one could diminish his accomplishments. In the space of just four years, in areas worlds apart, he had captained both history's first great oceanographic expedition and the expedition that had come closest to reaching the North Pole.

CHAPTER 16

The Midnight Sun. In his journal, William Gilder described the "strange" effects of living in an environment of constant sunlight. "In the spring, the sun never sets," he wrote. "There is no morning and no night. It is one continuous day for months. At first it seems very difficult to understand this strange thing in nature. One never knows when to sleep. The world seems to be entirely wrong, and man grows nervous and restless. Sleep is driven from his weary eyelids, his appetite fails, and all the disagreeable results of protracted vigils are apparent. But gradually he becomes used to this state of affairs, devises means to darken his tent, and once more enjoys his hour of rest. In fact, he learns how to take advantage of the new arrangement, and when traveling pursues his journey at night, or when the sun is lowest, because then he finds the frost that hardens the snow a great assistance in sledging.

"The sun's rays then, falling more obliquely, are less powerful, and he avoids somewhat the evils that beset his pathway at noontime. He is not so much exposed to sunburn or to snow-blindness. It may sound strangely to speak of sunburn in the frigid zone, but perhaps nowhere on the earth is the traveller more annoyed by that great ill. The heat of ordinary exercise compels him to throw back the hood of his fur coat, that the cool evenings and mornings preclude his discarding, and not only his entire face becomes blistered, but especially—if he is fashionable enough to wear his hair thin upon the top of his head—his entire scalp is affected about as severely as if a bucket of scalding water had been poured over his head. This is not an exaggeration. At a later period than that of which I am writing, Lieutenant Schwatka's entire party, while upon a sledge journey from Marble Island to Camp Daly, were so severely burned that not only their faces but their entire heads were swollen to nearly twice their natural size. And a fine-looking party they were. Some had their faces so swollen that their eyes were completely closed upon awakening from sleep. When one could see the others he could not refrain from laughing, so ludicrous was the spectacle. All dignity was lost. Even the august commander of the party was a laughing-stock, and though he knew why they laughed at each other, he could not understand why he should excite such mirth until he saw his face in a mirror. Then, when he tried to smile, his lips were so thoroughly swollen that the effect was entirely lost, and it was impossible to tell whether his expression denoted amusement, anger, or pain. The torture resulting from these burns was so severe that it was almost impossible to sleep. The fur bedding, which also served the purpose of a pillow, irritated the burns like applying a mustard-plaster to a blister. Then it was that the night was turned into day for the rest of the journey, and during the heat of the day the party were comparatively comfortable in the shelter of their tent. Straw-hats would have been the proper style of head-dress, but they had been omitted from the outfit, as was also another very important source of comfort, mosquito nettings. It is in the summer, however, that the necessity for the latter luxury is encountered.

"While the sun's rays pour down with all their force upon the devoted head of the traveler the reflection from the snow is almost as intense and still more disagreeable, for there is no possible escape from it. Not satisfied with producing its share of sunburn, it acts upon the eyes in a manner that produces that terrible scourge of the Arctic spring—snow-blindness. It is a curious fact that persons who are near-sighted are generally exempt from the evils of snow-blindness, while it appears to be more malignant with those who are far-sighted in direct ratio to the superior quality of their vision. Lieutenant Schwatka and his companion, the present writer, are both nearsighted, and during the two seasons that they were exposed to the disease neither were at any time affected by snow-blindness; while the other members of the party, and especially the natives, who have most powerful visual organs, were almost constantly martyrs to the disease whenever exposed to its attacks."

CHAPTER 17

The Search Continues. Relics of the lost expedition continue to turn up in the Arctic, reminding us of all that remains unanswered, riddles that continue to drive individuals and entire expeditions to the region in hope of solving what has been called "the mystery that has never diminished."

Some, like American historian and naturalist Bil Gilbert, who personally duplicated Franklin's 1820–21 overland trek from Great Slave Lake to the Arctic coast, have sought solutions by placing themselves in the explorer's footsteps. Others have combed particular sites central to the Franklin saga. The Lady Franklin Memorial Expedition of 1993, for example, led by Lieutenant Ernie Coleman of the Royal Navy and Dr. Peter Wadhams, former head of the Scott Polar Research Institute, thought they had made a major find when, on King William Island, they discovered what had all the characteristics of a burial mound. Could it be John Franklin's grave? To their disappointment, the "grave" turned out to be a large earthen mound with an empty air pocket beneath it.

Most of the modern-day searches have focused on finding the *Erebus* and the *Terror*. If, as several of the Inuit reports indicated, one of the vessels sank and the other was driven ashore, their remains have to be somewhere, waiting to be found. It's not that scores of famous wrecks, including at least two involved in the search for the passage and for Franklin, have not been located. In 1980, the *Breadalbane*, the ship that sank while attempting to bring supplies to the Belcher expedition almost one hundred years earlier, was discovered by a National Geographic expedition led by Joseph McInnes. Lying three hundred feet down on the ocean floor, the *Breadalbane* was found to be in "an excellent state of preservation," a condition attributable to the frigid waters in which she lies. Sonar picture reveal that the vessel's masts remain intact, and a hole in her side provides a glimpse into such historic articles as her compass, signal lantern, and other navigational instruments.

In 2004, a Royal Navy expedition, named Exercise Arctic Quest 1832, organized to retrace the route taken by John and James Clark Ross on their 1829–33 passage search, found the remains of the explorers' ship *Victory*, which they had abandoned before being miraculously rescued. "To be the first British expedition to reach the winter harbours is itself a great achievement especially in the worst ice conditions in sixty years," the team's leader, Don Mee, stated. "But to make such discoveries is beyond our wildest dreams."

BIBLIOGRAPHY

PRIMARY SOURCES

Armstrong, Alexander. *A Personal Narrative of the Discovery of the North-West Passage.* London: Hurst & Blackett, 1857.

Back, George. *Narrative of the Arctic Land Expedition to the Mouth of the Great Fish River . . . in the Years 1833, 1834, and 1835.* London: John Murray, 1836.

———. *Narrative of an Expedition in HMS* Terror *. . . in the Years 1836-37.* London: John Murray, 1838.

Barrow, John. *Voyages of Discovery and Research in the Arctic Regions, from the Year 1818 to the Present Time . . .* London: John Murray, 1846.

Beechey, Frederick. *A Voyage of Discovery Towards the North Pole . . . Under the Command of Captain David Buchan, R.N., 1818 . . .* London: Richard Bentley, 1843.

Belcher, Edward. *The Last of the Arctic Voyages.* London: L. Reeve, 1855.

Bellot, Joseph. *Memoirs of Lieutenant Joseph René Bellot . . . with His Journal of a Voyage in the Polar Seas in Search of Sir John Franklin.* London: Hurst & Blackett, 1855.

DeBray, Emile. *A Frenchman in Search of Franklin: DeBray's Arctic Journal, 1852–54.* Toronto: University of Toronto Press, 1992.

Franklin, John. *Narrative of a Journey to the Shores of the Polar Sea in the Years 1819, 20, 21, 22.* London: John Murray, 1823.

———. *Narrative of a Second Expedition to the Shores of the Polar Sea in the Years 1825-26-27.* London: John Murray, 1828.

Geiger, John and Alanna Mitchell. *Franklin's Lost Ships: The Historic Discovery of HMS* Erebus. New York: HarperCollins, 2015.

Gilder, William. *Schwatka's Search: Sledging in the Arctic in Quest of the Franklin Records.* New York: Charles Scribner's Sons, 1881.

Gill, Harold, and Joanne Young. *Searching for the Franklin Expedition: The Arctic Journal of Robert Randolph Carter.* Annapolis: Naval Institute Press, 1998.

Hall, Charles. *Life With the Eskimaux: The Narrative of Captain Charles Francis Hall . . . from the 29th of May, 1860, to the 13th September, 1862. . . .* London: Sampson Low, Sons and Marston, 1862.

Hayes, Isaac. *The Open Polar Sea: A Narrative of a Voyage of Discovery Towards the North Pole, in the Schooner* United States. New York: Hurd and Houghton, 1869.

Hendrik, Hans. *Memoirs of Hans Hendrik, the Arctic Traveller Serving Under Kane, Hayes, Hall and Nares, 1853–1876.* London: Trubner & Co., 1876.

Hutchinson, Gillian. *Sir John Franklin's* Erebus *and* Terror *Expedition: Lost and Found.* London: Bloomsbury, 2017.

Kane, Elisha Kent. *The United States Grinnell Expedition in Search of Sir John Franklin: A Personal Narrative.* Philadelphia: Childs & Peterson, 1854.

———. *Arctic Explorations: The Second Grinnell Expedition in Search of Sir John Franklin, 1853, '54, '55.* Philadelphia: Childs & Peterson, 1856.

Kennedy, William. *A Short Narrative of the Second Voyage of the* Prince Albert *in Search of Sir John Franklin.* London: W. H. Dalton, 1853.

Klutschak, Hendrik, *Overland to Starvation Cove: With the Inuit in Search of Franklin.* Toronto: University of Toronto Press, 1987.

Lyon, George. *Private Journal During the Recent Voyage Under Captain Parry.* London: John Murray, 1824.

M'Clintock, Francis Leopold. *The Voyage of the* Fox *in the Arctic Seas: A Narrative of the Discovery of the Fate of Sir John Franklin and His Companions.* London: John Murray, 1860.

McClure, Robert. *The Discovery of the North-West Passage by HMS* Investigator, *Capt. R. M'Clure, 1850, 1851, 1852, 1853, 1854.* London: Longman, Brown, Green, Longmans & Roberts, 1856.

McCoogan, Ken. *Searching for Franklin: New Answers to the Great Arctic Mystery.* Madeira Park, BC, Can. Douglas & McIntrye, 2024.

McDougall, George. *The Eventful Voyage of HM Discovery Ship* Resolute *to the Arctic Regions in Search of Sir John Franklin and the Missing Crews of HM Discovery Ships* Erebus *and* Terror . . . London: Longman, Brown, Green, Longmans & Roberts, 1857.

Miertsching, Johann. *Frozen Ships: The Arctic Diary of Johann Miertsching 1850–1854.* Toronto: Macmillan, 1967.

Nares, George. *Narrative of a Voyage to the Polar Sea During 1875–76 in HM Ships* Alert *and* Discovery . . . London: Sampson Low, Marston, Searle, and Rivington, 1878.

Osborn, Sherard. *Stray Leaves from an Arctic Journal: Or Eighteen Months in the Polar Regions in Search Sir John Franklin's Expedition in the Years 1850–51.* London: Longman, Brown, Green, Longmans & Roberts, 1865.

Parry, W. Edward. *Journal of a Voyage for the Discovery of a North-West Passage from the Atlantic to the Pacific . . . in the Years 1819–20 . . .* London: John Murray, 1821.

———. *Journal of a Second Voyage for the Discovery of a North-West Passage . . . in the Years 1821, 22, 23 . . .* London: John Murray, 1824.

———. *Journal of a Third Voyage for the Discovery of a North-West Passage . . . in the Years 1824–25 . . .* London: John Murray, 1826.

———. *Narrative of an Attempt to Reach the North Pole . . . in the Year 1827.* London: John Murray, 1828.

Rawnsley, Willingham. *The Life, Diaries and Correspondence of Jane Lady Franklin, 1792–1875.* London: Erskine MacDonald, 1923.

Rae, John. *Narrative of an Exploration to the Shores of the Arctic Sea in 1846 and 1847.* London: T. and W. Boone, 1850.

Richardson, John. *Arctic Searching Expedition . . . Through Prince Rupert's Land and the Arctic Sea in Search of the Discovery Ships Under Sir John Franklin.* London: Longman, Brown, Green, Longmans & Roberts, 1851.

———. *The Journal of John Richardson . . . 1820–1822.* Montréal: McGill-Queen's University Press, 1984.

Ross, James. *A Voyage of Discovery and Research in the Southern Antarctic Regions During the Years 1839–43.* London: John Murray, 1847.

Ross, John. *A Voyage of Discovery for the Purpose of Exploring Baffin's Bay and Inquiring Into the Probability of a North-West Passage.* London: John Murray, 1819.

————. *Narrative of a Second Voyage in Search of a North-West Passage . . . During the Years 1829, 1830, 1831, 1832, 1833*. London: Webster, 1835.

Scoresby, William. *An Account of the Arctic Regions with a History and Description of the Northern Whale Fishery*. Devon: David and Charles, 1969.

Snow, W. Parker. *Voyage of the* Prince Albert *in Search of Sir John Franklin: A Narrative of Every-Day Life in the Arctic Seas*. London: Longman, Brown, Green, Longmans & Roberts, 1851.

Stackpole, Edward. *The Long Arctic Search: The Narrative of Lieutenant Frederick Schwatka, U.S.S., 1878–1880*. Mystic, CT: Marine Historical Association, 1965.

Stefánsson, Vilhjálmur. *The Friendly Arctic: The Story of Five Years in Polar Regions* (reprint edition). New York: Macmillan, 1921.

GENERAL WORKS

Allen, Everett S. *Children of the Light*. Boston: Little, Brown, 1973.

Amundsen, Roald. *The Northwest Passage: Being a Record of a Voyage of Exploration of the ship* Gjöa, *1903–1907*. London: Constable, 1908.

Beattie, Owen, and Geiger, John. *Frozen in Time: The Fate of the Franklin Expedition*. New York: Dutton, 1987.

Berton, Pierre. *The Arctic Grail: The Quest for the Northwest Passage and the North Pole*. New York: Penguin Books, 1988.

Blake, E. V. *Arctic Experiences: Containing Capt. George E. Tyson's Wonderful Drift on the Ice Flow . . .* Harpers & Brothers, 1874.

Colby, Bernard. *For Oil and Buggy Whips: Whaling Captains of New London County, Connecticut*. Mystic, CT: Mystic Seaport, 1990.

Cookman, Scott. *Ice Blink: The Tragic Fate of Sir John Franklin's Lost Polar Expedition*. New York: John Wiley, 2000.

Fleming, Fergus. *Barrow's Boys*. New York: Grove Press, 1998.

McGoogan, Ken. *Fatal Passage: The Story of John Rae, the Arctic Hero Time Forgot*. New York: Carroll & Graf, 2001.

Newman, Perter. *Empire of the Bay: An Illustrated History of the Hudson's Bay Company*. Toronto: Viking/Madison, 1989.

Sandler, Martin W. *Shipwrecked: Diving for Hidden Time Capsules on the Ocean Floor*. New York: Astra, 2023.

Woodman, David. *Unravelling the Franklin Mystery: Inuit Testimony*. Montréal and Kingston: McGill-Queen's University Press, 1991.

BIOGRAPHIES

Corner, George. *Doctor Kane of the Arctic Seas*. Philadelphia: Temple University Press, 1972.

Dodge, E. S. *The Polar Rosses*. London: Faber and Faber, 1973.

Johnson, Robert. *Sir John Richardson: Arctic Explorer, Natural Historian, Naval Surgeon*. London: Taylor & Francis Ltd., 1976.

Loomis, Charles. *Weird and Tragic Shores: The Story of Charles Francis Hall, Explorer.* New York: Alfred Knopf, 1972.

Lloyd, Christopher. *Mr. Barrow of the Admiralty: A Life of Sir John Barrow, 1764–1848.* London: Collins, 1970.

Markham, A. H. *Life of Sir John Franklin.* London: George Phillip & Son, 1891.

Markham, C. *The Life of Admiral Sir Leopold McClintock.* London: John Murray, 1909.

Morton, A. S. *Sir George Simpson: Overseas Governor of the Hudson's Bay Company.* Toronto: J. M. Dent, 1944.

Parry, Ann. *Parry of the Arctic.* London: Chatto and Windus, 1963.

Simpson, Alexander. *The Life and Travels of Thomas Simpson, the Arctic Discoverer.* London: Richard Bentley, 1845.

Stamp, Tom, and Cordelia Stamp. *William Scoresby.* Whitby: Caedmon of Whitby Press, 1976.

Woodward, Frances. *Portrait of Jane: A Life of Lady Franklin.* London: Hodder and Stoughton, 1951.

PRINT ARTICLES

Beattie, Owen. "A Report on Newly Discovered Human Skeletal Remains from the Last Sir John Franklin Expedition." *Muskox* 33 (1983).

"Dr. Rae's Report." *Household Words* (December 1854).

"Joe and Hannah." *Beaver* 290 (Autumn 1969).

"Recently Discovered Traces of Sir John Franklin's Expedition." *Geographical Journal* 117 (June 1951).

Keenleyside, Anne, Margaret Bertulli, and Henry C. Fricke. "The Final Days of the Franklin Expedition: New Skeletal Evidence," *Arctic* 50, no. 1 (March 1997).

"The Last Voyage of the Resolute." *Boston Daily Advertiser* (June 11, 1856).

Dickens, Charles. "The Lost Arctic Voyagers." *Household Words* (December 1854).

"Was the Ill-Fated Franklin Expedition a Victim of Lead Poisoning?" *Nutrition Reviews* 47 (October 1989).

ONLINE ARTICLES AND SITES

"Abandoned 1854 Ship Found in Arctic," CBC News, July 28, 2010, https://bit.ly/3Nr7ES4.

Barton, Katherine, "No Camera, No Proof: Why Sammy Kogvik Didn't Tell Anyone About HMS *Terror* Find," CBC News, September 15, 2016, https://bit.ly/3zNqFv3.

Cecco, Leyland, "Inuit Oral Historian Who Pointed Way to Franklin Shipwrecks Dies Aged 58," *The Guardian*, March 29, 2018, https://bit.ly/40mbvI7.

Gannon, Megan, "Divers Get an Eerie First Look Inside the Arctic Shipwreck of the HMS *Terror*," *Smithsonian* magazine, August 29, 2019, https://bit.ly/3BHnGoB.

"HMS *Investigator*," *Archaeology* magazine, January 1, 2011, https://archaeology.org/issues /features/hms-investigator-banks-island-canada/.

Potter, Russell, "Remembering Louie Kamookak, a Wellspring of Inuit Traditional Knowledge," *Nunatsiaq News*, October 13, 2024, https://bit.ly/3zV0VNi.

ACKNOWLEDGMENTS

A BOOK OF THIS MAGNITUDE requires the help and support of many individuals and I have been blessed by being aided by the very best. It was my good fortune to have the gracious assistance of Russell Potter of Rhode Island College, whose guidance with the artwork proved invaluable. His marvelous foreword to this book proves once again that he is among the most perceptive and articulate of all Arctic experts.

I am most appreciative of what four highly talented individuals have brought to this book—Russell Hassell for his most appealing interior design, and Rich Hazelton for the revised interior design; Jared Oriel for his arresting cover design; and Nick Springer for his beautiful maps. Thanks are also due to project editor Christina Stambaugh, photo editor Linda Liang, and production manager Sandy Noman.

Very special thanks are due the following dedicated experts who provided assistance in the research and acquisition of illustrations: Sandy Johnson, Alaska State Library; Scott Currier; Paul Frecker; Kitty Kelley; Bill Peterson, Louisa Watrous, and Amy German at the Mystic Seaport Museum; Joanna Murray, National Library of Australia; Isabel Fernandez, National Library and Archives of Canada; Jeremy Mitchell, David Taylor, Doug McCarthy, and William Duguid at the National Maritime Museum; Matthew Bailey, National Portrait Gallery; Edward Baker, New London Historical Society; Sheila Carleton and Alan Walker at the Toronto Public Library; Gilbert Gonzalez, Rutherford B. Hayes Presidential Center; Perry Willett, University of Michigan Library; and Harmony Haskins, White House Historical Society.

As always, I am deeply indebted to my late wife, Carol Weiss Sandler, who not only contributed her considerable research skills, but once again accommodated to the schedule of a workaholic husband.

Finally, this book could not have been written without the continual guidance and invaluable contributions of Barbara Berger.

Barbara, all is forgiven for the outragous schedule, the weekend and late-evening emails and calls, and the Columbo-like "just one more thing." Your superlative editing, your skill and perserverence in picture selection, and, most important, your dedication and passion for excellence, have been an inspiration. There would not have been a book without you!

INDEX

Page numbers in *italics* indicate photographs and illustrations

PICTURE CREDITS

Courtesy Alaska State Library:
203: Schwatka, Frederick-1

Art Resource: National Portrait Gallery, London: Pl. 11

Bridgeman Images: Pl. 6: National Portrait Gallery, London, UKPhoto©NPL - DeA Picture Library / Pl. 26: Private Collection/Look and Learn/Valerie Jackson Harris Collection (Note: *Image depicts Lieut. John Powles Cheyne's three-balloon North Pole scheme of the 1870s (Cheyne was an officer on two Franklin search expeditions in 1850s). These balloons are larger in scale than the search balloons used in the Franklin search, although Cheyne was inspired by them.*)

Courtesy the Currier & Ives Foundation: Pl. 27

Getty Images: Pl. 30 / *229*: Bettman /*194*: Historical

Courtesy of Paul Frecker, London: Pl. 12: Adm. Sir Edward Belcher, 1861, by Camille Silvy

Courtesy Library and Archives Canada *W. H. Coverdale Collection of Canadiana:* Pl. 2: Acc. No, 1970-188-1946 / Pl. 7: Acc. No. 1970-188-1946 / Pl. 10: Acc. No. 1970-188-1945 / *39*: Acc. No. 1970-188-554; Purchased with the assistance of the Department of the Secretary of State *Library and Archives Canada:* Pl. 3: Acc. No. 1960-109-36 / *64*: ARCH Rare G650 1829 R8 fol. / Pl. 8, *80*: National Library of Canada *Peter Winkworth Collection of Canadiana:* Pl. 9: Acc. No. R9266-1032 / Pl. 22: Acc. No. R9266-2114 / *24*: Acc. No. R9266-3038 / *98*: Acc. No. R9266-1031

Courtesy of Prints & Photographs Division, Library of Congress: *xix*: from *The Frozen Zone and Its Explorers; a Comprehensive Record of Voyages, Travels, Discoveries, Adventures and Whale-Fishing in the Arctic Regions for One Thousand Years*, 1874 / Pl. 21: LC-USZC4-4671 / Pl. 24: LC-DIG-cwpbh-03348 / Pl. 25: LC-USZ6-422 / *217*: LC-USZ62-123892

Courtesy Mystic Seaport, The Museum of America and the Sea: Pl. 19: *Bark GEORGE HENRY of New London, Connecticut,* Engraving depicting the date: May 28, 1860; © Mystic Seaport Collection, Mystic, CT #1939-1244

Courtesy National Library of Australia: Pl. 5: Cooke, Edward William, Erebus *and* Terror, *Sir John Franklin's Expedition,* ca. 1850, nla.pican2282969 / 7: *Portrait of Sir John Barrow,* painted by John Jackson; engraved by W. J. Edwards, London: Published by Henry Graves & Compy., 1853, Rex Nan Kivell collection, NK11150, nla.pic-an9288312

Courtesy National Maritime Museum: *33, 264, 265*

Courtesy of the National Oceanic & Atmospheric Adminstration (NOAA): Pl. 16: NOAA Central Library / *Frontispiece*, Pl. 17, *12, 115 & 129*: Treasures of the NOAA Library Collection

Courtesy of the New London County Historical Society, New London, Connecticut: Pl. 18: Captain Buddington (in sealskins), 1862, from Giles Bishop Collection, NLCHS 799, N461, photograph by G. C.Waldo

Courtesy of Parks Canada: *252*: Thierry Boyer. 89M00517EF. 2014 / *255*: Wrecks of HMS *Erebus* and HMS *Terror* National Historic Site /*256*: Ryan Harris. 90M-2019-353. 2019 /*258*: Ryan Harris. HMS *Investigator* at 25 m range large format. 2010

MARTIN SANDLER has received many honors, including winning the 2019 National Book Award for Young People's Literature for *1919: The Year That Changed America*, two Pulitzer Prize nominations, and seven Emmy Awards. His Library of Congress American History series was a national bestseller, and he was creator and cowriter for the acclaimed twelve-part *This Was America* TV series. Sandler has taught American history and American studies at the University of Massachusetts and Smith College. He lives in Cotuit, MA.

I am a passionate tennis player, an avid moviegoer, and a lifelong, dedicated follower of the Boston Red Sox, an avocation which, until the miracle of 2004, threatened both my health and my mental stability. More than anything else, however, I love to uncover important but neglected stories in the human experience, particularly if they involve unimaginable heroism and surprising results. That is why researching and writing the saga of the *Resolute* has been such a joy. I feel extremely privileged to have had the opportunity to tell it.